About Being
A Priest

The Author

Federico Suarez was born in Valencia in 1917. He obtained a doctorate in history from the University of Madrid and in 1940 began his teaching career at the University of Santiago de Compostela. In 1948, the year of his priestly ordination, he was awarded the chair of Modern and Contemporary History at that university. In 1955 he became dean of the Faculty of Philosophy and Letters at the University of Navarre, where in 1957 he created the Seminar in Modern History dedicated to research and the training of historians. A result of this work has been the Historical Collection of the University of Navarre, which has published some forty volumes.

In addition to his work as a historian, Fr. Suarez has carried out an intense personal apostolate directed particularly to university students and priests. His best known work in English is *Mary of Nazareth*, first published in the United States and Ireland in 1959 under the title *Our Lady the Virgin.* A companion volume entitled *Joseph of Nazareth* was published in English in 1984. Among Fr. Suarez's other books that have been translated into English are *The Afterlife*, *The Sacrifice of the Altar*, and two collections of his talks to university students: *The Narrow Gate* and *When the Son of Man Comes.*

About Being
A Priest

Federico Suarez

Scepter Publishers
Princeton
Midwest Theological Forum
Chicago

Nihil Obstat: Stephen J. Greene, *censor deputatus. Imprimi Potest:* ✠ Dermot, Archbishop of Dublin, *May 31, 1978.* (The *Nihil Obstat* and Imprimi *Potest* are a declaration that a book is considered to be free from doctrinal or moral error. This declaration does not imply approval of, or agreement with, the contents, opinions or statements expressed.)

ISBN 0-933932-88-X

This book is a translation of *El Sacerdote y su Ministerio* (Ediciones Rialp, SA, Madrid), second edition, 1970, updated in conformity with the fifth edition of 1989. © 1979 Federico Suarez, © 1979 translation: Four Courts Press Ltd. This revised second English edition published in 1996 by Scepter Publishers, PO Box 1270, Princeton NJ 08542.

Foreword

THE GREAT VALUE OF FATHER SUAREZ'S BOOK *About Being a Priest* is that it shows in practical terms how the priest of today can be true to the exacting demands of his vocation. One of the outstanding contributions of the Second Vatican Council to the theme of priestly spirituality was to stress that it is in the actual carrying out of his ministry that the priest must acquire the holiness which his vocation requires. It is not in doing something other than, or apart from, his priestly duties that he is to develop a life of prayer and draw nearer to Christ in faith and love. It is precisely in giving himself unreservedly to the needs of others as minister of Word and Sacrament that he takes upon himself the Cross of Christ and grows in Christ's likeness. Time for personal prayer is, of course, indispensable; but such prayer must be closely linked to the priest's active ministry, combining with it to form a single unified design for growth in holiness.

This insight into priestly spirituality is fundamental. It provides the priest with the basic program by which to integrate his apostolic activity with his personal search for holiness. However, this program needs to be worked out in detail in terms of the varied activities and responsibilities of a priest's life. Many problems arise here, and if the priest is to cope with them successfully, he can scarcely dispense with the advice of an experienced and trustworthy guide. This becomes all the clearer once it is observed that the program in question, despite its apparent simplicity, entails a fundamental paradox: for it states that the priest, in order to

v

draw nearer to Christ, must devote most of his time and energy, not to seeking Christ directly, but to serving the needs of others.

Father Suarez addresses himself to this paradox, and shows how it can be lived out and bear fruit in the many duties and challenges of a priest's life. He has principally in mind the priest in the parish, and the diocesan priest in particular. He has a clear and consistent vision of the priestly office and, in a happy blend of theology and practical wisdom, provides helpful guidance on many questions that confront the priest engaged in the pastoral ministry in the world of today.

It is true, of course, that no author can provide ready-made solutions to suit all individuals and situations. Differences in character and temperament, as well as in concrete circumstances, have their part to play in determining the right course to be followed. Despite such differences, however, any priest who takes up Father Suarez's book may be assured that he will come away with a keener sense of the lofty requirements of his vocation and a clearer view of how he can meet them more effectively in his daily life.

⍟Kevin McNamara
Bishop of Kerry

Contents

Abbreviations of the Titles of Documents
of the Second Vatican Council

AA   *Apostolicam Actuositatem:* The Decree on the Apostolate of the Laity

AG   *Ad Gentes:* The Decree on the Church's Missionary Activity

GS   *Gaudium et Spes:* The Pastoral Constitution on the Church in the Modern World

LG   *Lumen Gentium:* The Dogmatic Constitution on the Church

OT   *Optatam Totius:* The Decree on the Training of Priests

PO   *Presbyterorum Ordinis:* The Decree on the Life and Ministry of Priests

SC   *Sacrosanctum Concilium:* The Constitution on the Sacred Liturgy

UR   *Unitatis Redintegratio:* The Decree on Ecumenism

Introduction

A S FAR BACK AS 1961 a Belgian priest, Louis Bouyer, published a book on the meaning of the priestly life in which he commented that the conditions in which the clergy live, and even more especially the circumstances in which they exercise their priesthood, have changed so much in the space of a few generations that it comes as no surprise when we hear that many of them are experiencing some unrest.

This is true. Mankind is entering upon a new era in its history, one of whose features is that profound changes are taking place all over the world and so quickly that they emerge almost before we have time to prepare ourselves to assimilate or adapt to them. Such rapid change has many consequences. One result is that it produces anxieties, contradictions and upheavals; these affect the priest like everyone else; indeed they probably cause him more concern than most people. We have only to look at the sermons and addresses of Popes Paul VI and John Paul II to see how widespread this phenomenon has become in the life of the Church and in the pastoral care of its visible head.

Unless a priest goes back to the very roots of his vocation to the priesthood, it is never easy for him to grasp the demands made by the Church on those who have responded freely and willingly to the divine call, those who have accepted that enormous task and taken on that tremendous responsibility. It can never be easy, but it is especially difficult in times of crisis, such as we are now experiencing.

The present book has been written as a reflection on the priest and his work, not a theological reflection—though it makes use of theology—but mainly ascetic and pastoral. I am not thinking of priests in general, but rather of those priests who spend their lives day after day in the care of souls, dealing with concrete problems, in real circumstances, with worries more closely related to practical life than to theory, those living and working in cities, towns and rural areas. I have in mind particularly the self-sacrificing and courageous secular clergy, laboring tirelessly and humbly to bring the Church home.

May the Blessed Virgin Mary, mother of Christ the Eternal Priest, obtain from her Son that these reflections may help us all to devote ourselves entirely to the fulfillment of our vocation as servants.

1

The Priest

IN HIS VERY FIRST ENCYCLICAL, *Ecclesiam Suam*, Pope Paul VI wrote: "We believe that it is a duty of the Church at the present time to strive towards a clearer and deeper awareness of itself and its mission in the world, and of the treasury of truth of which it is heir and custodian . . . the Church must here and now reflect on its own nature, the better to appreciate the divine plan which it is the Church's task to implement."[1]

Similarly we can say that now is also the time for the priest to consider his position, to reflect on the mysterious nature of his priesthood, to give serious thought to his mission, not forgetting his final destiny. In these times of profound renewal within the Church, of radical changes throughout the world and in the minds of the men and women among whom and for whom he exercises his ministry, a priest must also become deeply aware of himself, if he is to avoid being lost in the storms that inevitably emerge in times of crisis.

The priest and the Church

If he is to consider his position and think seriously about his priesthood, a priest must first of all approach the question from a point of view that will help him to see things clearly. If any deep thought is to be possible on the subject of the priesthood, we must situate the priest in the context in which he lives, works and justifies his existence, as well as examine the nature of the priesthood itself. We cannot think of him apart from the Church, for he is inconceivable without it. He is surrounded and penetrated with the Church's ethos; only the mystery of the Church can throw light on the mystery of his vocation.

The Church thinks of herself as "a kind of sacrament" by her relationship with Christ, a "sign of intimate union with God, and of the unity of all mankind. She is also an instrument for the achievement of such union and unity" *(Lumen Gentium* [hereafter cited as LG] 1).[2] Christ founded the Church, and it was he who entrusted it with the task of announcing the Kingdom of God and of "bringing all men to full union with Christ," for the Church on earth is the beginning, the seed, of this Kingdom.

There is only one people of God, one mystical body of Christ, one Church. She has only one mission, and it devolves upon the whole Church, the whole people of God, the whole mystical body. The fulfillment of this mission, then, is "entrusted to all the members of the people of God, who through the sacraments of initiation have been made sharers in the priesthood of Christ, to offer to God a spiritual sacrifice and bear witness to Jesus Christ before men. Each has his own role to play in this mission of saving and building up the community."[3]

This is a universal mission. It extends to all people of all times and all places. Christ died for each and every one of them. And for this one mission, there is but one priesthood, namely that of Christ, the eternal Priest, in which all the faithful share in different ways and to different degrees. By divine institution, some of those faithful who share in that common priesthood are called to something else, to the ministerial priesthood. This differs essentially and not just in degree from the other, although it presupposes it: "The ministerial priesthood confers a *sacra potestas* which enables its recipients to share in the authority with which Christ, the head of the Church, builds up, sanctifies and governs his Body."[4]

Only this ministerial priesthood gives one the right to offer the eucharistic sacrifice, forgive sins and publicly exercise the sacramental priesthood for the benefit of others, because it is the result of the special sacrament of Order, by which the Holy Spirit bestows on those who receive it a particular character which likens them to Christ the Priest, and enables them to act in the name of Christ, head of the Mystical Body.

The highest degree of priesthood was conferred by Christ on his apostles and, through them, on their successors, the bishops. But from very early times when the people of God were beginning to take their first steps forward, the apostles "legitimately handed on to different individuals in the Church various degrees of participation in this ministry. . . . Although priests do not possess the highest degree of the priesthood, and although they are dependent on the bishops in the exercise of their power, they are nevertheless united with the bishops in sacerdotal dignity. By the power of the sacrament of Holy Orders, and in the image of Christ the eternal High Priest, they are consecrated to preach the Gospel, shepherd the faithful, and celebrate divine worship as true priests of the New Testament" (LG 28).

Hence the priest is above all else a man of the Church and he can be understood, his position is meaningful, only within the context of the Church. His vocation is so closely linked to the Church's mission that it merges with it. Indeed, to a great extent the Church exercises her mission through and by means of the priest, so much so that not only the propagation of the message of salvation among those who do not know Christ but even the "renewal of the whole Church depends in large measure on a ministry of priests" (*Optatam Totius* [OT] preface).

However, "the mission of the Church is not only to bring to men the message and grace of Christ, but also to penetrate and perfect the temporal sphere with the spirit of the Gospel" (*Apostolicam Actuositatem* [AA] 5). So the priest's ministerial work and his vocation, that is, his divine calling, extend also to this life. God created the world; he made it spotless, well ordered and good, but it has been diverted from its true course by sin, while God's plan is to unite all things in Christ, "things in heaven and things on earth" (Eph 1: 10). Men cannot be saved outside their normal environment, outside the world in which they live, for that is not how they exist. The Church, and consequently the priest also, is concerned with real people, not with mere abstractions, and real people live on this solid earth, at a particular moment in time, involved in temporal things, in a civilization that has specific characteristics. These are the people who have to be saved; in fact, it is the whole world that has to be saved, the world which God loved so much "that he gave his only Son, that whoever believed in him should not perish but have eternal life" (Jn 3: 16).

The Church's action, through the common priesthood of all the faithful, aims to a great extent at bringing about a situation in which "the faith of Christ and the life of the Church will no longer be something extraneous to the society in which they live, but will begin to permeate and transform it" *(Ad Gentes* [AG] 21). And this is to be achieved "not in any external dominion exercised by merely human means" *(Gaudium et Spes* [GS] 42), but by bringing about the unity of all men through an application of faith and charity to their ordinary lives. This being so, the priest must make every effort to teach faith and charity, doctrine, and moral judgment to those members of the faithful entrusted to his care, so that they too may play their part in the mission assigned to them by the Church as a means of restoring the order distorted by sin.

Priests, therefore, constitute a section of the people of God to whom the Church has entrusted an extremely important and exceptionally delicate task, namely to transform the world by transforming men and women. However, they perform this task, not alone, but with the aid of the faithful who exercise the common priesthood and who also, as a part of the people of God, have an active role to play within the Church in spreading the gospel. All the faithful who make up the people of God (and priests must be among them as leaven, keeping their faith, hope, and charity alive and constantly growing) should show the world God's saving plan, the meaning of life and of creation, how all men and all things are directed towards God through Christ, the center of our entire history. They have to show the world the great mystery of redemption as well as the mystery of the Church, through which mankind's redemption has been achieved down through the ages.

Since the Church is a sign of unity, not only among people but between the supernatural and temporal worlds, the priest should also regard himself as a sign of unity. The wedge driven by modern philosophy between religion and life, between faith and temporal activity, between this world and the next, affects the minds and attitudes even of Christians and is one of the gravest errors of our time. If this error is to be rectified, the priest has a lot to say and a lot to do, for he is a consecrated man, situated on the frontier of both worlds, active on both levels and bringing them together.

In the light of these basic principles relating to the priest, showing his position in the Church and in the world, seeing him as a man of the Church entrusted with an important part of her mission, we can now begin to think about the priest and his ministry. We may start with a classic text on the subject, taken from the letter to the Hebrews: "For every high priest chosen from among men is appointed to act on behalf of men in relation to God, to offer gifts and sacrifices for sins. He can deal gently with the ignorant and wayward, since he himself is beset with weakness. Because of this he is bound to offer sacrifice for his own sins as well as for those of the people. And one does not take the honor upon himself, but he is called by God, just as Aaron was" (5: 1-4).

It is clear that these words are perfectly applicable to priests, for "by the sacrament of Orders priests are configured to Christ the Priest so that as ministers of the Head and coworkers of the episcopal order, they can build up and establish His whole Body which is the Church" (*Presbyterorum Ordinis* [PO] 12), a task they fulfill as living instruments of the eternal Priest.

A priest is a man, but a man taken out from among men, invested with a new and tremendous dignity through his ordination and then given back again to serve all men and women "in relation to God." He serves them by offering gifts and sacrifices for sins; for his own as a man—he is also a sinner—and for those of others, for all the sins of the world. And he does this, not as an exceptional man, isolated from all others, but rather in great sympathy with them, for his nature is their nature and, like them, he is full of defects and shortcomings.

It is not his virtues which invest him with this new and special dignity, with these powers that are not his by nature, with this unique mission; his virtues are as ordinary as those of anyone else. It is God himself who chooses him from among men, endows him with mysterious supernatural powers and then sends him back to his fellowmen with the task of saving them. Indeed no one can apply to himself as strictly as the priest the words of Saint Paul, "What have you that you did not receive?" (1 Cor 4: 7).

A consecrated man

Above all else, a priest is a consecrated man. There is a clear difference between a man as such and a Christian, for Baptism imposes on its recipient an indelible character, a permanent mark, so permanent and indelible that it can never be erased, and this makes him really and truly a new man. There is also a difference between a Christian as such and a priest, for the sacrament of Orders confers on the Christian who receives it a new character, a new mark which is also permanent and indelible, making its recipient a priest for ever—a *sacerdos in aeternum*. Just as anyone who has been baptized is saved or damned *as* a Christian, so the Christian who has been ordained is saved or damned *as* a priest. He has taken an irreversible step that leaves him marked out forever. When a Christian is ordained he receives and accepts something new that never disappears, something that changes him and makes him different from all others. God takes possession of him in a special way; he consecrates him to his service for the benefit of the rest of mankind, his brothers and sisters; he makes him a sharer in Christ's priesthood and gives him a new personality.

This man, who has been consecrated by the sacrament of Orders, is not a priest simply by virtue of the acts he performs when using the powers and faculties conferred on him, nor is he a priest merely when he is performing such acts. He is a priest continuously, internally, invisibly; he is a priest always and at every moment, whether he is performing the highest and most sublime office or the most vulgar and humble action of his ordinary life. Just as a Christian cannot leave aside the fact that he is a new man, that Baptism has given him a particular character, and act "as if" he were just a man purely and simply, neither can the priest leave aside his priestly character and behave "as if" he were not a priest. Whatever he does, whatever attitude he adopts, whether he likes it or not, it will always be the action or the attitude of a priest, because he is a priest always and at all times down to the very depths of his being, whatever he may do or whatever he may think. Just as a Christian cannot cast off the fact that he is a Christian as if it were an old coat, neither can a priest lose his priesthood even for a single moment, simply by dressing in lay clothes or by engaging in non-priestly activities; he is simply a priest dressed as a layman or engaging in non-priestly activities.

He is a consecrated man. A consecrated man is one who has given himself up and no longer claims ownership of himself: "I the Lord am holy, and have separated you from the peoples, that you should be mine" (Lev 20: 26). Consecration to God means surrendering to God, giving oneself, one's being, everything one has or may have, everything one is or may be, one's activity, one's intelligence, one's will, future, life and death. "None of us lives to himself, and none of us dies to himself. If we live, we live to the Lord, and if we die, we die to the Lord, so then, whether we live or we die, we are the Lord's" (Rom 14: 7-8). Therefore a consecrated man must be detached from all things; he must deliberately, willingly and freely have given himself up so that God may do with him whatever he wishes, using him in the service of others and shaping him to his own liking. As Pope Pius XII said, "He does not belong to himself, just as he does not belong to his family or friends or even to a particular country: universal charity must constantly surround him and emanate from him. His very thought, will, sentiments, are not his, but belong to Christ, his life."[5]

He is "pre-elected from among the people, privileged with divine charisms, a repository of divine power, in a word, *alter Christus*."

A priest is another Christ. This is so by virtue of the nature of the priesthood itself, which is a participation and continuance of Christ's priesthood on the cross, where he died to redeem man from the slavery of sin. A priest is another Christ also by reason of his function, for strictly speaking, as Saint Thomas says, "the characteristic function of a priest is to act as mediator between God and his people. This implies first that he communicates to the people the things of God."[6] Of course, there is no mediator in the true sense between God and man, or between man and God, except Christ Jesus, true God and true man, so if the priest is a mediator it is solely because he is *alter Christus* and shares in the eternal mediation of the Man who is God. This mediation of Christ, St. Thomas continues, is based on the fact that "as man his office is to unite men with God, which he does by setting before men the divine commandments and gifts and by atoning and interceding for men with God."⁷ This two-fold aspect of the mediator's task, offering the divine command-ments and gifts to men on God's behalf while interceding with him and making reparation for men, must be fulfilled by the priest acting as a delegate of Christ, as his instrument and col-laborator, an instrument in administering the sacraments and a collaborator in all his other functions.

From another point of view, the priest is also a prophet, that is to say, a spokesman for God, a herald of his divinity, a man of God. He ought to defend God's rights in the world, his plan of salvation, making sure that people are continually aware of the speed with which this temporal life passes, the importance of the moral order, their redemption and the divine realities. As a spokesman for God, he never speaks in his own name but simply transmits the word of God to men; it was for this he became a priest: "To all to whom I send you, you shall go; and whatever I command you, you shall speak. . . . Behold, I have put my words in your mouth" (Jer 1: 7, 9).

The priest is a minister of God. As an envoy and a minister, his faculties and powers came to him from the Lord, in whose name he speaks and acts. He is lent the strength necessary to allow him to fulfill his mission, for that purpose and for none other. He must never distort the divine message, he cannot relax in the fulfillment of his duty however many and however great the obstacles in his way. He must never give way in the face of human pressure, or compromise with falsehood, deceit, error or evil, neither may he dilute the teaching received through revelation. His task of passing on the precepts and gifts of God to others must be as continuous and permanent as his interces-sion and the atonement he offers to God for those same men and women. He has received tremendous faculties for the exer-cise of his function as a spokesman for God. "See, I have set you this day over nations and over kingdoms, to pluck up and to break down, to destroy and to overthrow, to build and to plant" (Jer 1: 10).

He is also an instrument of unity. It is the Lord's wish that they may all be one (Jn 17: 21). He clearly proclaimed that a kingdom divided within itself will be defeated and that a city or a household that loses its unity by internal divisions cannot survive. The Church is one and only one; to outsiders she reveals herself "as a sign raised above the nations. Under this sign the scattered sons of God are being gathered into one until there is one fold and one shepherd" (*Sacrosanctum Concilium* [SC] 2). So priests must be "eager to maintain the unity of the Spirit" (Eph 4: 3) and "this exhortation applies especially to those who have been raised to sacred orders so that the mission of Christ may be carried on" (*Unitatis Redintegratio* [UR] 7). So it is the priest who has to carry the burden of maintaining and extending this unity among his brothers and sisters, it is he who has to be on guard to ensure that their unity in the faith, in the Lord, and in Baptism shall be stronger than those divisions and antagonisms caused by different attitudes and opinions on accidental or earthly matters. We must never allow brothers and sisters to be divided by difference of ideas or temporal interests, when they ought to be united by the strength of their faith. By his conduct and example, by his word, his concern for others and his self-denial, the priest has to ensure that his brothers and sisters constantly realize that nothing in this life is of sufficient importance to be worth destroying the marvellous reality of that "one heart and one mind" (Acts 4: 32), that no sacrifice is too great if it might attract back those who have strayed from the bosom of their Mother the Church, who is suffering because of their absence.

However, if divine grace is to bear fruit, it needs the cooperation of man. He has to accept it freely and respond without reservation. Each individual must behave in accordance with what he is. The priest, a consecrated man, has a special quality, the quality of something holy, for his sacramental consecration endows him with a sacred character. He can no longer behave as if this special quality did not exist. He is a man of God, belonging no longer to himself but to God alone. His life is not his own, for he surrendered it when he responded to the divine call, so he cannot act as if it still belonged to him. He has no right to attempt to gain his life, for if he does, he will unquestionably lose it. On the other hand, if he gives it up completely, keeping nothing back for himself, then indeed he will gain it forever, both here and hereafter. If he really lives for the fulfillment of God's will in himself and in others, if he makes his priesthood his whole life, if his dedication to the mission entrusted to him genuinely occupies every fiber of his being, then he will truly experience how the divine promise of a hundred-fold return becomes an authentic reality.

Since he is "another Christ"—a mediator between God and man—the priest can hope for no better treatment than his Saviour received, for it is written: "A disciple is not above his teacher, nor a servant above his master; it is enough for the disciple to be like his teacher, and the servant to be like his master" (Mt 10: 24-5). And we know the treatment Jesus received in the world and how he was rewarded for his mediation: he had nowhere to lay his head (Mt 8: 20), his life was one of hard work with scarcely any time to himself (Mk 3: 20), he was slandered and criticized, rejected by his own people, condemned and crucified. But he overcame sin and death; he rose victorious from the dead. We were saved by him, and through him hope poured out endless light on a world enveloped in the darkness of despair.

The priest must hope for no human compensations or rewards in the fulfillment of his duties. He is not to seek fame, prestige, reputation or comfort. He cannot measure supernatural work by purely human yardsticks or by the standards of this world. There is only one way to yield the fruit that God expects, and Christ showed it to us clearly. "Truly, truly, I say to you, unless a grain of wheat falls into the earth and dies, it remains alone" (Jn 12: 24). The priest does not look for success in the world's eyes, but for a lasting, supernatural, success in the eyes of God. He must always be ready to welcome and embrace the cross of Christ, for if Christ the eternal Priest blesses us with the cross, what greater reward can the priest expect than to feel the Lord's blessing on his shoulders?

A prophet, a divine herald, a man of God. Cardinal Emmanuel Suhard of Paris in his book *God, the Church and the Priesthood* tells us that "the priest is an envoy, a messenger, an official invested with God's powers in dealing with men, and hence the apostolate is founded, not so much on a command from Christ, as on Christ himself: 'As my Father has sent me, even so I send you'

(Jn 20: 21)."[8] The Father sent his only-begotten Son, "not to condemn the world but that the world might be saved through him" (Jn 3: 17). The priest is God's envoy sent to the world to preach the word of salvation. He receives his power and his mission from God, whose messenger he is. Therefore, as Pope Pius XII reminded us in *Mediator Dei*, he is not an official elected by the community. The community cannot give him his instructions, nor can he say the things the community likes or wants to hear. It is only from God, through his Church, that the priest receives his powers and the words he is to utter, whether people like them or not. For this reason he cannot be surprised at times to find himself undergoing the same experiences as those other divine heralds, the prophets—resistance from those in authority, misunderstanding on the part of the people, being treated as if he were a leper, contempt and fear. Have we forgotten that God commanded Isaiah, "Cry aloud, spare not, lift up your voice like a trumpet, declare to my people their transgression, to the house of Jacob their sins" (Is 58: 1)? The priest is bound to find that he has to do just this now and again, perhaps often or even very often. Can he expect such words to sound pleasant or to be received with great joy always and by everyone? Can he expect it to be easy to shake people out of their sleep when their souls have been numbed by the gentle comfort of letting themselves be carried along by the good things of this world, firmly attached to this present life and afraid of anything that might remind them of death or hell?

Finally, if the priest is to be a genuine instrument of unity, he must begin by practicing it himself. On this point he must be careful to relax no more—and indeed perhaps much less—than on other points. Without ceasing to be very human—and unless he is human he will be unable to understand everyone and everything—he must nevertheless remain on a transcendental or supernatural level. Consequently he has to strive with all his strength to keep his brothers and sisters closely united around their common shepherd, Christ's vicar, remembering that a priest entrusted with the care of souls must practice charity first and foremost by looking after the faithful. But he must always remember also that there are many lost sheep straying far from the fold, separated from the Church, and that she loves them dearly and suffers for them. If he is to unite these separated brothers and sisters while at the same time keeping the others united, he will be successful only on condition that he himself remains identified, united, fused with his own shepherd, and through him, with the visible head of the Church. This, however, will be impossible without a deep desire for holiness, because "there can be no ecumenism worthy of the name without a change of heart. For it is from newness of attitudes, from self-denial and unstinted love, that yearnings for unity take their rise and grow toward maturity" (UR 7).

This is so because the priest is not there to cause division or to bring death, but to impart unity through that charity which is Life. The bond of union is love, charity, and whenever there is division, it can safely be said that the Spirit of Christ is absent, for there is no charity—if there were, there would be no division. The priest's responsibility in this respect is tremendous, for it is a terrible thing to destroy the Mystical Body of Christ, to tear its members apart, when his function is precisely to mold the faithful into the unity of the total Christ.

Obviously the priest is a special person and his position is one beset with difficulties. He is the ambassador of a world distinct from the one in which he lives, sent to remind people of many saving truths (which at times are repellent to their fallen nature), invested with extraordinary powers, bearing a message of salvation and yet subject for that very reason to a hard and lonely life.

It is very difficult to express adequately the priest's great dignity or the greatness of his vocation. Much has been given to him but much is also demanded of him. If there is anyone who is not allowed to live his own life, that person is the priest; if there is anyone denied the right to have personal problems, that person is the priest; if there is anyone to whom all human reward or any kind of selfishness is forbidden, that person is the priest, for, as Pope Paul VI said, he is a man who lives not for himself but for others, he is a man of the community. There is no more heroic task than his, no more difficult situation, no greater responsibility. Neither, however, is there anything more sublime, more self-sacrificing, more exciting than the priesthood.

The priest's place

The place and the function of the priest are clearly outlined in those brief words already quoted: he is "appointed to act on behalf of men in relation to God" (Heb 5: 1). Now, if he is to act on behalf of men he must be in contact with them, living among them, therefore he has to live in the world. The diocesan priest is not someone who lives apart from everyday reality; on the contrary, he is profoundly and fundamentally secular. If he is to fulfill the function for which he was chosen and consecrated, his place is with other men, wherever ordinary life is going on in the midst of the world; for the world is his place, the environment surrounding him, the atmosphere in which he breathes and which he must purify.

When he does this, he is only following in the footsteps of his Master. Whether in Nazareth, where he was busy working as a carpenter until he reached the age of thirty, or in Jerusalem, Judea, Samaria, Galilee and the Decapolis, where he spent the public stage of his life, Jesus lived among people, surrounded by the things of the real world. And if the priest is to imitate him in this respect, he must imitate him also in the other. For Jesus was undoubtedly in the world but he was not *of* the world. He himself clearly laid down the attitude his disciples should adopt on this point: "They are in the world. . . . They are not of the world, even as I am not of the world. . . . As thou didst send me into the world, so I have sent them into the world" (Jn 17: 11, 16, 18). So the priest neither is, nor can be, in the world like other human beings: he is there because the Lord has sent him, just as He himself was sent by his Father. He must be in the world, not as someone belonging to the world, but as Jesus was, namely as an envoy belonging to a region different from the world in which he lives.

He is in this world to act "in relation to God." His whole purpose, the justification for his being here at all, the reason why he has been sent by God, is that he may be concerned with the things of God while dealing with people living in the world. He is concerned with divine things, not human things. Here, as elsewhere, he has to follow the Lord's example. On a certain occasion when he was surrounded by a crowd—as often happened—Jesus was teaching the people. During a pause in his speech, one of his listeners intervened to put forward a personal problem of his own: "Teacher, bid my brother divide the inheritance with me." This might have seemed a good opportunity for the Lord to give a lesson on how an inheritance should be divided, to do a good deed and make peace between two brothers by dividing their property fairly between them. He has only to say a few words and the problem would have been solved. But the words he spoke were of a very different kind and were probably quite unexpected: "Man, who made me a judge or divider over you?" (Lk 12: 13-14). He dissociated himself completely from the problem put to him, for the simple reason that he was sent to mediate, not between men, but between God and men, between men and God. Problems arising between men should be resolved by men.

Similarly the priest must assiduously avoid getting involved in purely human disputes, arguments, problems or affairs. Like his Master, he is not here to mediate between individuals in their disputes, as if he were just another man, but only to act on behalf of them in relation to God. If, on the other hand, he does get involved in matters of this kind as a mere man among men, he should scarcely be surprised if his prestige and his dignity as a priest should suffer as a result; for it is he himself who reduces them to such a low level by concerning himself with problems which he was not sent to solve. As Pope Pius XI wrote in *Ad Catholici Sacerdotii*, the object of his mission is not human or transitory things, however important or lofty they may seem, but divine and eternal things. The second Vatican Council stresses the same point when it tells us that "it is true that those in holy orders can at times engage in secular activities, and even have a secular profession. But by reason of their particular vocation they are chiefly and professedly ordained to the sacred ministry. . . . But the laity, by their very vocation, seek the kingdom of God by engaging in temporal affairs and by ordering them according to the plan of God" (LG 31). Any other attitude would be wrong and would lead, not to the conversion of the world, but to its "clericalization."

What he can and should do whenever a human problem of this kind arises, as at all other times, is to carry out the mission entrusted to him by giving doctrine and raising people up to a supernatural level, rather than lowering himself to the purely human plane. This is what the Lord did, for he made use of the man's request concerning the inheritance to show how sad and indeed foolish it is to be anxious and to fill your heart with things which you may have to leave behind that very night if your soul is required of you (Lk 12: 20).

It's not easy, at least it's seldom easy, to explain simply and precisely something complex in itself, such as the relationship between the priest and the world. Possibly due to the influence of the spirituality proper to religious orders, from an ascetic point of view a very specific attitude to the world has traditionally been stressed, namely the idea that it is the enemy of the soul, an earthly city standing in opposition to the heavenly city.

This view of the world is certainly not the result of old, out-dated, extremist or medieval ideas, as perhaps we in the last decade of the twentieth century might think. The Gospel shows us two worlds on earth existing side by side simultaneously. This is evident especially in Saint John, where our Lord himself clearly points out a difference between the earthly city, governed by the "ruler of this world" (Jn 12: 31), and the place of those redeemed by faith and grace, between "this world," to which God's kingdom does not belong (Jn 18: 36), and the kingdom of God, which nevertheless is "among you." "This world" is not yet saved, not yet brought into the fold in actual fact, though capable of being saved, for of course the redemption has made its salvation possible; it is a world still governed by the law of sin, with its back turned towards God. It is a world turned in upon itself.

The priest is in this world. He has to live and perform his duties, therefore, in an adverse environment. As Pope John XXIII put it, his position obliges him to live in a world permeated by an atmosphere of excessive liberty and sensuality, often morally alone, seldom fully understood. It matters little whether he lives in a city or area with many Catholics, for they too are submerged in the same climate and the priest's role is to help them breathe the pure air above him, lest they die of suffocation. In this sense the world is understood as the earthly kingdom standing in opposition to the heavenly kingdom, the kingdom of sin as distinct from that of grace, the kingdom of fallen nature. It is a world that will last as long as there is life on earth.

Throughout its history, this world has been seen in many different guises, although in substance it has always been the same. "For all that is in the world, the lust of the flesh and the lust of the eyes and the pride of life, is not of the Father but is of the world" (1 Jn 2: 16). The temporal circumstances determining the character of earthly realities have varied along the course of this unended path which men have been treading from the appearance of the earth to the present day. There have been enormous variations in the structure of society—if we contrast, for instance, the Roman Empire with the critical period of the Barbarian invasions or the Middle Ages and the profound differences ranging from the barbarian kingdoms to the monarchies of the fourteenth century, the Renaissance, the "Enlightenment" of the eighteenth century, the era of industrialization and now the atomic era—nevertheless, beneath them all, nothing has changed as far as the deepest reality of life on earth is concerned. There always has been, and until the end of time there always will be, a conflict between grace and sin, and the question of how redemption is to reach all men. There is only one real problem, namely salvation or damnation. Whatever guises it may have adopted in the course of human history, life is simply a battle-ground. And the priest is at the heart of the battle.

These considerations explain his peculiar position in the world. First of all, like his Master he is a sign of contradiction. Whenever he appears, as Cardinal Suhard says, passions immediately crystallize, coalitions are formed, love and hatred spring up instantaneously and concentrate around him, he is the touchstone of consciences.[9] He is never ignored, for his very nature makes him a living witness to the "other world" and his mere presence speaks to men and women of that hereafter which they would so often like to forget.

He is a strange man and a lonely man. This is inevitable since he is situated on the boundary between those two worlds. He is in this world and yet he belongs to another world which he has not yet entered. Consequently "he is the everlasting outsider who is supposed to be not of this world, a man who has been removed from the purely human sphere, one whom men think of as alien and peculiar. He is a being signed and separate, a man who stands at the margin of life, and who is yet continually drawn to its center."[10] He is a strange man, at the center of life and and yet somehow apart from life, for he represents the permanent element in the continuous ebb and flow of living situations. Indeed, he could not be a minister of Christ if he did not dispense and bear witness to another life distinct from this earthly life, yet neither could he serve men if he remained alien to their life and their circumstances. So he lives and remains amid the noise and activity of this world, while at the same time having his roots firmly fixed in eternity. He is here and yet he is not here, he lives and yet he lives not, he is present and yet he is absent.

Undoubtedly he is a man, a man like other men, participating in everything human, yet he is not at all like other men, he cannot and must not be like them. After all, he has been singled out from among them, consecrated and sent back to them. The consecration which impresses this particular character on him makes him different from others and places him apart from them. It does not dehumanize him, however, it does not change his human nature or affect the stirrings of his heart. Nevertheless, even here his way of loving is different from that of other people. It is a love in Christ which, however great—or precisely because it is so great—leaves the heart always free, free because it has been given to God and cannot be monopolized by any mere creature.

In the world of today the priest is seen as an enemy by all those who are intent upon building a paradise on earth, for whom religion is the opium of the people, for whom God is a myth and the Church an outdated institution. With this mentality, it is only natural that the priest should be considered a deceiver and a fraud. However, this attitude to priests is nothing new; in fact, it is an anachronism, for Jesus was also regarded as a deceiver and a fraud; he was accused of cheating the people. He was treated as a deceiver precisely because he came to destroy all hopes of an earthly messianism.

For many other people, of a more superficial type perhaps, whose objective seems to be to drink the delights of this world to the lees, selfish to the core, with no problems of any kind apart from the inherent difficulties of deriving as much personal enjoyment as possible from all the pleasures this life can offer, the priest is only an embarrassment, an obstacle to their enjoyment. For, as Sellmair says, "the world sees that he places at the very center of existence something which, even when it recognizes it, it will only tolerate at its periphery—God and his reality. He appears to the world as the representative of that other world which is invisible and full of mysteries which, almost without their knowing it, the majority of men fear."[11] They cannot look happily on someone whose very presence reminds them that we have no lasting city (Heb 13: 14), that the journey through this life is only a step towards eternity. He is bound to be an embarrassment if he upsets the superficial, calm and inert nonchalance of people who have put their souls to sleep, if he denounces the veneer that conceals injustice and shame, dishonesty and selfishness, vice and evil. They want no one to come along who might stir the stagnant waters, lest any of the mud stick to them. And the priest's function is precisely to make himself heard, to remind people of what they must and must not do, what is not allowed, what is unjust— to arouse desires of purification. He has to preach the spirit of poverty in a climate where greed and possession of wealth have become ends in themselves, he has to preach chastity in a world where sex-appeal is used even to sell toothpaste, washing-machines or soap, he has to preach love of the truth when people all around him tell lies, behave hypocritically and turn their back on the truth. He has to preach humility, patience, meekness, love (genuine love, not what the world means by that word), self-denial, penance for sin, mortification and the cross. It is not surprising that for many people, the Sadducees of today, the priest is nothing but a nuisance to be avoided at all costs.

Then there are the mean, calculating types, for whom religion is first and foremost—not to say almost exclusively—a pillar of the establishment, of the *status quo*, and the priest, being a minister of religion, is just a prop that helps to support the established order and keep things as they are. These are people who have learned to serve two masters, as anxious to avoid the risk of becoming saints as to preclude the danger of being damned, afraid of going too far in the love of God, lest it diminish their love for the good things of this world. They have made the golden mean into an unobtrusive compromise with mediocrity. Selfish people like this who love, or say they love, and respect the priest, because they know what he is and what he stands for, but yet cannot quite refrain from involving him, the Church and religion in so many outward manifestations of support, have been largely responsible for causing the Church to be accused—though quite falsely—of keeping her members in feudal subjection.

The priest must be fully aware of where he is and what he is doing there. "This world," by definition, will never be on his side, it rejected the Lord and it cannot but reject his ministers: "If the world hates you, know that it has hated me before it hated you. If you were of the world, the world would love its own, but because you are not of the world, but I chose you out of the world, therefore the world hates you" (Jn 15, 18-19). So the priest must be fully aware also of what he can, and must, expect from this world.

Far from frightening him, however, all these factors which go to make his situation so difficult and so strange, so full of contrasts and so beset by problems, ought to inspire him with supernatural courage capable of overcoming all the obstacles he may find in his way: "Behold, l send you out as sheep in the midst of wolves" (Mt 10: 16), "if they persecuted me, they will persecute you" Jn 15: 20). There is one very powerful reason why he should be courageous and that is the word of God: "I have said this to you, that in me you may have peace. In the world you have tribulation, but be of good cheer, I have overcome the world" (Jn 16: 33).

As another Christ, the priest will always overcome the world, whatever tribulations he may encounter. He will always triumph, in spite of everything, if only he remains faithful to his mission, if only he offers no resistance to the grace of his priesthood, but lets it penetrate him and transform him, if only he makes his priesthood his whole life. His most powerful enemies

—the world, the flesh and the devil—have no power over him: "Be not afraid of them, for I am with you to deliver you, says the Lord" (Jer 1: 8). Opposition, indifference or even flattery are of no avail; nor are any attempts to escape from the word of God and its messengers: "But you, gird up your loins, arise, and say to them everything that I command you. Do not be dismayed by them, lest I dismay you before them. And I, behold, I make you this day a fortified city, an iron pillar, and bronze walls, against the whole land, against the kings of Judah, its princes, its priests, and the people of the land. They will fight against you, but they shall not prevail against you, for I am with you, says the Lord, to deliver you" (Jer 1: 17-19).

A word of caution, however, is necessary. Too much emphasis on this particular view of the world, however accurate, might lead to a wrong attitude, because a judgment may be correct but may nevertheless be one-sided, it may be the truth, but not the whole truth. Therefore it would not be right for a priest, or even for any Christian, to have an aversion to the world or regard it as an enemy to be defeated—among other reasons because if God so loved the world as to give his only-begotten Son that it might be saved through his mediation, how is the priest to hate what God so loved? It is to save this same world, the real world in which we live, and not to condemn it, that priests have been ordained.

It would be wrong for a priest to be so naive as to be ignorant of the real circumstances of the world in which he has to exercise his duties; to avoid this mistake he must be careful not to forget these basic facts. Unless he knows them and is aware of them, he may well be captivated by the world to such an extent that his work as a priest becomes fruitless. Neither, however, should he allow himself to be so totally and exclusively influenced by this view of the world that he decides to abandon it to its fate. "When things are seen in this way, churches become the setting par *excellence* of the Christian life. And being a Christian means going to church, taking part in sacred ceremonies, being taken up with ecclesiastical matters, in a kind of segregated 'world,' which is considered to be the ante-chamber of heaven, while the ordinary world follows its own separate path. The doctrine of Christianity and the life of grace would in this case brush past the turbulent march of human history, without ever really meeting it."[12]

That quotation is from Blessed Josemaria Escriva, a secular priest who showed us what the priest's secularity is and what it ought to be. "I have taught this constantly using words from holy Scripture. The world is not evil, because it has come from God's hands, because it is his creation, because Yahweh looked upon it and saw that it was good (see Gen 1: 9-31)." Therefore "your ordinary contact with God takes place where your fellow men, your yearnings, your work, and your affections are. There you have your daily encounter with Christ. It is in the midst of the most material things of the earth that we must sanctify ourselves, serving God and all mankind."[13]

A substantial part of the priest's saving mission consists of giving back to the world that cleanliness of which sin deprived it. However, that world which has its own "ruler," that world for which on one occasion our Lord deliberately did not pray (Jn 17: 9), is not the *whole* world. The priest cannot confine himself to looking with pessimistic indifference at those impersonal crowds, masses of people separated from God, inert multitudes seeking nothing but the daily satisfaction of their physical needs, like flocks of sheep or herds of goats. "What noble passion there is in this apparent indifference, what hidden possibilities! He must serve them all, place his hand on each one of them as Jesus did, to return them to life, to enlighten their mind and strengthen their will. . . . And we shall then make of the flock an army, of the herd a regiment, and we shall single out of the drove all those who are not content to be unclean."[14]

To restore all things in Christ, everything in heaven and everything on earth" (Eph 1: 10)—if this is God's wish, then no priest can allow himself to have such a totally negative opinion of the world, of this world in which he lives and has to encounter Christ, that he considers it lost even before seeing its immense possibilities, before finding the mark which God the Creator, Redeemer and Sanctifier has left on it. Neither, of course, can he have such an exalted idea of the world that he thinks it is the gospel or the Church that should be reformed for the world's sake, as if this were the stable element while the gospel could vary and fluctuate. This would not save the world but would undoubtedly lose the priest.

Every period of history requires a new effort, a different emphasis, on the part of the priest. Our own particular era, like all times of crisis, demands a greater effort than most. Shortly after the Second World War, Cardinal Suhard described the situation as follows: "The crisis now affecting the world greatly surpasses the causes which provoked that crisis. The war is part of it, with its resultant calamities. But the disorder unleashed by the war did not end with the war: it comes from further back and goes further on. The ruins are a disaster, they are also a symbol. Something has died on earth that will not rise again. The conflict that has ended thus acquires its true sense: it is not an intermission but an epilogue. It signals the end of a world. But at the same time the era initiated after the conflict has the characteristics of a prologue; it takes us into the drama of a world in the process of being made."

The birth of a new world: here we have a situation similar to that at the time of the Renaissance or at the end of the ancient world and the beginning of the medieval period. The Church emerged from each of these crises with very different results. At the end of the ancient world, in the crisis provoked by the decay of the Roman Empire and the Barbarian invasions, she had men of spirit and learning capable of infusing that spirit and that learning, which they had received from the gospel through the Church, into the world they saw emerging. Thus, in spite of all the human deficiencies and all the vicissitudes, the new world was a Christian world. But the men whom the Church had at her command during the Renaissance were very different: a hierarchy which had long been over-worldly and not very competent in matters of doctrine, a decadent and rather uncultured clergy, including some popes who were lax and careless in observing the signs of the times, tending their flock, and fulfilling their function. So the modern world was not modeled by the Church; the new era of history was not shaped by the supernatural spirit of the gospel, but by a human spirit. The Counter-Reformation produced many saints, introduced new methods and institutions, promoted countless zealous works, but—in human terms—it came too late. The gradual secularization of life, which reached a low point in the worldliness, secularism and general religious ignorance at the end of the nineteenth and beginning of the twentieth centuries, was possible largely because of the same conditions that brought about the triumph of the Reformation, namely the worldliness of the consecrated men whom the Church had at her command.

Once again today the Church finds herself in a situation where she can win back large numbers of souls for Christ, where she can repossess everything worth saving, everything good and true in the thought and culture of the modern world, as she did with the pagan culture in the latter period of the ancient world, where she can use all the techniques, all the advances, all the discoveries of our civilization as instruments of salvation in the service of God and of souls.

The Church is quite prepared for this. To prove it, if proof is needed, we have the documents of the Second Vatican Council, to mention but one clear example. Indeed she has always been prepared: today, as well as at the time of the Renaissance and during the crisis of the ancient world. The Church has never failed, for she is holy, she is Christ's spotless bride. It is men who have so often failed, consecrated men in whom she had put her trust and on whom she relied, men who, in one way or another, have not responded adequately and have been found wanting, men devoted to her service who have not always reached the spiritual and human standards required for that service. It is the Church's servants who have so very often failed to serve her.

The struggle to remain faithful

"This is how one should regard us, as servants of Christ and stewards of the mysteries of God. Moreover it is required of stewards that they be found trustworthy" (1 Cor 4: 1-2).

Trustworthiness. Above all else that is what is required of a priest, Christ's minister and dispenser of God's mysteries: trustworthiness and fidelity to his priestly character, faithfulness to his mission, loyalty to the doctrine he has received, sincerity even to his own humanity, to his human qualities.

However, trustworthiness, faithfulness, is not a gratuitous gift which one possesses and retains without effort, without any act of the will, independently of the circumstances or the situation. Rather, it is a treasure which has to be protected against all the enemies attempting to snatch it away, it comes only after a struggle and it is the prize conferred on the victor. The life of a priest in the world—in a world which is hostile, by definition—is far from being a soft and comfortable existence. Ordination to the priesthood does not bring comfort but conflict, for "Has not man a hard service upon earth?" (Jer 7: 1), and this is especially true of the priest because of his special mission and indeed because of his priesthood itself.

Joseph Sellmair poses the problem from a personal point of view in a rather forceful way. In effect, he says, the priestly profession implies the sharpest contrasts—heaven and earth, nature and supernature—while between them both is the priest, a mediator between these two worlds. Can he, then, achieve interior harmony and soften these contrasts, or must he rather be an example, a victim of the universal discord in which all creation has been moving ever since the primitive order was broken down? In his position as mediator, Sellmair continues, the priest runs the risk of adopting an equivocal attitude, never finding his rightful place, never properly working out the correct relationship with his environment and with mankind. He runs the risk of seeing the very center of his being swung to one side, his character distorted and deformed, his very nature falsified.

He cannot allow the center of his being, to use Sellmair's expression, to gravitate excessively to the human side or become so "humanized" that in fact nature obscures, stultifies or annihilates the supernatural element of his priestly character. Neither must he move to the other side, however, becoming so "dehumanized" as to be reduced to a caricature of a man—after all, his nature will never allow him to be an angel. So, above all, he has to achieve that balance, that equilibrium, that harmony, so perfectly achieved by the Man who was God, his master and model, and this is precisely the purpose of his training, as we shall see later.

The first thing and, we could truthfully say, the most important thing required of a priest is that he should not "be conformed to this world" (Rom 12: 2). He must not allow the world to change him; rather, it is he who should change the world in accordance with the spirit of the gospel—that is why he is in the world and that is why he is a priest. If the world changes the priest, if he conforms to the world, then the world has triumphed over him; he cannot be another Christ, for the ruler of this world had no power over Christ (Jn 14: 30). He is a creature modeled by the world in its own image and likeness, a person whom the world has made its own. He is no longer another Christ, for he does not bear his seal. He cannot be a mediator, for he has taken sides with those who have no wish to be saved. He is not a man of God, but a man of the world. No longer is he someone who has given himself up but rather someone who has been made a prisoner, for he has exchanged the freedom of Christ for vile servitude by letting the world take possession of him; in short, he is a broken instrument, a useless collaborator. There is nothing more sad than a worldly or world-dominated priest. In the conflict between God and the world to win his trust and loyalty, he has chosen to let himself be captured by the world. Anyone who has read Graham Greene's novel *The Power and the Glory* will have seen something of the tremendous inner sadness weighing so heavily on the priest who has allowed himself to be trapped by the world.

The pressure brought to bear on the priest by all those factors jointly known as "the world" is total, for it embraces everything. All that exists is composed, in fact, of what is either outside a man or inside him or in the area separating the one from the other. And since the disciple is not above his Master, the priest is not exempt—nor is there any good reason why he should be—from the test which (because his love for us forbade him to dispense himself from anything that might be a help, a consolation or an encouragement to us) the Lord willingly underwent.

The "ruler of this world" twice tried to tempt Jesus away from his loyalty to his Father, and both of those occasions were decisive ones in his life—when he was about to commence his ministry and when he was about to undergo his passion. It is particularly interesting to notice the lesson involved in the first temptation, which took place in the desert when Jesus had ended his forty-day fast in the wilderness. Matthew (4: 1-11) and Luke (4: 1-13) tell of this episode, which is so well known to priests because they preach on the subject at least once a year.

"If you are the Son of God, command these stones to become loaves of bread" (Mt 4: 3). The temptation seemed an innocent one. Jesus was hungry after forty days of prayer and fasting. Was there anything very wrong in satisfying his need, in using his power to change those stones into food in order to sustain him physically? Surely he had a right to revive his strength? Nevertheless, he chose not to do so. There was a hidden trap laid to ensnare his trustworthiness: the temptation was, in fact, to use the supernatural for the benefit of the natural, to place high things at the service of low appetites, to exercise for his own personal good the powers conferred upon him as an envoy for the fulfillment of his mission. If he had yielded to that temptation, he would have been using supernatural faculties to obtain temporal benefit.

This is the way of the "lust of the flesh," a way which the priest must always keep carefully guarded. We shall bear not only the burden of our bodies, until the moment of death, but also the weight left by original sin and the instincts which, because of that same sin, tend to be accomplices of all kinds of temptation, if not the main cause of the temptation itself.

The struggle to counterbalance that dead weight of our nature must be as continuous as the pressure exercised on us by the weight itself, and it must be as continuous as the attacks of our disorderly instincts. The temptations we have to undergo are not just of the crude, carnal type which are easy to identify and whose very coarseness would put any priest's sense of delicacy on its guard. These are certainly not the most dangerous kind. Obviously the temptation in the desert was anything but crude in this sense.

One temptation that can slip in almost unnoticed is that of "professionalism," the tendency to make the service of God and souls—not deliberately, of course—into a business, a way of earning a living. In "Catholic" countries more than in others the priest enjoys a status which perhaps he would not have as a layman. He has a certain security, however precarious, and a certain, usually not so precarious, prestige. To use his priesthood to obtain benefits of a temporal kind, to make use of it as a way of earning a livelihood—perhaps even an easier way than others, in that it involves no competition or rivalry, and there is always support if necessary—would be almost to prostitute his vocation and profane something holy. Love of comfort, lowering of standards, the line of least resistance and carelessness are all symptoms and consequences of losing the priestly spirit, which can be suffocated by the stench of the world in its most vulgar form. And "Ho, shepherds of Israel who have been feeding themselves!" (Ez 34: 2). Such a priest changes from a man with a mission into an official, in the worst possible sense, a paid religious official. Instead of serving the Church, he makes the Church serve him. He rests comfortably on his status and sits back to enjoy whatever he can get, inevitably taking whatever compensations he can find along the way and exploiting them to the full. Since he is a lonely man (for he is not allowed human love like other men), his loneliness begins to weigh heavily upon him and the danger of forming certain attachments begins to raise its ugly head. His celibacy becomes a burden, sometimes borne ungracefully or in a way that shows nothing of the joyful gift of the love which he has offered to God. Certainly he carries out his duties—what less could he do?—but making a mean distinction between duties in justice and duties in charity. He becomes more and more involved in temporal affairs and in things of this world.

Such a man is like the living corpse of a priest, for he has lost all his enthusiasm and energy, his spirit of faith, his supernatural view of the Church. He may sometimes retain some vestige of dignity, like the main character in Georges Bernano's novel *L'imposture*. Sometimes he loses even this and then presents to the eyes of the world around him the sad spectacle of a priest reduced to the condition of a poor wretch who sinks so low as to pick up with great eagerness the crumbs that fall from the world's table, so laden with attractive things for its own intimates. He reaches the stage of being totally void of any inner impulse; he may still adore God with his mouth and his lips, but his heart is far from him and his concern for souls is nil.

"If you are the Son of God, throw yourself down, for it is written, 'He will give his angels charge of you,' and 'on their hands they will bear you up, lest you strike your foot against a stone.'" (Mt 4: 6). Jerusalem was built on Mount Sion, the temple stood at the highest point in the city and the pinnacle was the highest part of the temple. Let us imagine for a moment an expectant crowd, with all eyes raised to the top of the temple. Suddenly they see Jesus throw himself into space; angels come and guide him gently to the ground; the multitude is delighted and excitedly acclaims the Messiah; there is a mass conversion—Pharisees and Sadducees, scribes and priests, all included—a quick, spectacular and overwhelming success.

This would have been very easy for Jesus. Without prompting from any tempter, he could have achieved the same effect by a similar method any time he chose. But on this occasion, too, the ruler of this world was disappointed. The Lord could not use his supernatural powers to crush men's most noble faculties which make them like God—namely their intelligence and their will. He could not wrest from them, by undue influence, something they ought to give freely; for to act freely the will must be moved by reason.

This is the lust of the eyes. Here the means used by the world to worm its way inside the priest, to empty him of all his supernatural spirit and set itself up in its place, is not his own body but external things. The temptation to seek success in the world is one of the strongest of all, because it is directed at a particularly sensitive point, namely, human vanity. The priest is "a man without arms or money, a living opposer of the world's common law, an exception to the rule, an irritating witness to what the world regards as an outworn past," as Cardinal Suhard says; and there is a danger that he might attempt to abandon a position in which his apostolate may have had little success and adopt a different one which he might consider more effective and capable of yielding faster and better results. If he gives in to this temptation, he will come to regard success as depending on human means, on his own ability, technique or attractive personality.

Such a man tries to win the world by cajoling it, using "modern" methods acceptable to the world, making concessions as a bait on the hook, diluting the true doctrine wherever it seems a bit too harsh or rough for the worldly palate. In his desire to get close to the world in order to win it over to Christ, he runs the risk of becoming as "modern" and carefree, as "advanced" and as merely human as anyone else, making many imprudent errors and being saved only by a miracle from doing much worse. All this action takes control of him, to the grave detriment of his spiritual life. Chautard portrayed this type of deviation from the priestly ideal very cleverly in a really useful book which every priest ought to read carefully and in detail. The danger of allowing secularity to degenerate into worldliness is almost inevitable if a priest's center of gravity swings away from the inner to the outer life. For want of stability, he is then carried along by what Kipling might call the wheel of life and ends up being ground to pulp. He may sometimes even feel tempted to ask the world's forgiveness for what he regards as the Church's failure, or to apologize for what he sees as other priests' conservatism. Genuinely concerned for the fate of the world and worried by its estrangement from God, he may feel himself more closely identified with it than with other priests, his brothers, whom he considers to be lacking in understanding, reluctant to move with the times and still living in medieval stagnation.

This kind of temptation hangs over the priest particularly today and is so subtle that it is capable of causing many problems. Indeed in all times of crisis when there are praiseworthy and arduous attempts at renewal, there is the danger—as Pope Paul VI has pointed out—that some people should feel "tempted to believe that only what is new, what is modern, what coincides with the hopes of the contemporary world is alive. The temptation at once arises to reject what was done and thought yesterday, to abandon traditional discipline and theology, to regard everything as impugnable—as if we had to begin to establish the Church today, to reformulate its teaching not so much on the basis of revelation or tradition as of the temporal realities among which contemporary life goes on, in order to give life to new forms of thought, of spirituality and customs, on the pretext of endowing our Christianity with an authenticity only now discovered and comprehensible only to the people of our own time." This would undoubtedly be one way of attaining that *aggiornamento* sought by the Second Vatican Council, but a way in which, to use the words of Pope Paul VI, the Church, "far from deriving therefrom new forms and virtues . . . would end up by resembling this world which, on the contrary, looks to her for a ray of her light and a taste of her salt, rather than a complacent acquiescence in its own questionable theories and profane customs."[15]

When the world captivates the priest through the lust of the eyes, it puffs him up with pride and blinds him; he becomes a blind man leading the blind (Mt 15: 14), and both he and they come to a sad end. He may still have some warm feelings—more sentimental than real—for souls, but he has no light to impart.

"All these I will give you, if you will fall down and worship me" (Mt 4: 9). There is nothing subtle here, the devil no longer says "if you are the Son of God." He now attacks from the front, concealing nothing. He had shown Jesus "all the kingdoms of the world and the glory of them," and here he offers them all in return for one act of adoration. This is his last card, he is gambling to win all or nothing. This is obviously a different approach from those he had tried before. If Jesus possessed all the kingdoms of the world and had complete control over them, surely it would be easy for him to impose his message, and lead them along the path of salvation using his power and influence to achieve his ends.

This is the third way of the world: the "pride of life." Pride, the root of all sin, huddling quietly deep down in every one of us, never totally destroyed and always ready to raise its head—pride, the will to power, the desire to dominate. This is another testing-ground on which the priest's trustworthiness and fidelity may be tried, also in a surreptitious way, although this seed is so strongly rooted in us all that the Enemy seldom has to deceive us to ensure that this temptation gains entry to our soul. Here the basis of the problem is not the body or external things, but something already inside us.

The world's victory over the priest by this method leads to "clericalism.'" The "clerical" priest actually wants the Church to dominate the world. Rather than the world's conversion to

God, he is seeking the subjection of the world to ecclesiastical control.

By some unconscious mental process, such a priest regards the Church as a power attempting to gain control of the world, rather than as the bride of Christ or his Mystical Body. Far from restricting her activity to the kingdom of God, he would extend it to include dominion over temporal affairs of the type in which the Lord himself studiously avoided becoming involved. He is not content that the Church should act exclusively from within, from deep within the world by transforming people, as grace works in the soul by transforming human qualities. He wants her to operate in a more direct way, dominating and determining society and the State, institutions and customs, just as the old Calvinist system attempted to do. It is as if his gospel were confined to the Old Testament, not the New. His idea of a hero is closer to the Pharisee, forcing orthodoxy on everyone, than to Jesus Christ, who so deliberately respected the freedom of others. His strength is not his humility, but his pride; his weapon is not the cross, but the power of authority. This produces the kind of authoritarian priest, full of his own importance, who governs rather than feeds his flock, inspires fear and terror rather than confidence, gives orders rather than patient and courteous advice. This type of man is portrayed in sacred scripture: "The weak you have not strengthened, the sick you have not healed, the crippled you have not bound up, the strayed you have not brought back, the lost you have not sought, and with force and harshness you have ruled them. So they were scattered, because there was no shepherd" (Ez 34: 4-5).

It is remarkable how clearly the Council has corrected this error for anyone who reads the conciliar documents carefully and properly. In particular, the detailed treatment of the laity's vocation to the apostolate is highly significant, for they "share in the priestly, prophetic, and royal office of Christ and therefore have their own role to play in the mission of the whole People of God in the Church and in the world" (AA 2). This role consists of "penetrating and perfecting the temporal sphere of things through the spirit of the gospel."[16] Therefore, as Msgr. Escriva pointed out, "we must reject the prejudice that the ordinary faithful can only confine themselves to helping the clergy in the Church's apostolic undertakings. The apostolate of the laity need not always consist merely of participating in the hierarchical apostolate; since they have a divine calling, as members of the people of God they have a duty to be apostles. This is not because they have received any canonical mission, but because they are part of the Church. And they fulfill that mission through their occupation, their work, their family, their colleagues, their friends."[17]

Pride may also cause a priest to fall into another danger, the danger of fanaticism. In this case he runs the risk of becoming intransigent, uncompromising—not with error or distorted ideas, but with anyone who deviates from his own particular way of looking at things. He may become inflexible to the point of seeing treason in every dialogue, dogmatic to the extreme of wishing to suppress every possible nuance of discrepancy, every area that is not totally black or totally white, confusing and equating the truths of faith with mere pious beliefs, the permanent with the transient, divine teaching with ecclesiastical customs, habits and traditions. He may become passionate to a degree that his reason is blurred, harsh to the point of condemning all adversaries, stubborn to the extreme of total obstinacy. When a priest is overcome by the world through his pride, some light may still remain flickering in him, but there is absolutely no warmth, and he reaches the stage of repelling the very people whom he sets out to attract.

To remain faithful at all costs, through all the temptations and attractions of the world, in all places and in all circumstances, whatever may happen and whatever the situation, is an attitude truly worthy of a priest, a man of God. A priest is "the salt of the earth; but if salt has lost its taste, how shall its saltiness be restored? It is no longer good for anything except to be thrown out and trodden under foot by men" (Mt 5: 13). A priest is "the light of the world" (Mt 5: 14). So what is to become of the world if it immerses the priest in its own muddy waters and puts out the only light that can guide it through the darkness? God relies on the priest to give taste to a tasteless world, to act as a beacon for those lost on the high seas, trying to find their way through the raging storm. The Church looks to him to distribute the bread of life and the word of salvation to many of her children languishing far from her bosom, hungry for life and for truth, even though they are often unaware of it themselves.

The priest must be faithful and trustworthy. He cannot cheat God; he has no right to fail the Church; he must not abandon all those people who are crying out to have their frozen inner vacuum filled by the warmth of the divine presence in their soul. What does all the power of this world matter or all the strength of the spirit of darkness? Has not the Lord said "Let not your hearts be troubled, neither let them be afraid?" (Jn 14: 27). For the priest is never alone. God himself gives him all the strength he needs, provided only that he places no obstacle in its way but accepts it and is willing to use it. To overcome the lust of the flesh he has to fulfill the first of the conditions laid down by Jesus for his disciples: "If anyone would follow me, let him deny himself" (Mt 16: 24). After all, he is of no significance, he counts for nothing; only God and his will are of any importance. To overcome the lust of the eyes, he must embrace the cross and expect no human success other than that which the Lord himself reaped as the fruit of his love for men— the gallows and shame, solitude and failure. He cannot attempt to advance any faster than his Mother the Church, nor must he try to push her along paths of his own choosing or use any means other than those she puts at his disposal, for she is a Mother, a teacher, a faithful spouse. To withstand the temptation of pride, above all else he should try to be humble, wishing to obey rather than to command, to offer suggestions rather than to impose his will. For he must realize that his strength lies in meekness, patience, love, generosity, and respect for all who are made in the image and likeness of God and for their freedom. His sphere of activity is not the social, political, economic, administrative structures of a country, but the souls of people redeemed by Christ with his own blood. Let him never forget that he is there to act on behalf of men in relation to God, not to improve the organization of temporal affairs. It is not institutions or structures he has to transform, but people, and they themselves will do the rest.

Nothing is impossible for the priest who is faithful to his priestly mission and function. As an envoy of God, he can rely on God for support. "If God is for us, who is against us? He who did not spare his own Son, but gave him up for us all, will he not also give us all things with him? Who shall separate us from the love of Christ? Shall tribulation, or distress, or persecution, or famine, or nakedness, or peril, or the sword? . . . For I am sure that neither death, nor life, nor angels, nor principalities, nor things present, nor things to come, nor powers, nor height, nor depth, nor anything else in all creation, will be able to separate us from the love of God in Christ Jesus our Lord" (Rom 8: 31-39).

On a priest's faithfulness many important things depend—perhaps the salvation of millions of souls, their peace and happiness even in this life, their joy. Many people who are lost rely on him to show them the goal of their journey. Countless others, overwhelmed by confusion in the great wide world, depend on him to point out to them the meaning of their life, the purpose and object of their existence. The devil knows all these things, for he genuinely exists, he is very active and truly terrible, and he takes careful aim at the instrument in order to destroy it, because he is powerless to touch the Force behind the instrument. If he can corrupt or disable a single priest, his joy is comparable only to the sadness—if we may use such an expression—felt by our Lord. Therefore the struggle to be trustworthy and faithful is hard, arduous and very demanding. However, there is a great reward and great honor to be won. "Now, therefore, if you will obey my voice and keep my covenant, you shall be my own possession among all peoples; for all the earth is mine, and you shall be to me a kingdom of priests and a holy nation" (Ex 19: 5-6).

2

The Ministry

WHAT IS THE PURPOSE, the function, the nature of this unusual man, living as he does in such difficult circumstances, surrounded by so many dangers that his whole life is one long battle, destined for such great things that no other person on this earth can surpass him? Why is it that he has to remain alone and isolated on the frontier between two worlds, has to fight bravely on, full of understanding and love for all men, who after all are his brothers and sisters. He is beset by all kinds of tribulation, yet never losing courage, "afflicted in every way, but not crushed, . . . persecuted, but not forsaken, struck down, but not destroyed . . . always carrying in the body the death of Jesus, so that the life of Jesus may also be manifested in our bodies" (2 Cor 4: 8-10).

If, as Alvaro del Portillo said, *nature* and *mission* are the two complementary and inseparable aspects of the Church's overall outlook, then we must consider the priest's mission if we are to understand and grasp his priestly nature, for this is the aspect that complements and explains it. We can understand someone fully only when we know his purpose, the function he has to exercise. The same is true of the priest: he is quite incomprehensible if taken separately from the mission, the purpose, which he was ordained to fulfill, for only this explains why he is a man sealed with a divine destiny.

As Pope Paul VI said, "above all else, the priest has been ordained to celebrate the eucharistic Sacrifice in which, in *persona Christi et nomine Ecclesiae*, he offers to God sacramentally the passion and death of our Redeemer and at the same time makes them into food for his own supernatural life and that of the faithful, to whom he must make every effort to distribute it widely and worthily; the ministry of the word and of pastoral love must converge on the ministry of prayer and sacramental action where they will find inspiration and support."[1]

The priest's nature and function are thus determined by the fact that he is a man chosen to participate in Christ's eternal priesthood. From the beginnings of time, there has been no event so important, so great or so decisive as the redemption. And in comparison with these events—the incarnation of the Word, the life, passion, death and resurrection of Jesus—all other happenings in the world, from the invention of fire or the wheel to the great philosophies of Aristotle or Hegel, are as children's games, transparent shadows, fleeting figments of the imagination with no real texture.

The object of the redemption was to reconcile man to God, an object, therefore, with a two-fold aspect, namely God's glorification and men's salvation. And what impelled the only-begotten Son of God to humiliate himself to the extent of assuming our human nature was his love for us.

The priest, therefore, as another Christ, can on no account set himself an objective other than that set by his Master, the eternal Priest. That same two-fold purpose which determined the action of Christ must also guide the priest's conduct, activity and ministry. As far as he is concerned, God's glorification and the salvation of souls must be translated into the search for personal holiness—giving glory to God directly—and the exercise of his ministry, the apostolate: bringing souls nearer to their Creator. These objectives are not really different things, but only different aspects of one and the same thing, for personal holiness and the ministry are so intimately connected that they can hardly be separated.

An example from physics may help us to see the relationship between holiness and the apostolate, between life and the ministry, a little more clearly. There is a principle which says that when two bodies come together they generate heat. So if a man hits a table very hard with an iron bar, he will undoubtedly produce some heat. But the amount of heat generated will be very slight, in comparison to the effort expended and, if it is struck hard enough, the table may well break into pieces—cold little pieces. On the other hand, if the person in question takes a little time, puts the iron bar into a fire, waits patiently until it becomes red hot and then brings it into contact with the table, the effects will be seen immediately, a fire will begin to blaze and it may even spread in all directions.

A priest whose heart is cold, who has lost all his supernatural warmth, can still carry on a great amount of apostolic activity, but he will soon feel exhausted from the effort expended; and the souls with which he is dealing, once the initial effect of his efforts has worn off, will probably be as cold at the end as they were at the beginning. On the other hand, if he concerns himself first and foremost with his spiritual life, if he makes that the most important thing, if his heart is burning with love of God, then wherever he is, whatever apostolic work he does, he is bound to set souls ablaze with his own interior fire.

No one can give what he doesn't have. The soul for which the priest has to answer to God, before any other, is his own. One who, on the pretext of doing apostolic work, is careless about offering to the Creator the tribute of his own total self-surrender, who neglects to make every possible effort to seek union with God by all the means at his disposal, or who fails to follow eagerly St. John the Baptist's example: "He must increase, but I must decrease" (Jn 3: 30), is not giving glory to God.

Scripture tells us that Jesus began "to do and to teach" (Acts 1: 1) and *The Way* comments: "First, action: so that you and I may learn."[2] The man who fails to practice what he preaches is portrayed in very harsh terms in the gospel: "The scribes and the Pharisees sit on Moses' seat; so practice and observe whatever they tell you, but not what they do; for they preach, but do not practice. They bind heavy burdens, hard to bear, and lay them on men's shoulders, but they themselves will not move them with their finger" (Mt 23: 1-4). They are blind guides, however alert their mind may be, for action is indispensable for the fulfillment of the ministry; it is essential to do as well as to teach. "You brood of vipers! How can you speak good, when you are evil? For out of the abundance of the heart the mouth speaks" (Mt 12: 34).

Thus a holy life is an essential prerequisite for any apostolate and this, in turn, will be an expression of the love of God which the priest bears in his heart. Therefore the apostolate is not, and cannot be, an occupation, a mere activity, something cut off from his life. Either it is the overflow of his life "within"[3] or else it is not genuine apostolate however much actual activity is carried out. A priest cannot lead a double life, a two-faced existence. If his apostolate, the exercise of his ministry, is not the expression of a soul that loves God and that feels the same compassion as Christ did for the crowd, "harassed and helpless, like sheep without a shepherd" (Mt 9: 36)—if it is instead just a job to be done like any other human occupation, then its chances of bearing fruit are slight and the risk the priest runs of finding himself figuratively torn apart is very great.

When speaking of the priest's ministry, his apostolate, we can hardly overemphasize the importance of pleasing God primarily through personal sanctity, for this is so closely connected with his mission. Probably nothing can do so much harm to souls as seeing a priest whose ministry and behavior seem to go their separate ways or even to contradict one another—a priest whose actions and the tenor of whose life seem to belie the very things his lips are preaching. The most important thing for him is to practice what he is going to preach: then he will is in a position to pass on the teaching which he has lived

What gives a priest apostolic zeal is his love of God, his spiritual life. When St. Paul was in Athens, waiting to be joined by Silas, "his spirit was provoked within him as he saw that the city was full of idols" (Acts 17: 16). He didn't rest until he found a way of preaching the Lord Jesus to those people, taking advantage with supernatural skill of the opportunity offered him by a basic characteristic of their life—their curiosity—for "all the Athenians and the foreigners who lived there spent their time in nothing except telling or hearing something new" (Acts 17: 21).

It is this zeal, this energy, that makes the priest an apostle, endowing him with a kind of sixth sense which allows him to take advantage of any situation, the slightest opening, to bring souls to God. And he is able to do this in such a way that it neither tires, nor upsets nor bores, as an artificial or imprudent zeal often does. This is what gives apostolic work a certain spontaneity, because for the priest with enthusiasm and energy, the term "doing apostolate" has practically no meaning—just as to say that a healthy person is "busy breathing" would be meaningless—it is simply the expression of an inner life which expresses itself (and nourishes itself too) in caring for the welfare of souls.

We can see the same attitude in the emphasis which the Second Vatican Council lays on the close connection between life and work, glorification of God through personal holiness, and glorification of God through the salvation of others. "Priests will attain sanctity in a manner proper to them if they exercise their offices sincerely and tirelessly in the Spirit of Christ" (*Presbyterorum Ordinis* 13). The priest's work, the exercise of his office, is a source of sanctification. But "priestly holiness itself contributes very greatly to a fruitful fulfillment of the priestly ministry . . . . ordinarily God desires to manifest his wonders through those who have been made particularly docile to the impulse and guidance of the Holy Spirit. Because of their intimate union with Christ and their holiness of life, these men can say with the Apostle: 'It is now no longer I that live, but Christ lives in me' " (PO 12). The priest's holiness, his spiritual life in Christ, is a source of apostolic activity.

Preaching

Preaching the word of God forms part, and an extremely important part, of the priest's special mission. St. Paul shows this with some very convincing logical arguments in his epistle to the Romans: "For 'every one who calls upon the name of the Lord will be saved.' But how are men to call upon him in whom they have not believed? And how are they to believe in him of whom they have never heard? And how are they to hear without a preacher? And how can men preach unless they are sent?" (Rom 10: 13-15). As far as people are concerned, the purpose of the priest's mission is their salvation. But there can be no salvation for anyone other than through Jesus Christ; he is the only way that leads to God, he alone can save. Our desire to be saved is expressed by invoking the name of the Lord, but for this an essential requirement is that we should believe in him. We call upon someone when we think he can be of help not when we are convinced he can do nothing for us. And how are people to believe in him if they do not know him, if he is a complete stranger to them? Obviously it is necessary that someone should speak to people about God, otherwise they will never hear of him, will never get to know him, will never believe in him, or call upon him and be saved. Therefore "priests, as co-workers with their bishops, have as their primary duty the proclamation of the gospel of God to all" (PO 4).

Authority is demanded by the very nature of the word to be preached and proclaimed. It is not just any word, but the word of God, who is *The Word.* Jesus pointed out that he himself had been sent and that he spoke only what the Father had taught him (Jn 8: 28). He assures us that "he who sent me is true, and I declare to the world what I have heard from him" (Jn 8: 26). This is the word which makes those who hear it clean (Jn 15: 3), the word which nourishes them (Mt 4: 4), the saving word which Jesus Christ, Son of God, preached and deposited in his Church. Only the holy, Roman, catholic, and apostolic Church, the Church of Christ, has the fullness of the word of salvation and only she, who possesses it in its fullness, can teach it in its fullness.

This task of teaching the word of God was explicitly entrusted by Christ to his apostles: "Go therefore and make disciples of all nations . . . teaching them to observe all that I have commanded you" (Mt 28: 19-20). This magisterial faculty is exercised by the Church through the apostles' successors; they alone possess it by express delegation from the Lord.

Priests, then, have been sent to teach, they have been sent in the same sense and in the same way as the apostles. "As the Father has sent me, even so I send you" (Jn 20: 21). All their power is based on the fact that they have been sent by him who has supreme authority, and it is from him that their authority comes, not from their own personal qualities, their eloquence, their preparation, or even their training. These personal qualities—eloquence, preparation, and training—obviously influence their way of expounding the word of God, Christ's message, but in no way do they affect the essentials, for these are independent of any human authority.

There is another point to be clarified here also. The priest has been sent with a very specific commission, namely to preach Jesus Christ and to make his message known. This is stated quite explicitly. "Preach *the gospel* to the whole creation" (Mk 16: 15). By virtue of the command he has received, the priest's commission is precisely to preach the gospel, the good news of our salvation, and nothing else. It is a mission that refers to *all* creation, all mankind. Whether people are willing to listen to him or not has no effect whatever on the exercise of his mission: he has been sent to *all* men by Christ who is God, and whose redemption embraced all men.

The fact that he has been sent to preach the gospel must form the basis of all our thoughts and reflections on this aspect of the priest's ministry. This aspect is important, more important perhaps than is often realized. This is not difficult to see if we examine carefully that passage in the Acts of the Apostles which deals with the appointment of the first deacons. When the numbers of Christians in that first church at Jerusalem began to grow and the complexities of government consequent upon those numbers also began to increase, the apostles came to a decision: "It is not right that we should give up preaching the word of God to serve tables." To avoid this, seven deacons were appointed and then the apostles could say, "We will devote ourselves to prayer and the ministry of the word" (Acts 6: 2,4). Thus if the apostles considered prayer and preaching to be so important as to oblige them to delegate other duties, then these two activities are certainly important enough to constitute the priest's primary duties among the tasks involved in his state and his ministry.

On the subject of preaching, Pope Paul VI said, in his encyclical *Ecclesiam Suam*, "We want to stress once more the very important place that preaching still has, especially in the modern Catholic apostolate and in connection with the dialogue which is our present concern. No other form of communication can take its place, not even the exceptionally powerful and effective means provided by modern technology: the press, radio and television. In effect, the apostolate and sacred preaching are more or less synonymous terms. Preaching is the primary apostolate. Our ministry, Venerable Brethren, is before all else the ministry of the word."[4]

So there is a certain equivalence between apostolate and preaching. To be an apostle means to be sent but, as St. Paul explains, "Christ did not send me to baptize but to preach the Gospel" (1 Cor 1: 17). Every priest is an apostle and has been sent to spread the message of salvation, the gospel, which is our hope in Christ, as St. Paul again reminded the Ephesians, who were also filled with hope when they had heard "the word of truth, the Gospel of your salvation" (Eph 1: 13).

Preaching the word is not just an honorary prerogative which the priest enjoys; it is also, and most especially, a duty, a grave obligation. The word of salvation must be spread and made available to everyone, for God "desires all men to be saved and to come to the knowledge of the truth" (1 Tim 2: 4). The priest must therefore never slacken in urging himself, in driving himself, to fulfill this duty, for people's salvation depends on the word of God. And how strongly the Lord expressed this through the words of St. Paul: "For if I preach the gospel, that gives me no ground for boasting. For necessity is laid upon us. Woe to me if I do not preach the gospel! For if I do this of my own will, I have a reward; but if not of my own will, I am entrusted with a commission" (1 Cor 9: 16-17).

"Woe to me if I do not preach the gospel!" Priests do not always fully realize the responsibility they have in mankind's salvation or condemnation; perhaps the world around them worms its way gradually into their hearts and weakens their enthusiasm. The ignorance of religion in the world is immense, however, millions of people do not know Jesus Christ. The truth which could set them free, the teaching of Christ (Jn 8: 31), is still available to only a very small proportion of mankind, in spite of the fact that it was revealed for all. No priest can be complacent when he remembers that in Athens, St. Paul's "spirit was provoked within him as he saw that the city was full of idols"(Acts 17: 16). In the world today, there are still many people who have never heard of the Truth. Many more turn their back on God to adore a new image of man based on some ideology or other, though perhaps not daring to abandon God completely. Some try to forget him by filling their hearts and their minds with things of the earth; while still others know no better than to live in a very hard world, totally separated from the supernatural, without light in their life, without warmth in their hearts, easy prey to any pseudo-redeeming doctrine that promises them a wisp of hope even in this life. A large part of mankind "struck with wonder at its own discoveries and its powers . . . often raises anxious questions about the current trend of the world, about the place and role of man in the universe, about the meaning of his individual and collective strivings, and about the ultimate destiny of reality and of humanity" (GS 3).

Without complexes of any kind, without fear of anyone or of anything, with every right—for the truth has a right to be taught—and with total freedom, for "the word of God is not fettered" (2 Tim 2: 9), the priest must make contact with all these people and teach them the doctrine of salvation. He has no right to remain silent. Woe to him if he does not preach the gospel! "Wherever the message of the Lord is taught, there is the Lord himself" (Didache).[5] To abandon the ministry of the word would be to hinder the presence of the Lord in many places; to neglect it would be to merit grave punishment, for scripture says: "cursed be he who does the work of God halfheartedly" (Jer 48: 10).

This is where the priest must be especially careful in the matter of faithfulness, for it is Christ's teaching, not his own opinion, that he must make known, and Christ's teaching as it has been handed down through the Church, without any personal interpretations or additions. Both these points are of great importance.

As far as the first point is concerned we may quote a very clear and expressive passage by St. Vincent of Lerins: "'Guard what has been entrusted to you' (1 Tim 6: 20). But what is something that has been *entrusted* to you? It is what has been given to you, not what you yourself have found; what you have received, not what you thought up; not a matter of invention but of doctrine; not of private use but of public tradition . . . whose author you should not be, but its guardian. . . . Preserve inviolate and spotless the talent of the Catholic faith. What was entrusted to you, you should keep and you should hand over. You have received gold: deliver gold; . . . do not shamefully replace the gold with lead. . . . Teach the same things as you have learned, though you may say things in a new way, do not say new things."[6]

Neither was St. Vincent saying anything new when he wrote this; he was only practicing what he preached by passing on the teaching laid down by St. Paul: "So then, brethren, stand firm and hold to the traditions which you were taught by us, either by word of mouth or by letter" (2 Thess 2: 15), and "even if we, or an angel from heaven, should preach to you a Gospel contrary to that which we preached to you, let him be accursed" (Gal 1: 8). "If any one teaches otherwise and does not agree with the sound words of our Lord Jesus Christ and the teaching which accords with godliness, he is puffed up with conceit, he knows nothing; he has a morbid craving for controversy and for disputes about words" (1 Tim 6: 3-4).

Here lies a danger for the priest when engaged in this ministry—the danger of becoming involved in controversies and disputes about words. This danger would arise if he were to lose his simplicity either through excessive zeal, desire for recognition and applause, or over-confidence in his own intelligence. The human spirit is very ingenious and can easily tarnish the supernatural purity of Christ's message with its own effervescence. In this regard, the priest should be careful not to trust his own ideas unduly, however brilliant or clear they may seem. He should not be over-anxious to keep up to date by reading every article that appears; for the message of salvation, which has been complete for many centuries, doesn't change; and it is the message, not the theories, hypotheses or interpretations surrounding it, that has to be taught. This danger seems especially endemic today due to the many books of the "theology-fiction" type that are being published, the many personal and subjective interpretations of the mysteries of faith that do not emanate from the Church's magisterium, and the publicity given in the press to trends and attitudes presented as mature reflections which in fact are no more than the untested theories of individuals or small groups. But there is no need to insist any further on this point, Popes Paul VI and John Paul II have dealt with it repeatedly in recent years and their views are well known.

Sometimes a priest may unconsciously allow himself to be carried away by a desire to adapt Christ's teaching to the historical circumstances of his time, and he may end up quite far from his initial starting point. In this he may often be motivated by praiseworthy intentions but at the same time be unduly influenced by the climate of the world around him. St. Paul considered it necessary to leave Timothy in Ephesus simply to "charge certain persons not to teach any different doctrine, nor to occupy themselves with myths and endless genealogies which promote speculations rather than the divine training that is in faith" (1 Tim 1: 3-4).

The priest is a minister of the word; he is not, and cannot be, an argumentative person. He is a man who has received the command to teach the truth and who teaches it. Therefore he has no need to quote scientific authorities to support his statements. The Church's authority is all he needs, for the Church has sent him and it is the repository of truth. On the other hand, he must take great care that the doctrine he preaches should be—at the very least—the Church's "common teaching." For the personal opinions of this or that theologian, this or that school, group or movement are supported by no authority other than that of their authors, and however holy or wise those may be, their ideas in themselves have no value whatsoever as far as salvation is concerned, for they are merely the ideas of men and valid only in so far as they coincide with the teaching of the Church's magisterium. As the German bishops pointed out in a pastoral letter issued not long after the close of Vatican II: "uncertain theories should not be the subject of preaching. Theological controversy has its rightful place in the Church, but it is not a fit topic for preaching. If it mingles with the Church's teaching it frequently provokes confusion."[7] In the course of time, the Church, whose magisterium on matters of faith and morals is infallible, may adopt certain ideas either wholly or in part, because they satisfactorily illustrate, clarify or explain some points of the revealed truth—never because they add or change anything, for no man can extend or alter the word of God. Then, when these ideas have become part of the "common teaching," the priest may use them, confident that he is not deviating in the slightest from the Church's views or embarking on intellectual adventures.

We can never sufficiently emphasize that it is the Gospel, the word of God, and not the word of men, that must be preached. The Lord himself had to reprimand the Pharisees rather sadly on this point: "In vain do they worship me, teaching as doctrine the precepts of men" (Mt 15: 9). Historical and temporal circumstances are mere forms and we are concerned with doctrine, the unique and invariable doctrine, valid for all men and for all times, destined to condition the lives of men whatever the historical circumstances in which they live—it is this doctrine that has to be preached. Otherwise we run the risk of seeing our preaching become so influenced by the passing fashions of each particular period of time, that Christ's message may be contaminated by human trends alien to it, disturbing and polluting the truth which is permanent and timeless. In the thirteenth century, for example, sermons frequently dwelt on people's duties towards the king, the duties of subjects, respect for the established social order, obedience, and submission. Today the danger lies in going to the other extreme: becoming demagogues when we should be preaching detachment; stirring up class strife by pointing out social injustices when what we should foster is love, understanding and generosity; using the Church's social teaching as a bait to win the workers and the poor and deprived. Yes, we have to be careful about our fidelity to Christ's teaching lest, as a way of salvation, instead of the living word we offer nothing but a dead letter.

Although priests ought to be careful about this point at all times, there is one situation above all others in which they have to be particularly aware that their task is not to teach their own wisdom but God's word" (*PO* 4). This situation arises each time a priest has to preach at a liturgical act, and particularly during the liturgical act *par excellence,* the sacrament of the altar.

In those circumstances the liturgy of the word takes the form, not so much of preaching, as proclaiming. The priest reads the sacred texts officially chosen as readings, he puts them forward in the name of the Church, which thus offers the faithful the saving word, of which she is the repository, through the ministry of the priest acting on her behalf. The manner in which the proclamation is made deserves careful attention. The priest should give the texts their proper meaning and read them with the tone and feeling of a man pronouncing sacred words, with all the seriousness and respect due to God's message to men.

The homily should set out above all else to instruct and edify the faithful by Christ's teaching. Preaching at Mass is not an interruption in the holy sacrifice, a blank space in the liturgy to be filled in by the priest; rather, "the two parts which, in a certain sense, go to make up the Mass, namely, the liturgy of the word and the Eucharistic liturgy, are so closely connected with each other that they form one single act of worship" (SC 56). The priest is not supposed to preach on his own personal ideas or on subjects alien to the liturgy itself, however important or topical they may be, much less read parish notices, for precisely "by means of the homily, the mysteries of the faith and the guiding principles of the Christian life are expounded from the sacred text during the course of the liturgical year" (SC 52). The passages of scripture chosen by the Church for the readings are not allocated at random, but are always related to the liturgical period of the year and specially selected as appropriate to prepare the souls of the faithful for the contemplation of one or other of the great mysteries of our redemption.

It is not a question, therefore, of using the scripture to say something good which the priest thinks would be useful or suitable. On the contrary, his teaching and his subject matter must be deduced from the word of God. This word is not to be reduced to a mere excuse or some kind of ornament for the lesson the priest has decided to teach. Here we see precisely where he has to avoid any attempt to achieve personal recognition, but must seek only the good of his listeners. He must *sentire cum Ecclesia*, be of one mind and heart with the Church, for on these occasions he is the Church's spokesman in a particularly solemn and official way.

Since the ministry of the word is such a delicate and important matter and the priest has so many limitations, how is he to fulfill such a task? Perhaps we may answer again that, as in everything else the priest has to do, it is a question of collaboration between God and the man he has chosen as his instrument. With this in mind, the priest has to play his part to the best of his ability and leave the rest in God's hands, secure in the knowledge that his Master will not leave the work unfinished. And, at least at first sight, it would seem that his own part consists of competence, simplicity and love.

Competence means preparation. There is no need to insist on the importance of this. But how is it to be done properly? The immediate procedure is easy, it consists of studying the subject, consulting books, looking at, for example, the homilies of St. Augustine or St. John Chrysostom or the sermons of the Curé of Ars, using some of the books of sermons for the various liturgical periods, or manuals with suggestions on the Gospels and epistles, commentaries and quotations from theologians and the Fathers, even models and stories to illustrate points. There is no shortage of suitable material.

However, there must also be a less immediate type of preparation, otherwise the result, at best, may be nothing more than an excellent, even erudite, piece of sacred oratory and, at worst, the recital of a well learned lesson, like a conscientious schoolboy. This less immediate preparation is the more important of the two: "I believed, and so I spoke" (2 Cor 4: 13), says St. Paul very forcefully. Certainly the immediate preparation must not be neglected. Obviously we must think of what we are going to say to our congregations. But first we must *have* something to say. And the person most likely to have something to say is normally, not the person who needs to study the topic each time, but the man who is filled with the teaching of Jesus Christ and, like the good scribe, at any given moment can produce from the storehouse of his heart new things and old. Only the priest who lives a deep spiritual life has this kind of basis, because daily reading of the scriptures and spiritual books, the truths of which he transforms into life through his daily prayer, keeps the Truth, which is Christ, constantly before his eyes. When a piece of doctrine is so fully assimilated that it has become part of our life, when the Gospel is familiar to us because we have contemplated the Lord a thousand times in our reading and in our prayer, then our words are saturated with faith and ring true, because "out of the abundance of the heart the mouth speaks" (Mt 12: 34). What we then have to offer our congregation is not just a lesson well learned, but truths which are living and well lived.

Let us turn once again to the authoritative words of Pope Paul VI. "We must return to the study, not of human eloquence or of empty rhetoric, but of the genuine art of proclaiming the word of God. We must search for the principles which make for simplicity, clarity, effectiveness and authority, and so overcome our natural ineptitude in the use of this great and mysterious instrument of the divine word, and be a worthy match for those whose skill in the use of words makes them so influential in the world today and gives them access to the organs of public opinion."[8] The difficult art of speaking is the instrument which the priest must use if he is to make Christ's message available to the ears and the hearts of his listeners. But we are not living in a period favorable to rhetoric or eloquence, which far from making it easy to pass on the divine word in all its purity, frequently obscures it, drowns it in tremendously florid images, metaphors, quotations . . . and verbiage. Sometimes the doctrine is so wrapped up, so heavily disguised, that it is quite invisible. "Is not my word like fire, says the Lord, and like a hammer which breaks the rock to pieces?" (Jer 23: 29). If this is so, why then do we have to replace the Lord's word with unnatural language, since the language of scripture is so simple in itself that we can scarcely make it any clearer? It was Bossuet who said that a single word from the Gospel has more power over souls than all the vehemence and all the ingenuity of human eloquence.

The priest must always remember that his object is, or at least should be, the spiritual welfare of his listeners, their edification in doctrine and in faith, never his personal success. St. Paul established this very clearly: "We speak not to please man, but to please God who tests our hearts" (1 Thess 2: 4). And this holds true both for what we say and for how we say it, for the teaching itself and the way we present it. It would be very difficult to imagine the Lord's disciples, or the priests of the churches founded by St. Paul in Asia Minor, Macedonia and Greece, or those first seven deacons, being concerned with composing pieces of oratory. Indeed we may say that if their preaching— which we know from the Acts of the Apostles—had any formal feature at all, it was its simplicity, the total absence of any artifice. Instead of speeches, they gave explanations; rather than practicing oratory, they simply spoke or talked.

If the priest genuinely wishes to edify his listeners, and if he fully realizes that his function is to teach them the good news of salvation, he will try to find the best means to reach their minds and their hearts. He will go by the straightest way, which is always the shortest, that is, the way of simplicity. He will simply tell his hearers what the Lord said and, if necessary, explain it to make sure it is properly understood. And the explanation he gives will be the Church's explanation, not his own personal or subjective interpretation. For if he is simple he will follow the example of his Master: "With many such parables he spoke the word to them, as they were able to hear it" (Mk 4: 33). Even a summary reading will show us the different methods used by Jesus when dealing with the theologians in Jerusalem, with the scribes and Pharisees who knew the scriptures, and with the simple villagers and fishermen in Galilee.

If he is to be faithful to his mission, it is not sufficient for the priest to *possess* the word of salvation. He must also be able to *express* it in a way that will make it comprehensible at all times, whatever the circumstances of his hearers. He must be able to state the truth of the gospel and make Christ known, adapting his words in each case to the mentality of his listeners and their particular situation. In short, he must possess and practice what Blessed Josemaria Escriva called the "gift of tongues."

Furthermore, he must honor the word he preaches and make every effort to live in accordance with the truth he teaches. And he must do so with love, which is the soul of preaching. "Of no avail is the speech of him that teaches," says St. Gregory the Great, "if he cannot show the incentive of love."[9] The priest who exercises the ministry of the word is not a galley-slave making forced labor out of what Paul VI called "the primary apostolate." If he is genuinely an apostle, that is, an envoy, with every fibre of his being, then he cannot but share those sentiments which St. Matthew tells us the Lord felt: "When he saw the crowds, he had compassion for them, because they were harassed and helpless, like sheep without a shepherd" (Mt 9:

36). If he has interior life, he will have love of God; if he has love of God, he will love his fellow men; if he loves his fellow men, no effort, no trouble will seem excessive if it might help or benefit them. St. Peter says: "If you speak, speak as one who utters oracles of God" (1 Pet 4: 11). This is precisely how the priest should speak, for if he is a man of God, wisdom should speak through his mouth, and, as another Christ, he should be filled with compassion for everyone, as was his Master.

If there is love in him, he will seek the welfare of those who hear him. Forgetting himself, realizing his limitations, he will rely on the grace of God more than on his own human capabilities. If he has love of souls, he will take the steps necessary to ensure that his preaching yields fruit. And knowing that natural means can never produce supernatural effects, he will have recourse to prayer and mortification so that the word of salvation may penetrate into the minds and hearts of his hearers. St. Paul proceeded in this way; he confessed that he preached the Gospel "not with eloquent wisdom, lest the cross of Christ be emptied of its power" (1 Cor 1: 17). How, then, are we to explain the fact that he had so little success in Athens, although he had probably never delivered a more thoughtful, well structured, logical or convincing speech? On other occasions, in other places, people embraced the faith in sufficient numbers to allow him set up a church; and that was because, as in the case of Lydia, the Lord opened their hearts "to give heed to what was said by Paul" (Acts 16: 14). For this same reason St. Gregory the Great could truly say "that if the Spirit of God does not inwardly assist the heart of the hearer, the word of the teacher is of no avail."[10]

The priest is first and foremost a sower, a tireless sower of seed. His work consists of sowing, watering, weeding, and doing all the work the field requires for its cultivation, but never forgetting that it is God "who gives the fruit" (1 Cor 3: 6). The two instruments he has to use in order to obtain this fruit from God are prayer and sacrifice. Without them there is a grave danger that he will produce nothing, whatever his eloquence, however detailed his preparation. If fruit does appear despite his indolence, he can only conclude that it has grown, not because of him, but in spite of him, and his conclusion will not be wrong.

Administration of the sacraments

Another of the priest's essential functions is to administer the sacraments, the signs which both signify and produce grace. "Sacrament" is a word meaning "mystery." In fact, both refer to things which are sacred, and at the same time mysterious, because their nature, their operation, and their effect on people are realities whose deepest essence can't be grasped by reason alone.

"Christ is always present in his Church, especially in her liturgical celebrations. . . . By his power he is present in the sacraments." If "the liturgy is considered as an exercise of the priestly office of Jesus Christ . . . every liturgical celebration, because it is an action of Christ the priest and of his Body the Church, is a sacred action surpassing all others. No other action of the Church can match its claim to efficacy, nor equal the degree of it" (SC 7). Man's attitude to the sacred, to the mysterious, should be one of great veneration, respect and attentiveness. He cannot treat lightly or casually realities whose greatness and whose very nature are quite frightening. The priest's demeanor in administering the sacraments should in itself be a living lesson to the people; his attitudes and conduct should reflect the holiness of the mysteries whose minister he is.

Of course the sacraments are effective independently of the priest who administers them. They work *ex opere operato* and therefore one could almost say that the priest is of little significance. This is certainly true as far as the sacraments themselves are concerned, but it is not quite accurate with regard to the faithful, for these receive grace according to their capacity, which the priest could decrease by any attitude that weakens their faith.

It should also be mentioned that what really matters is not the external demeanor, but the inner attitude, for "not what goes into the mouth defiles a man, but what comes out of the mouth, this defiles a man" (Mt 15: 11). However, we must remember that the priest is not divided into air-tight compartments, all adopting different or even opposing attitudes. He is a single unit, whose outward attitude and behavior is always the result of an inner frame of mind. Anyone who is careless about his external conduct is unlikely to be careful inwardly, for coarse behavior can never be compatible with delicate and refined sentiments—and this applies to a priest as much as to everyone else.

It is a human trait that constant repetition of a particular action creates a habit. A priest, being human, is no exception to this. Anything we do over and over again eventually requires very little real attention on our part, the habit can easily degenerate into mere routine. If he is not careful and constantly on the alert, the priest runs the risk of becoming accustomed to sacred things to such an extent that even the most magnificent aspects of his ministry may deteriorate and become almost mechanical. If he mumbles the words of the ceremony when administering Baptism, looking around him (for constant repetition has taught him the formulas by heart); if he intersperses instructions to those helping him, the sacristan, or the people; if he conducts the ceremony hurriedly or in a way that shows even the least observant of the congregation that he is thinking about something else; or if he looks bored and shows that he is doing it just because it is a duty and that he has little interest in what he is doing; he is very probably weakening the faith, the respect, the humility and even the patience of those present. His behavior proclaims aloud that he has no interest in the ceremony; it is a chore he has to carry out whether he likes it or not, and his heart is far away; he does only the minimum to give the sacrament its validity. Sometimes the faithful wonder if such a priest really believes what he himself teaches about the sacraments (actions of Christ, who performs them through men, as Paul VI reminds us in *Mysterium Fidei*), for his attitude does not reveal the respect and veneration that such holy things should arouse (especially in him), nor does his way of administering them show the delicacy and diligence due to things which really should be touched only with the tip of one's soul, as has been said.

All of these considerations become especially important when we realize, as the Church teaches, that "because they are signs they also instruct. They not only presuppose faith, but by words and objects they also nourish, strengthen, and express it;

that is why they are called 'sacraments of faith' " (SC 59). As a minister of the sacraments, the priest has to do his best to be both imbued with the transcendental importance of the liturgical act he is performing and conscious of his obligation to edify the faithful by placing the meaning of the sacramental signs within their reach. But it would seem unlikely that he will be very successful unless he pays attention to everything he is supposed to do, down to the slightest detail—from the gravity and dignity of the gestures down to the deliberate and intelligible pronunciation of the words used.

Let us pause for a moment to pay special attention to one of the sacraments in particular, both because of the frequency with which every priest administers it, and because his human personality has a more significant role to play in its administration than in the others. We should go into this particular sacrament in some detail for, of them all, "penance occupies an outstanding place in the ministry of priests" (Alvaro del Portillo). It is probably when hearing confessions that the priest can best fulfill a function commended to him by the Second Vatican Council, namely that of helping the faithful to see "what is required and what is God's will in the great and small events of life" (PO 6). He can have no better opportunity than confession and spiritual direction to educate people in their faith and to give them sound ideas so that, as Christians, as disciples of Christ, they can go out and 'Christianize' the world through their work, their family life, their social and political activities. Here the priest is able to direct each of his penitents according to the particular circumstances of the time and place in which he or she lives, and to help them insofar as he can with any specific problems they may have.

Every priest, and indeed every Christian, knows that the sacrament of reconciliation is first and foremost a court hearing, the tribunal of penance, but with very simplified formalities and procedure. The defendant, the sinner, is both prosecutor and accused, the priest hears the case, judges and imposes a penance, a punishment, for the offenses committed. However, this tribunal is much more than just that, for unlike secular courts, it is an instrument not of justice —fortunately for us—but of mercy. Its purpose is not to safeguard or protect society, but to save sinners, and instead of condemning the offenders to jail to make them pay their debt to society, it absolves and frees them from the bonds with which sin had been holding them prisoner. When a priest exercises the office of confessor he knows that he is, above all else, a judge. But it would be an error—and one which might have grave consequences—to think that he is nothing more than a judge. Moral theology has taught him that to exercise fully and properly the office of confessor, he must also be a father, a teacher, a physician, that is, a shepherd full of concern for his flock. His function, therefore, is not simply to judge actions or conduct, coldly and in accordance with certain objective rules, a certain moral code. If a priest acts merely as a judge, forgetting that Jesus Christ, in whose place he stands, loves us so much that he constantly intercedes for us, "then" as Karl Adam says, "spring up in the impoverished soil of the soul the arid growths of mere morality, and with them all of that contorted virtue, extreme asceticism, and intense scrupulosity which now and again turn the glad tidings of the Gospel into tidings of terror."[11]

Not all the factors involved are purely objective, that is, actions to be judged and moral rules to be applied, for it is important to consider subjective elements also. The rules do not change but people are all different, so much so, that one and the same violation of a rule, and one and the same sin, may be extremely grave in certain cases and almost insignificant in others.

The priest is undoubtedly a judge and has to decide on the degree of blame or the gravity of the offense. But he is also a father and, as a father, he must be understanding, he must delve into the complexities of the soul with whom he is dealing, take its circumstances into account, consider its past history, know the details of the person's life, weigh up all the factors—and all this with a father's heart.

As a teacher, he must teach. People often know so little about the things relating to God! So he must point out the obstacles, open up new horizons, suggest useful ways.

He is also a physician and, as such, must heal the sick. Some souls are gravely ill and he must attend them with infinite patience, treat wounds and bind them up, as the good Samaritan did to the man who had been set upon by thieves (Lk 10: 30-37).

A confessor's whole attitude must be impregnated with understanding and concern, fairness and compassion, for he is a shepherd, a good shepherd; and this means that, if he fulfills his function as our holy Mother the Church wishes, then he always acts as a spiritual director, whether he likes it or not, indeed whether he realizes it or not. If he understands, teaches and heals, then he is guiding souls towards God and this is precisely what is meant by spiritual direction. Obviously the more he knows about human nature, about the circumstances in which people live at this time, their habits and environment—and obviously too the better he knows himself, the deeper his spiritual life, the more widely he has read—the more easily will he understand, teach and heal, in other words, the more easy will he find it to direct souls. This is another good reason for him not to neglect himself, for he will have to render an account not only of the evil he has done, but also of the good he could have done and failed to do.

The first thing a confessor must learn is that he has no right to be shocked or scandalized by anything he hears in the confessional, however awful it may be. Clearly the author of the epistle to the Hebrews knew this when he wrote that the priest "himself is beset with weakness" (5: 2). No sin, however enormous, should surprise a priest. Apart from the fact that Jesus, his model, was never shocked by anything—not even by the supreme sin committed by his people. The priest, as a man, in spite of all the special attention and exceptional graces he has received from God, is himself capable of anything, even the most abominable things, if once he lets go of God's hand. So how can he be scandalized by the weakness of his fellow-men? He has only to meditate on our Lord's attitude to the woman taken in adultery (Jn 8: 3-11), to the Samaritan woman (Jn 4: 5-30), or to the good thief (Lk 23: 42-43) to know what attitude he himself should adopt.

Consequently every priest must be very careful how he treats the penitent who kneels before him. We can unhesitatingly assert that the frown or the reprimand, however justified, is not an effective method. The normal result of this attitude, unless the penitent is very humble indeed, is that he is frightened away forever, or at least thinks twice before returning to the confessional. The priest must remember that it is God who has been offended and God understands, waits patiently and without punishing, encourages and forgives. What right has he, then, who has not been offended at all, to be hard on the sinner, who may have had to overcome countless difficulties and endless shame before making up his mind to tell things that make him feel like the lowest creature on earth? Then, instead of the helping hand which he expects to reach out to him in his difficulty to make it a little more bearable, when he trusts his conscience to the understanding of the priest placed before him by God to heal and help him, he gets a reception which, far from encouraging him to open up his soul, makes him think it would be better to have stayed away. The priest may be in a bad mood for any number of reasons, he may be suffering from nervous tension brought on by his work—all sorts of explanations are possible. Nevertheless, in spite of everything, we must always try to be as open and encouraging as our Lord was, when despite his fatigue, he saw the needs of the people, was moved to pity for them and healed their sick (Mt 14: 14).

The priest can scarcely be surprised, then, that those who come to him should be the needy. Like his Master, he must know that "those who are well have no need of a physician, but those who are sick." And, therefore, like Jesus, he must go out to meet the wretched and the downfallen, for he is another Christ, and Jesus "came not to call the righteous, but sinners" (Mt 9: 12-13).

It is no exaggeration to say that every priest needs a lot of patience. To be a good listener is not only an art but a sign of exquisite charity. People must be allowed to pour out their troubles, however insignificant, to tell everything that is worrying them, everything that weighs heavily on their soul, even things that are of no importance from an objective point of view. For the confessor many things may seem insignificant, but he is not the person involved, he is not suffering under their weight. He must let all his penitents speak in their own way as best they can. He must never lose his patience, interrupt sharply or give the impression that he is in a hurry by urging the penitents to be brief. If we spend a little time in showing people how to confess properly, explaining what is important and what is irrelevant, we may waste, so to speak, a little bit of time, but we'll regain it in the future, for ourselves and for others, and no one will have been hurt.

If at all possible, absolution should never be refused except in cases of genuinely bad will on the part of the penitent, that is, when there is no purpose of amendment. If there is actual sorrow and he or she is willing to do whatever they can to improve, why should he be deprived of absolution which might be his salvation? And not just once, but as often as the penitent feels actual sorrow and is ready to put up a struggle, however weak he or she may be, or perhaps precisely because of this weakness. "Then Peter came up and said to him, 'Lord, how often shall my brother sin against me, and I forgive him? As many as seven times?' Jesus said to him, 'I do not say to you seven times, but seventy times seven'" (Mt 18: 21-22). If the Lord is willing to forgive as many times as a sinner goes to him, how can any priest refuse to wash away the stains of his fellowman as often as he returns, however unclean each time, to the sacrament that washes away sins?

We must not of course, equate understanding with weakness or complicity. The priest must make demands, heavy demands, but he ought to do so tactfully and at opportune moments. "Those who transgress frequently in very little things are to be admonished to consider anxiously how sometimes there is worse sin in a small fault than in a greater one. For a greater fault, in that it is the sooner acknowledged to be one, is so much the more speedily amended; but a smaller one, being reckoned as though it were none at all, is retained in use with worse effect as it is so with less concern," says St. Gregory the Great.[12] A priest who regards everything as all right and nothing as very wrong provided that there are no mortal sins is not a good confessor. He might as well tell the sinner that he can go on lying, being proud, dishonest, sly, unchaste, lazy, intemperate, calumnious, slanderous and many other things provided he keep within reason and not go beyond the limits that mark the boundary of mortal sin.

Naturally there is no point in expecting a sinner to be cured instantaneously, almost miraculously. This is possible, of course, but very improbable. If changes are to be enduring and lasting, they need time, perseverance, efforts repeated over and over again. A tree has to sink its roots deeply into the ground if it is to be strong and healthy: "The plants lay hidden under the snow. And the farmer, the owner of the land, observed with satisfaction: 'Now they are growing on the inside.'"[13] "To grow on the inside" takes time and effort; we cannot expect to see the fruit spring up minutes after the seed has been sown. But there are no hopeless cases: "God is able from these stones to raise up children to Abraham" (Mt 3: 9). So the priest should always be receptive, do his best, wait patiently and quietly for the grace to penetrate and produce its effect for, like his Master, he must not "break a bruised reed or quench a smoldering wick" (Mt 12: 20). He must not push; apart from the fact that nobody likes to be pushed, "in creating souls, God never repeats himself. Each individual is as he is, and must be treated as God has made him and leads him along. 'I made myself all things to all men so as to save all' (1 Cor 9: 22). We must be all things to all men. There are no panaceas. We have to educate, devote to each soul whatever amount of time it needs, with the patience of a medieval monk illuminating a manuscript, page after page, help people to grow up, to develop their consciences, feel their personal freedom and the responsibility that follows it."[14] Therefore time is never wasted if it is spent helping a sinner to improve, to rise again, and to fight against his or her inner hopelessness, that despair that tempts one to abandon the struggle. Far from being wasted, it is time gained.

The priest is bound to be understanding of the weaknesses and shortcomings of others if he remembers his own. This will also encourage him not to be hard when it comes to the question of a penance. Obviously the penance imposed, however harsh it may be, is never directly proportionate to the sins committed. For if all offenses, even venial sins when committed deliberately, involve some degree of contempt for God's infinite majesty, clearly a few Hail Marys are very small satisfaction and totally disproportionate to the outrage committed. Thus the sinner is always and necessarily in God's debt; his penance is a gesture of good will and an acknowledgement of his indebtedness, a token of his desire to make reparation and pay something back, rather than adequate satisfaction which would cancel the debt and leave no balance in his disfavor. Nevertheless, the actual penance itself has to bear proportion to the gravity of the sins; what is not necessary is that the penitent himself should fulfill that actual penance. The priest, as a father, should assess his strength and not load him with a burden he cannot bear, for this might crush him completely. In theory he *should* be able to bear it, but in fact he cannot do so. For instance, a man of thirty is at his peak as far as strength is concerned and he should be able to lift a certain weight; but if he has just come out of a coma that kept him prostrate for many days, even if he is now quite well again, there is no point in loading him with anything but a very slight burden. To be another Christ and carry the cross for the sins of his fellowmen, the priest has many resources open to him. These range from offering the holy sacrifice or the divine office, through self-denial and prayer, to corporal mortification (such as taking the discipline), leaving the penitent to say a Hail Mary or perform a similar part of the penance. Is it not the priest's duty to make confession, access to our Father God easy? What price did the father in the Gospel impose on his prodigal son when he returned home, after years of wasting his patrimony abroad, and humbly confessed his folly?

A very important aspect of the confessor's role is that he should teach. His attempts to exhort the penitent and encourage him along the right path may either be genuine and effective or may consist of a few vague conventional remarks. He doesn't have the human race in front of him, but a concrete individual, a real person of a particular age, married or single, with a particular job situation, living in a particular environment, surrounded by circumstances peculiar to himself, with a mentality and standard of education unique to him. A general kind of exhortation given out to everyone equally, however they may differ from one another, will probably be of little use to any of them. The same thing cannot, or should not, be said, or the same manner used for a child as for a married woman, for a working man as for a schoolgirl, for a student as for the mother of a family with a husband causing her problems, even if the actual words used are universally and eternally true. The confessor has to give each individual what he needs, taking his or her circumstances, mentality, and particular difficulties into account. Obviously it is a good thing to advise everyone to have devotion to our Lady, whatever the occasion, the danger, or the problem. Nevertheless, to say: "Above all, have a great devotion to the blessed Virgin, help of sinners, so that she will obtain for you the grace not to sin any more" to a child who tells lies, to a boy who has difficulties with purity, to a man with a bad temper who often annoys his wife, to the mother of a family who spends her day trying to get through the thousand small chores that exhaust her, is not the same as suggesting to each of them some specific way in which they could show their love for our Lady that would have a direct bearing on the defect they are trying to correct. But even this should be done with an indication of some short time limit, such as "Try it, and if you come back next week you can tell me how you got on," for, in a way, a resolution covering too long a period is no longer specific enough. The whole of one's life has no real existence, not even tomorrow exists. Suffice it to make a resolution just for today; if tomorrow comes, and if we are there to see it, it will also be today.

The priest should never forget that he is only an instrument. He is not a model for anybody. No one has set him up to be imitated; on the contrary, the Church has always pointed to Christ as the only model for every Christian to imitate. Similar to the sense in which we say a potter's fingers mold the clay, the priest can regard himself as being used by the Holy Spirit, whose grace sanctifies, molds and shapes the soul to bring it closer to Christ, its model. Overenthusiasm and insufficient education on the part of some people, coupled perhaps with a certain lack of prudence on the priest's part, may sometimes give rise to embarrassing situations or relationships, for they can lead to a kind of hero-worship which is fatal. The priest may come to consider himself indispensable if a particular soul is to improve and the person himself also may think—or, what is worse, may tell others—that he owes it all to a particular *man*, rather than to the *priest* acting on behalf of the Church.

Apart from being embarrassing, these ideas are completely false. A priest will fulfill his function only to the extent to which he follows John the Baptist's motto: "He must increase, but I must decrease" (Jn 3: 30). Otherwise he can hardly hope to direct souls to Christ, and, instead, will either send them in the opposite direction or, at best, make them feel attached to himself, both of which extremes are erroneous. Only if he makes himself another Christ will he succeed; and that is why personal sanctity is so important—it will limit him to giving doctrine and passing on the counsels the Church has taught him, for it is the Church that must direct the lives of her children towards Jesus Christ, and the priest is only the means she uses to do so. The priest must avoid the danger of bringing things down to a personal level; his own self must enter into things as little as possible. It is not a question of influencing the penitent through the use of his own personality, or of substituting his own will for that of the sinner, turning him into some kind of puppet, a mere performer of pious practices and devotions.

He should never give orders—except perhaps (for their own good) in the case of people suffering from scruples—for his function is not to issue commands to anyone. On the contrary, he should deliberately limit himself to pointing out facts, helping the penitent to form his own judgments, drawing his attention to real or possible obstacles between him and God, opening up new horizons. For we all know that many people do as little as they do, not because of unwillingness, but because they are unaware of the possibilities. The priest is not there as a substitute for grace; neither should he be so over-active or so over-anxious that he leaves nothing to the Holy Spirit or to the penitent who, after all, has a mind and a will of his own, which the priest ought not to weaken or destroy by forbidding its use. A child may find it difficult to stay on his feet when learning to walk, but he will never learn unless he is allowed to try. A confessor or a spiritual director—and this applies to both—is a guide, not a crutch for cripples, or a support for people with no will of their own. He is not the owner of the souls entrusted to him. He must ensure that they remain totally free and unfettered so that at any moment they may change confessor without feeling they owe him any apologies or explanations. It would be worse still if they did not even dare to change, lest they hurt or offend him.

Neither, however should a confessor adopt a purely inactive attitude, listening impassively, just uttering some pious words of advice and giving a penance. On the contrary, he should make it easy for the penitent to confess his sins and pour out everything he feels rotting inside. His way of living and treating the people who go to him may help in this respect. If he is wise, he will know that there is a "dumb spirit" (Mk 9: 17) that tries to bring back at the moment of Confession the sense of shame it took away when the sin was being committed. He will realize that confession is a deeply humiliating experience for the person involved, who kneels down in the confessional, not to sing his own praises, but to expose all his foul rottenness, to speak of vile things, shameful things, dirty things, that lower him even in his own estimation. None of this is easy. The mere fact of approaching a priest in itself is a courageous act, an act of love of God, equivalent to holding out a hand to beg for help. The confessor must reach out his own hand in return and enquire into the state of that soul. If he has the art of asking questions, he will not only make confession easy—in so far as it can ever be made easy—but will offset the dumb spirit's efforts to make use of groundless fears and absurd timidity to ensure that all is not told. But he has to proceed with great tact and tremendous respect for people's privacy. The sanctuary of conscience, where the relationship between God and the soul is enacted, must never be violated. It is not a question of forcing one's way into a soul, as a thief forces a safe with an iron bar, but of discovering the roots of the trouble with the gentleness and tact of a doctor examining a patient to find what organs have been damaged, relying on the patient's good will only insofar as is absolutely necessary, and always respecting his freedom. In matters of purity, especially, extreme care has to be taken, and no amount of caution will ever be excessive.

The precautions recommended by the Church in this connection are well known to every priest, and if he takes them he has nothing to fear. "And for the most part," writes St. Gregory the Great, "it comes to pass that, while the ruler's mind becomes aware, through condescension, of the trials of others, it is itself also attacked by the temptations whereof it hears. . . . But of this the pastor ought by no means to be afraid, since, under God, who nicely balances all things, he is more easily rescued from his own temptations to the extent that he is more compassionately distressed by those of others."[15]

In practice it is quite impossible for a priest to instruct the penitent fully. He will often feel extremely upset when he sees possibilities in a soul which cannot be developed because of lack of knowledge, a knowledge which he simply cannot supply because of the insufficient time at his disposal. This is a situation where he should make use of books: they may help where he is powerless. If he is living a deep spiritual life and has been doing some spiritual reading every day for a number of years, from among the books he has read he could recommend the one most suitable for the mentality and needs of the person concerned. In this way, slowly and gradually the penitent's supernatural horizon will be widened, his ideas clarified, his objectives better defined, his judgment made more reliable, and his opinions more Christian. The result of this method, though indirect, will be no less effective for, apart from the actual good it does, it will leave the priest more time to attend to other souls.

Of all the functions which the priest has to perform as a shepherd of souls, there is probably none that gives him greater satisfaction than this. Possibly no other task offers him so many and such clear opportunities to do direct and effective apostolate, to practice charity and humility, faith and hope in God, patience and meekness, self-denial, compassion, tact, and the art of becoming "all things to all men" (1 Cor 9: 22). There is no greater compensation, even humanly speaking, than to see the joy, the relief and the sensation of peace experienced by the sinner when he receives absolution and feels free of the terrible weight that was burdening him, his soul liberated from the despotic power of the devil. The joy that fills the priest inwardly when he restores lost peace to the soul and sees it rise again through Christ's power is, as it were, a reflection of the joy felt in heaven when "this . . . brother was dead, and is alive; he was lost, and is found" (Lk 15: 32).

It is not true that the task of hearing confessions is monotonous. Certainly sin is monotonous, it is always the same. A priest may find hearing confessions boring if he only listens to lists of sins and gives penance and absolution on days when there are many people and little time. But there is no monotony when he can attend to them properly, for each individual is different, the spiritual life is amazingly rich and varied, it is exciting to try and understand each one of those different worlds. To look for an opening through which to inspire the love of Christ in an indifferent, routine-ridden, ignorant or hard heart, or one attached to the things of this world, demands all one's energy, knowledge and love of God and of souls. To console the afflicted, to give light to the blind, to show the way to those who are lost, to wash the dirty, heal the sick, comfort the weak, strengthen the lax, raise the fallen, give back joy to the sad, give rest to the restless, stimulate the downfallen, encourage the depressed; can these things be monotonous?

But there is more to hearing confessions than this. Each soul has been redeemed by Christ and is full of potential perfection, love of God, sanctity. If a priest is genuinely devoted to his ministry and living a spiritual life, he knows that he is there to lead the souls in his care "to God the Father," to sanctify and govern them "as fathers in Christ" (*Lumen Gentium* 28). Therefore his task is not simply to forgive sins and exhort the sinners to avoid them in the future, but also to help them grow in the love of God, to develop whatever talents God has given them, to "persuade everyone to the discharge of the duties of his proper state in life," to "see to it . . . that the faithful are led individually in the Holy Spirit to a development of their own vocation as required by the Gospel, to a sincere and active charity" (PO 5-6).

Blessed Josemaria Escriva has written something which, though addressed to the members of Opus Dei, also throws light on the priest's work in relation to his flock: "With the humility of people who know they are sinners and of little significance— *homo peccator sum*, we say with St. Peter—but with the faith of people who allow themselves to be guided by the hand of God, we have come to say that sanctity is not something for the privileged few, that the Lord calls us all and expects love from all of us, wherever we may be, whatever our state in life, our occupation or our work, for that ordinary, everyday, unpretentious life can be a means to sanctity: there is no need to leave one's position in the world to seek God, if the Lord does not give a particular soul a religious vocation, for all the ways on the earth are places where one can meet Christ."[16]

God "through Christ reconciled us to himself and gave us the ministry of reconciliation" (2 Cor 5 18). Just as he reconciled the world to himself through his Son, so also he wishes to reconcile the sinner to himself by making use of other Christs, his priests. It is in the sacrament of forgiveness and mercy that the meeting of the son with his Father takes place again, when, in the depths of a human heart, the divine supplication has been heard: "For I know the plans I have for you, says the Lord, plans for welfare and not for evil, to give you a future and a hope. Then you will call upon me and come and pray to me, and I will hear you" (Jer 29: 11-13).

This is also the sacrament of freedom for, if "every one who commits sin is a slave to sin" (Jn 8: 34), then to wipe out sin means breaking a chain that enslaves and giving the slave back his liberty. It is the sacrament of joy, for there is no joy without peace, and we are at peace when we have cancelled our debt with God. For these reasons the priest should have a great love for the duty—the hard duty, perhaps, from a human point of view—of hearing confessions.

(The Roman Catechism tells us that all devout people are convinced that the sanctity, piety and fear of the Lord which flourish within the Church are due in large measure to the sacrament of confession, and that if sacramental confession were removed from Christian life, vice and immorality would take control everywhere. Indeed, it is quite a remarkable fact that where confession is least used, psychiatry is most needed.)

The priest should also know that, if he spends regular periods on particular days at fixed times in the same confessional, he will soon be amazed to see how God sends him souls to purify and teach, encourage and strengthen, understand and heal. All the hours he spends in the performance of this duty, all the energy he uses, all the tiredness that builds up, will eventually be a precious garment with which to clothe his soul at the hour of truth, for whatever he does for the least of these, he does for the Lord.

Offering sacrifice

Through original sin, man cut himself off from God. The human mind is too small and limited to grasp the full significance of this free and deliberate act on the part of Adam, our first parent. Nature was grievously wounded; man was estranged from God; the human race was guilty of an unjustifiable crime. Mankind's conscience was deeply engraved with an awareness that it was in a state that needed salvation, and as a consequence of a vague memory of Adam's grave sin, men of all kinds have always felt a profound longing to be purified, a desire to pay off a debt that could never be paid, because no human creature could put together what man had torn asunder. Throughout the history of the world, it is interesting to notice in (albeit in a confused way) the custom of offering sacrifice to the divinity in order to be in favor and cancel debts with a view to salvation. This also implies, in a way, an acknowledgement of God's sovereignty, and man's dependence and desire to pay homage to the divine majesty. This was how mankind, separated from God, manifested its helplessness and its good will.

In his infinite mercy, God determined from all eternity to restore the harmony which man had broken. In fact the first ray of hope began to shine at the very moment when Adam and Eve were expelled from Paradise. The reference to the seed of the woman who would crush the head of the serpent (Gen 3: 15) is the first sign of a promise. Many years went by and then, at the opportune moment, God took a people to himself by calling Abraham, with whom he made a pact, which he later renewed. This is the old covenant made with Abraham and his descendants. God used it to begin to prepare men for their redemption, instructing them and raising them up again towards the supernatural world which they had lost, preparing them for the coming of the new Adam who would reconcile men to God again and restore the order and harmony of creation disrupted by the first Adam. This covenant was based on nature, for Abraham's descendants, and they alone, constituted the people of God, and they belonged to it by the formal initiation which took the form of circumcision. "Now even the first covenant had regulations for worship and an earthly sanctuary" (Heb 9: 1); this is the Holy of Holies which the priest alone can enter only once a year, "and not without taking blood which he offers for himself and for the errors of the people" (Heb 9: 7).

However, this old covenant was only a shadow of the reality, a figure and preparation for the new. According to the old law "gifts and sacrifices are offered which cannot perfect the conscience of the worshipper, but deal only with food and drink and various ablutions, regulations for the body imposed until the time of reformation" (Heb 9: 9-10).

When the "time of restoration" came, God became man and dwelled among us. Jesus Christ, true God and true Man, offered himself to the Father as a spotless and perfect Victim in the unique sacrifice which restored the order disrupted by sin and adequately, indeed excessively, compensated for the offense committed by mankind. For "Christ appeared as a high priest of the good things that have come, then through the greater and more perfect tent (not made with hands, that is, not of this creation) he entered once for all into the Holy Place, taking not the blood of goats and calves but his own blood, thus securing an eternal redemption" (Heb 9 11-12). Thus "he is the mediator of a new covenant, so that those who are called may receive the promised eternal inheritance, since a death has occurred which redeems them from the transgressions under the first covenant" (Heb 9: 15).

Jesus Christ, therefore, established a new covenant, a new pact, with a new people of God, not founded on nature, as the old one was, but on grace. This new people was constituted, not by flesh and blood, but by faith in Jesus Christ, and is composed of the multitude of believers, and not of the descendants of one chosen man. This is the people to which we belong, not through any accidental and extrinsic rite, but through the renewal which Baptism brings about by the death of the old, carnal man and the birth of the new, spiritual man in his place.

The sacrifice of the cross is the fullness of time; everything that went before was only a preparation; everything that follows is a continuation and a consequence, an application and a development. "All have sinned and fall short of the glory of God," but "by his grace as a gift, through the redemption which is in Christ Jesus, whom God put forward as an expiation by his blood" (Rom 3: 23-25), man has returned to friendship with God, the human race has been reconciled with its Creator and that which had been violently torn asunder has once again been put together. The time of grace has replaced the time of sin.

Shortly before giving himself up to be sacrificed, when Jesus Christ was instituting the Eucharist, the sacrament of his flesh and blood, he pronounced these words: "This is my blood of the covenant, which is poured out for many for the forgiveness of sins" (Mt 26: 28).

Influenced no doubt by Heb 9: 16, Schmaus says that "the Eucharist is the application of Christ's saving death to those who have a share in it. This is proved by the fact that Christ calls the chalice a *testament*, or will, which is a distribution of a dying person's property among his inheritors. It comes into force only on the death of the testator. Therefore, when Jesus refers to his death as a chalice, as his testament, he declares his death to be a saving gift to mankind and the Eucharist to be the distribution of that saving gift."[17] The Eucharist, the holy Mass, is the sacrament of the sacrifice of the cross.

"Do this in remembrance of me" (Lk 22: 19), "for as often as you eat this bread and drink this cup, you proclaim the Lord's death until he comes" (1 Cor 11: 26). The relationship between the sacrifice of the Mass and the sacrifice of the cross was clearly laid down by the Council of Trent: "In this divine sacrifice which is performed at Mass, that same Christ who once offered himself in a bloody manner on the altar of the cross is contained and immolated in a bloodless manner"(Denziger 940). Both have one and the same Victim, for he who offers himself at Mass through the ministry of the priest is the same Man as once offered himself on the cross. Both the sacrifice of the cross and that of the Mass are essentially identical, accidentally different. The identity lies in the Victim, who is Christ, and in the officiating Priest, who is also Christ. Christ offers himself to the Father as a propitiatory Victim. The difference lies in the manner: bloody on the cross, bloodless at Mass. The Mass is therefore the sacrifice of the cross made present now, and each time we celebrate this sacrifice the work of our redemption is repeated.

But the object of the redemption, as of everything Christ did, was to give glory to God through the restoration of his dominion over creatures and to save mankind. It is therefore a sacrifice of praise and expiation. It is also an act of thanksgiving—in fact, that is precisely the meaning of *eucharist.*

But how is man to give thanks to God? Undoubtedly by raising up his heart to him, in an attitude that acknowledges his gifts. However, as St. Augustine says, if he had not raised us up, we should still be lying on the ground. Christ, "the first-born of all creation" (Col 1: 15), has taken us into himself and through him, with him, and in him, we are capable of praising, giving thanks and offering atonement. Born children of Adam, the old man, we became God's enemies; reborn in Christ, the new Adam, rather than friends, we have become the adoptive children of God. This deep and radical change in our condition was made possible by our redemption through the sacrifice of the cross.

"By baptism," St. Thomas Aquinas says, "a man is incorporated in the Passion and death of Christ. . . . Hence it is clear that the Passion of Christ is communicated to every baptized person, so that he is healed just as if he himself had suffered and died."[18]

Since there is undeniably a fundamental relationship between sin and sacrifice, between guilt and reparation, the sacrifice of the Mass is more intensely lived by those priests who have become deeper persons because of their contact with the world of sin. Whatever else it may be, sin is not in the least shallow, despite being so widespread all over the world and despite being committed so often. Only people who are themselves superficial think its importance is also superficial; only those who treat God and everything referring to the world of grace lightly, take sin lightly. St. Teresa was amazed that any Christian could deliberately offend God—and she was referring to venial sin! That tormented priest, who spent the greater part of his life converting people who lived almost like pagans into genuine and consistent Christians, suffered intensely when he saw the nauseating ugliness of sin. Indeed the Curé of Ars had such a clear vision of the diabolical malice of sin that he felt afflicted—and suffered physically—on account of the havoc it caused in souls and the contempt for God it involved.

If a priest truly loves God and, as a consequence, loves souls, if he feels genuinely responsible for his "little flock," then he can never be very understanding or very tolerant with *sin*. He must, however, as we have already said, be immensely understanding with *sinners*, with those people who have the misfortune to be dead to life. Indeed, to gain for them the grace of their spiritual resurrection, as a mediator between them and God, as another Christ, he must sacrifice himself and, through his life of sacrifice and acts of expiation, pay their debts, thus making up for the sins of the world. It is when he tries to rescue sinners by his prayer and sacrifice, self-denial and penance, understanding, gentleness and love, that he appreciates the immense value of the Mass, the sacrifice of the cross. For it is then he realizes his own inability to cancel any of the debt which men have contracted by sinning; then he sees with a very convincing clarity the frightening disproportion between the scant means at his disposal and the magnitude of the offenses given to the Lord of creation. It is as if to pay a debt of several millions, he managed, at the cost of incredible sacrifice, to save a few dollars each year. If we consider the damage caused so often by sinners to perfectly innocent people—frequently damage which is irreparable, which the priest cannot remedy however hard he tries, for it is far beyond his powers—we shall begin to understand how great must be the disorder brought into creation by sin, how wide the abyss opened up between the sinner and God, and how helpless the priest is to repair it.

When the priest reaches the stage of realizing his own limitations, whether in regard to the sinner (how often he would change him completely if he could!), or in regard to sin (countless offenses are committed every day with the greatest of ease and the priest by himself cannot prevent a single one of them), or in regard to God (when he would dearly like to compensate for all the sins committed against him), then the Mass acquires supreme importance for him and becomes absolutely indispensable. For anything the priest can do by himself is as nothing, and, whatever efforts he makes, the chasm between the sinner and God persists. But there is, in fact, something he can do to redress the balance, there is a sacrifice he can offer which fully repairs the havoc caused by sin, for it offers to the Creator the immolation of a spotless Victim, whose very innocence and holiness more than compensates for the sins of the world. As St. Thomas says, the passion of Christ is sufficient satisfaction for all the sins of all mankind. And as Eugene Boylan adds: "All the worship we owe God was given to him in that one Sacrifice; all the satisfaction we owe God was given to him there also. All that we need from God, was merited for us there; and all the thanks we should give God are given there. Nothing remains but to make that sacrifice our own."[19]

And we make it ours through the Mass. Therefore, through the holy sacrifice we can not only offer to our Father God a sacrifice worthy of him, but also obtain for our own poor offerings and sacrifices a new and special quality that makes them acceptable. For when we offer them, and offer ourselves, in union with the Victim who assumed our own nature, they are fused into the sacrifice of Christ, the eternal Priest, and are thereby raised up, purified and sanctified. It is Christ himself who offers them to the Father as the firstborn of all creatures, and it is he who, by joining them with his own offering, makes them acceptable to him.

One aspect of the eucharistic sacrifice which the documents of the Council repeatedly emphasize, and with which the priest ought to be very familiar, is the fact that the Mass is the center and highest point of the Christian life. The Eucharist is the sacrament of unity, the sacrament of the body of Christ. We read in the *Summa* that "a priest exercises a two-fold action: the one, which is principal, over the true body of Christ; the other which is secondary, over the mystical body of Christ. The second depends on the first, but not conversely."[20] Not only is it true that "as often as the sacrifice of the cross in which 'Christ, our passover, has been sacrificed' is celebrated on an altar, the work of our redemption is carried on," but also "in the sacrament of the eucharistic bread the unity of all believers, who form one body in Christ, is both expressed and brought about" (LG 3).

Hence all the sacraments, as indeed all the priest's functions and all the works of the apostolate, are directed to the Eucharist.

It is the "summit of the spiritual life and all the sacraments are ordered to it."[21] "For the most blessed Eucharist contains the Church's entire spiritual wealth, that is, Christ himself, our Passover and living bread. Through his very flesh, made vital and vitalizing by the Holy Spirit, he offers life to men. They are thereby invited and led to offer themselves, their labors, and all created things together with him. Hence the Eucharist shows itself to be the source and the apex of the whole work of preaching the Gospel" (PO 5).

The celebration of the Eucharist gathers and unites the faithful around the priest who presides and offers to God, in the name of the Church, the perfect sacrifice of praise, propitiation and thanksgiving, and all the faithful should unite in him and with him. Hence active participation of the faithful in the liturgy of the Mass is encouraged so that they may exercise their share in Christ's priesthood by offering the divine Victim and offering themselves in the oblation, for they all form one body with the Head, "because there is one bread, we who are many are one body, for we all partake of the one bread" (1 Cor 10: 17).

Thus the priest, as well as being a minister of the Church, offering the eucharistic sacrifice, is also the delegate and representative of the bishop, presiding over the assembly of the faithful gathered to participate in the liturgical act *par excellence*, as a section of the people of God consciously and deliberately fulfilling their primary duty, namely that of giving praise, by offering their "bodies as a living sacrifice, holy and acceptable to God" (Rom 12: 1).

"Exercising within the limits of their authority the function of Christ as Shepherd and Head, they gather together God's family as a brotherhood all of one mind and lead them in the Spirit, through Christ, to God the Father" (LG 28). Priests must therefore be aware of the greatness of the eucharistic sacrifice, the magnitude of the mystery and its deep significance. At one with the Church's sentiments, we must be conscious of our role before the congregation of the faithful, presiding over the most perfect act of praise, expiation and thanksgiving that man can offer to God.

We are human and—once again we must repeat this point—consequently exposed to the danger of allowing the actions we perform day after day to degenerate into mechanical routine and mere habit. Therefore we must take great care with the details, precisely those which prevent us from falling into thoughtless routine. We can't approach the altar as if we were going to perform just another one of many actions we carry out in the course of each day. It's true, to a certain extent at least, that our human condition simply doesn't allow us to realize fully and totally the sovereign greatness of the Mass. It is very probable that were it not for this veil drawn by our nature over the supernatural, we would be incapable of looking directly into the depths of the mystery without being overwhelmed by what we see.

Nevertheless, we could expect a little more—indeed a lot more—from the priest as he approaches the altar of God to engage in such an extraordinary act. We could suggest, for instance, an act of faith before the Mass begins, a deliberate act of will which would force all the human faculties—understanding, memory, imagination—gently but firmly, to play their part in the mystery about to take place. A priest certainly does not show that he is following this or any other advice if, when putting on the sacred vestments, he continues to carry on a conversation he has begun, or chats about unimportant matters with the sacristan or other priests—meanwhile mechanically and unthinkingly saying the prayers laid down by the Church to be recited, or rather spoken (for they are a conversation with our Lord), precisely in order to give him a minimum of recollection before Mass.

At the very least we could hope and expect that he would attach to the sacrifice at which he is officiating a degree of importance sufficient to allow him to perform his part of the function correctly and properly. For if the Church considers what happens at Mass so significant as to provide for every gesture, every movement, every posture, every action—to ensure that everything is done with dignity and decorum; then the priest should realize that attention to the liturgy, extreme care and obedience to the norms prescribed, is not a luxury, but a basic duty. Therefore, reading hurriedly, undue freedom in the gestures, carelessness in making the sign of the cross and other signs, rushing through everything without decorum, naturalness, or even intelligibility in the prayers (sometimes reducing them to artificial or meaningless muttering), are all clear signs of boorishness towards God and of negligence—a sign of a lack of interested in what one is doing. And this certainly indicates what little importance one attaches to a task which he performs so casually.

There is no liturgical ceremony in the Church that can compare with the Mass in greatness, none as sacred in character as the sacrament of the body and blood of Christ; therefore none demands more extreme devotion, more exquisite veneration, or more profound respect. We cannot trifle with something as holy as the body and blood of Christ. It should never be used for liturgical experiments based on the whims or theories of some so-called theologian. Much less should it serve as a pretext for testing or trying out something not only differing from, but even opposed to, the Church's sentiments or any norms she has explicitly laid down. No, we cannot play games with the Holy of Holies; it would be too blatant a sign that we have no genuine priestly spirit, for we are neither seeking the glory of God, if we go against or show contempt for the Church's Magisterium, nor are we helping souls if we take a path other than the way of salvation.

Since it is Jesus Christ himself, true God and true Man, who comes down to our altar, we should hope that any refinement, any care, any attention we can lavish on this mystery would always be considered insufficient. It says little for the faith and love of a priest if he allows altar cloths with wax or wine stains or other spots to appear on the altar of his church, if he allows corporals so soiled and crumpled that it is shameful to think that, even for a few minutes, they are going to be like the swaddling clothes which covered the Child Jesus or that "clean linen shroud" (Mt 27, 59) in which he was wrapped when taken down from the cross, if he puts up with lavabo towels whose appearance shows they have been in use for weeks on end, or worn purificators, folded again and again without being washed. Can it be that in some parishes there are no persons with sufficient love of Jesus to perform these little services for him? Or is the cause of the problem the carelessness of a priest who has no interest in such "petty details," and celebrates Mass day after day without even noticing the uncleanliness and the neglected state of certain things whose very closeness to the sacrifice in a way makes them sacred?

Perhaps we could also make a brief mention here of the refinement, good taste and decorum we should expect to find in the house of God itself. One sometimes gets the impression that priests—or some priests, at least—are ashamed to give the Lord the best. Everywhere there is talk of human dignity and proper housing conditions. Everyone hopes for a certain minimum standard of comfort to make a house habitable and pleasant, so that the people who have to live in it can be happy to spend their time there. Yet we seem to want to send the Lord back to a stable and deprive him of all company by keeping churches so cold and empty of anything cheerful, so unwelcoming because of the sometimes dramatic decor (it is called modern art and we are told it means something to the people of today, but we are never told *which* people of today), that at times it is difficult to stay there a moment longer than is strictly necessary to fulfill our duty. This is one of the disadvantages of doing things according to the latest theory but with one's back turned on reality. That blatantly bad taste which used to make our churches look like makeshift theaters, with painted scenery, paper flowers, gaudy colors and bulbs, was preferable, I think, to some modern buildings which look like factories. At least they were more homelike, more friendly and also more humble. There is a golden mean, which is what we should try to achieve, because churches are houses of God, and deserve a certain minimum of dignity, and they are also houses of the faithful, the children of God, who have a right to feel at ease in them. They are not dead objects to be used for experiments in new styles or *avant garde* decorations—styles which are out of fashion almost as soon as they appear.

However busy a priest is and however urgent the things he has to do, the time devoted to thanksgiving after Mass should never be shortened. What has been consummated on the altar, and the immense privilege he has been granted, demand some response. It is only a question of good manners to express our thanks to someone who has done us a favor. That God himself should not only come down on our altar to offer himself in sacrifice for the sins of the world—including our own!—but that he should also have decided to become food for our souls in a profound and unique union, is something for which we shall never be able to show enough gratitude. The least we can do is devote some time to the Guest we have just received. If elementary courtesy demands that we be attentive to those who visit us in our home and take an interest in them, can there be any excuse whatever for indifference, discourtesy or bad manners towards our Lord? On his return to the sacristy, when the priest is still, as it were, a living tabernacle (for the sacramental species are still within him), if he begins to deal with other matters or to chat with people even before removing the sacred vestments, is he not proclaiming aloud that deep down—as well as on the surface—he has little realization of what he has just done or what is happening within him?

He cannot be shocked or surprised if the faithful are not always as docile or devout as they might be. Sometimes it is he himself who, by his behavior and example, diminishes their faith and fervor by his attitude to the sacred mysteries. It is he who instills doubts and arouses disconcerting thoughts concerning the truth of what he preaches; for people are bound to compare his preaching with his conduct, and they may often find that his actions belie his words. The accusation of hypocrisy sometimes levelled at priests, arises out of the levity, superficiality, and lack of spiritual life clearly manifest in some who are careless and too attached to the things of this world. Only God knows the harmful effect a lukewarm or cold, negligent, or pedantic priest can have on souls, and how large a part he may play in estranging them from the Church and the faith.

When instructing the faithful on the subject of the holy Mass, we usually point out the importance it has for a Christian and emphasize that it is "the center of the spiritual life." This very expression has been repeated so often that it has become almost a cliché and perhaps for some people (not excluding priests), it may be no more than a nice phrase.

When we say that our spiritual life should revolve around the Mass, what do we mean? Do we mean that throughout the day we should remember we have said Mass today and are going to say Mass again tomorrow? Obviously that in itself would not be a bad thing. But perhaps it is not exactly what is intended. Indeed, if thinking about that idea were to hinder our concentration on the duty of the particular moment, if remembering the Mass continually were to reduce the standard of our ordinary work, then perhaps we should have to deduce that, since it hinders the perfect fulfillment of God's will, it can scarcely be what he wants.

To make the Mass the center of our spiritual life is not to reduce it to a mere question of memory. It's something deeper and more vital than that, more essential to each one of us. Rather than meaning a number of pious practices, the expression refers to an inner attitude which can give rise to those and other acts, or, to be more accurate, the inner attitude that colors everything the Christian does.

Christ is the center of human history and the center of our life. If we now live supernaturally, it is because of his redemption for only through him, with him, and in him can our actions be pleasing to God or have any value in regard to eternal life. Only to the extent to which we are united with Christ can our deeds acquire a divine seal, a seal that comes, not from the person who performs them, but from the grace which Christ merited for us and which makes us capable of acting on a supernatural level. Since the redemption allows us to live a supernatural life, and since—like all living creatures—we manifest that life in actions and deeds, then the redemption is the center of every Christian's life, for all activity—a sign and expression of life—revolves around the principle that produces it. Since the Mass is the sacrifice of the cross, offered in a bloodless manner, in which the priest acts as a minister of the principal celebrant, it is the center of his life in an even more particular way than it is for Christians in general. Through the Mass we make the sacrifice of the cross, the culminating point of the redemption through which we were born to a new life, our own sacrifice.

What matters, therefore, is that the priest's relationship with Christ should not be reduced to mere memory work but should be an active and humble collaboration with the divine will throughout each day, with the same awareness of being a son of

God, the same spirit of praise, thanksgiving and reparation, which Christ, the eternal Priest, had on the cross and has at Mass. The priest should try to increase his consciousness of the fact that, like his Master, he has to make a holocaust of his whole life, but a holocaust without melodrama without useless or pretentious gestures—a holocaust, in a word, like our Lord's, a total and unconditional surrender to the will of God, having no will but God's will, for he himself has declared that "to obey is better than sacrifice" (1 Sam 15: 22). It is by this relationship with Christ, through obedience and docility throughout each minute of each day, that the priest must become one with him, for this union is achieved principally through the will. If he becomes so united with Christ as to be able to say with St. Paul "it is no longer I who live, but Christ who lives in me" (Gal 2: 20) then he will offer himself also with Christ in the sacrifice of the Mass and, since the sacrifice of the cross constituted the center of Christ's life—he lived for the supreme glorification of his Father by reconciling man to him through the redemption—so the Mass also becomes the center of the priest's life, for he lives (or should live) for the glorification of God by working ceaselessly for the reconciliation of sinners to him through his ministry.

If the priest lives such a deeply spiritual life as to be keenly and actively conscious at all times of the reason for his whole existence—not only as a *priest* but as a *man* created and chosen by God *to be* a priest—so that saying Mass never becomes a matter of mere routine, then his part in offering the sacrifice to God will have all the emotional freshness of someone carrying out the most sublime task that could ever be entrusted to any man. When offering the Mass, at the moment of sacrifice, he does so as a priest, that is, as a mediator acting on behalf of the Church, the community of those who believe in Christ Jesus. And it is Jesus Christ himself who, for a certain period of time, is really, truly and substantially present on the altar, for he has come down by reason of the words of consecration pronounced by his minister. We cannot be surprised, then, that Paul VI should so earnestly ask that the Mass be celebrated every day, even privately if there is no one to attend other than the server, for "any Mass, even if celebrated by a priest in private, is not private; it is the act of Christ and the Church. The Church, indeed, in the sacrifice which she offers, is learning to offer herself as a universal sacrifice; she is also applying to the whole world, for its salvation, the redemptive virtue of the sacrifice of the cross, which is unique and infinite."[22]

No words can adequately express the greatness of this mystery or the honor which God does to a man in allowing him to perform such a function, much less in actually choosing him for such a function. Therefore every priest should pay great attention to the manner in which he prepares to celebrate the mystery. Naturally, as we have already said, the best preparation is humble submission to the will of God in each and every act of our day, whether it be something very demanding or something ordinary and human, but not so as to exclude all other types of preparation. If we teach the faithful who are about to receive the Eucharist that it would help them to do so better if they tried to *know* and *think* about what they are going to receive, then with all the more reason should a priest be strongly encouraged not only to know, but particularly to think deeply and actively about what he is going to do. He could devote part of his morning prayer to this subject, for he should meditate on the goodness of God, who has left us such a marvellous proof of his love. He should reflect on the love of his Son, who humbles himself daily at the signal from the priest and gives himself to us in the food which unites us with himself and in his passion. This in turn should remind us, in a new bloodless manner, of the blood with which we were rescued and of all the graces we can obtain both for ourselves and for those whom God has placed in our care. The more the priest thinks about all these things, the more devotion and concentration will he put into them, the greater will be his gratitude and his desire to be united with the Victim of the altar, and the greater will be the value of his recollection.

3

Training

WHEN WE SPEAK OF TRAINING, we refer in a general sense to various kinds of educational processes, and, more particularly, to education for a specific purpose. We speak of training teachers, lawyers, doctors or scientists. We can also quite properly speak of ascetical training. In the priest's case, the object of the training involved is to educate him in such a way that he is adequately prepared to exercise properly the ministry to which he is devoting himself.

In every case, however, it is the whole person who performs an action, practices a profession, or fulfills a function, and since each person is individual and unique, a complete unit, not composed of independent or separate compartments, education is concerned with the whole person and not just with one particular aspect. Certainly, education may be directed towards one specific area of the personality which needs special attention at a given moment. We speak, for instance, of developing someone's willpower or someone's sensitivity. But in fact what is always meant is that the *person* is developed in one aspect or another. It is the *person* who is educated, and the person, as Pope Pius XI said, is constituted both in the order of nature and in the order of grace.[1]

So when we speak of training for the priesthood, we mean the process through which a man must go in order that, when he is stamped with the seal of the priesthood, he will be prepared. He will have the human and supernatural foundation needed to be the instrument God wishes him to be, that is, another Christ. In this sense he develops in a new and special way, in a particular and specific way, so as to become more and more capable of fulfilling that function for which he has been called. If any of the fundamental aspects of this training are neglected, the result will be defective and unsatisfactory.

Obviously the priest undergoes his training primarily while he is studying in the seminary. During that period his chief concern is to prepare himself to occupy the position to which the Church may assign him and to carry out his duties as a priest, working among people and for people. "The whole training of students ought to provide for the development of true shepherds of souls after the model of our Lord Jesus Christ, who was Teacher, Priest, and Shepherd"(OT 4). However, it would be wrong to imagine that one's training ends with the seminary years. A man's life is much longer than his adolescence and part of his youth. Does a doctor, for example, consider himself fully and finally trained when he gets his degree from medical school?

We all have to do our best "to attain to . . . the knowledge of the Son of God, to mature manhood, to the measure of the stature of the fullness of Christ" (Eph 4: 13), but the priest has to try harder than anyone else. Can any of us presume to have reached that fullness, beyond which it is impossible to go, in this life? Can anyone believe, while he is still a *viator*, a wayfarer, that he has achieved the science and the love of God so completely that no further improvement is possible? Obviously not. Therefore every priest and every Christian can go on advancing in the knowledge of Christ's doctrine and in human culture until the very moment of death; he can always improve his abilities as an instrument, developing new and greater possibilities. He can love a little more and a little better every day. He can always make further progress in his understanding of people, of divine things and human things. He can be more patient. He can do his work more perfectly. The words of St. Augustine, "Did you say 'Enough'? You have perished," apply also to the human aspect of the priest, for if he believes he has made sufficient progress, he is unlikely to take steps to make any further advance.

The new impulse given to the life of the Church by the Second Vatican Council affects the seminary, the methods of training priests, too. The Council has laid down directives referring to major and minor seminaries, the selection of teachers, the courses of studies and the textbooks to be prescribed. It would probably be no exaggeration to say that something very important in the life of the Church depends on the successful application of the Council's guidelines relating to seminaries. Furthermore, the training of students depends in no small measure—indeed the decree says "to a very large extent"—on the quality, holiness and dedication of the superiors and teachers. It is not by accident that, in choosing those on whose shoulders the responsibility for training future priests should rest, the Church asks that they "be chosen from among the best" and also that they "be painstakingly prepared by solid doctrine, appropriate pastoral experience, and special spiritual and pedagogical training" (OT 5). The teachers should not merely be well qualified in philosophical or theological subjects, they must also have "appropriate pastoral experience." Neither is it sufficient that they have wide pastoral experience, they should also be well qualified in the subjects they teach. Nevertheless, above all these considerations, they must be devout men with "special spiritual training."

The main purpose of every priest's training must be to achieve that unity of life which is the most perfect imitation of his Master and only Model. In the Person of the Word, the union of the divine nature and the human nature was such that everything he did, from the highest to the most humble and ordinary action, was always both divine and human. The divine Person was the principal, acting through the human nature. Grace must so permeate the priest also; it must perfect, raise and make use of his human qualities to such an extent that it is truly Christ who lives in him and inspires all his actions through that grace, that divine life.

The Council has emphasized this point, which is so essential for priests, to "seek for a way which will enable them to unify their interior lives with their program of external activities. No merely external arrangement of the works of the ministry, no mere practice of religious exercises can bring this unity of life, however much these things can help foster it" (PO 14). Nevertheless, if they are to be true men of God they must achieve a harmony and unity of life such that the interior and the external aspects not only do not hinder or interfere with one another, but actually complement one another, and do so in such a way that their devotion helps their ministry and their ministry in turn nourishes their devotion. Otherwise, their personality will, in a sense, be torn asunder, for neither the pious priest, diligent in his prayers and his reading but lacking in apostolic zeal, nor the man who spends all his time in ceaseless activity but is totally empty inside, can be free of anxiety and worry in the exercise of their duties. Hence the training given in the seminary is of great importance, for no small part of the priest's future may depend on it.

Human development

The first requirement for the reception of Baptism is obviously that the recipient should be human, and every member of the human race, male or female, is capable of receiving that sacrament, that is, of being raised to the supernatural order. However, for someone to be ordained to the priesthood, it is not sufficient to be human and to have been baptized: one also has to be male, one has to be a man. If sex is not a mere physiological accident but, as Michael Schmaus has said, involves a number of qualities which stamp the whole personality down to its very roots with their seal, then the fact that only males can be priests is of particular, and not merely generic importance.

Therefore when we refer to human development, we not only include that part of the priest's training which he shares with all other Christians, but also something more, namely the development of those qualities which are proper to his personality as a man.

This human aspect is an integral part of the priest's training, though not the most important by any means. It refers to the man, the *human being*, taking holy Orders. Its purpose is to prepare the natural foundation on which the whole supernatural structure of the priesthood is to be erected, and there are obviously good reasons why the human education of the priest should reach a high standard. First of all, there is the imitation of Jesus Christ, *perfectus Deus* but also *perfectus homo*, a perfect man. Indeed it's possible for us to imitate Christ precisely because, and only because, although he was God, he assumed our nature and became man in the spotless womb of the Virgin Mary. True God and perfect man, he appears throughout the Gospels as deeply human: energetic, strong, truthful, moderate, a man of character, serene, morally well balanced, firm, understanding but uncompromising, kind, just, honest, noble, sincere, compassionate. . . . The list could be extended almost indefinitely not just out of a pious wish to attribute every possible good quality to Jesus, but simply by deduction from the testimony of people who saw, heard, and spoke to him.

Perhaps the common habit of thinking of Jesus Christ primarily as God has hindered us at times from seeing the full exemplary force of his sacred humanity. Certainly the Person was divine, but his human nature played a substantial part in everything he did: his intelligence, his manner, his voice, his glance, his behavior. He dressed according to the fashion of his age, he ate as everybody else did, he behaved according to the customs of the time, place, and nation to which he belonged. He imposed hands, he ordained, got angry, smiled, wept, talked, became tired, was sleepy and exhausted, felt hunger and thirst, grief and joy. And the union, the fusion, of the divine and human was so complete and so perfect that every one of his actions was both divine and human. He was God, yet he liked to call himself the Son of Man.

Certainly the priest, a man of God, should act for supernatural motives, yet his own nature must provide him with as perfect an instrument as possible. In this way, instead of being a barrier or obstacle to the manifestation of the supernatural, it will be a vehicle through which others may be touched by divine grace. An electric current is always capable of giving light, but if a piece of string replaces the tungsten filament in a bulb, there is unlikely to be much light, not because the power is in any way deficient, but because of the poor quality of the instrument. Every soul is capable of thought, but if the brain, instead of being healthy, is damaged in some way, then only God knows what will pass through such a filter.

Another reason why every priest should be concerned about his human development and education is that he has a mission to perform among men, as a messenger sent to show them the way to God. We have already seen how difficult and delicate his position is. Being among men and occupying this special position, whether he likes it or not he is like a city built on high ground, like a lighted candlestick, exposed to everyone's gaze. If he fails to integrate the supernatural and the human, if either of these factors fails him, his personality will suffer. Clearly a great human personality is insufficient in itself, but on the other hand if there is any kind of deficiency here, then the *total* personality is necessarily weakened and the priest might find himself facing great insecurity or even anxiety and worry, which only a deep spiritual life could redress. Hence the danger that when such a problem arises, he may attempt to rectify it in inappropriate ways; then artifice and conventionalism appear, nature and grace part company, the threat of pharisaism, of developing a dual personality, looms up ahead. It is difficult to behave with supernatural naturalness—of which the Lord gave us a perfect example—when there is artificiality. Sellmair speaks of the "ecclesiastic's unctuous manner," when he tries to compensate externally and artificially for a non-existent spiritual life. But we could also speak of the careless attitude of a priest who lacks even the most elementary sense of secularity, whose human development is inadequate, who tries to be secular and "modern" and in fact only succeeds in being unpriestly.

Taking the circumstances of the real world into account, then, the priest needs good human qualities to fulfill his function. After all, in the economy of salvation God has decided that people should be saved with and through the help of other people, whom he has chosen specifically for that purpose. No two souls ever come into direct contact with one another because, on this earth, there are not souls, but people. Souls make contact through things which can be perceived by the senses, for it is through the senses that all knowledge is acquired. Therefore the supernatural needs the natural as a kind of bridge, so to speak. The human element, this bridge, is the first thing one sees, and if a priest fails to make access to the supernatural easy and attractive on this primary level, then he is failing in his responsibility. Instead of taking people to God, he may actually be keeping them from him, if they are put off by his own lack of human virtues.

We must now ask what form this development or education should take, keeping in mind, however, that the slightest gift of God's grace surpasses all the natural qualities in the world. We are not suggesting that absolute value be attributed to the human virtues or the natural factor in the priest, because there may still survive today, as a relic of philosophical trends of the last century, a certain danger of wanting to "naturalize" the priest. Nevertheless, as Alvaro del Portillo says "we must reject any tendency to dehumanize those who aspire to holiness as ministers of the Lord. It is impossible to believe in the holiness of people who lack the most basic human virtues."[2]

Though wounded in his nature by original sin, man has a number of natural gifts and qualities given to him by God to help him fulfill his purpose. Human virtues, then, are "all those moral habits which any man should have—even if he isn't a Christian—and which a Christian raises to the supernatural level through grace" (del Portillo). These virtues are not just external forms or appearances, therefore, unconnected with our deeper selves, but rather specific qualities manifested in our actions, which, in the priest's case, must not be merely *human*, but also specific to *men*.

As St. Thomas Aquinas says, grace perfects nature according to the nature in question and therefore the more qualities the nature has, the easier it will be for grace to perfect it. St. Antoninus deduced from this statement that whoever has the greatest nature, when moved by grace, does that which is perfect with the greatest perfection.[3]

Human development consists of harmoniously cultivating all those qualities which God has given us, all those moral habits that are founded on our human nature. This requires an effort, for it involves smoothing off the rough edges, correcting deformities, rectifying errors. Everything positive placed in our nature by God must be reinforced, while everything negative, which does not come from God but from original sin, or from the mud that has stuck to us as we have gone through life, should be eliminated.

For this reason, the human side of our education is an ascetic exercise and should not be undertaken in a pagan way. It is not an end in itself, much less the final goal of our training as priests, but one of many goals, and not even the most important—there are much more essential objectives. However, this does not mean that the human basis should be neglected or despised. The Second Vatican Council has stressed this facet of the priest's training and has mentioned some of the more important points it should include. "By wisely planning training there should also be developed in seminarians a due degree of human maturity, attested to chiefly by a certain emotional stability, by an ability to make considered decisions, and by a right manner of passing judgment on events and people. They should be practiced in an intelligent organization of their proper talents; they should be trained in what strengthens character; and, in general, they should learn to prize those qualities which are highly regarded among men and speak well of a minister of Christ. Such are sincerity of heart, a constant concern for justice, fidelity to one's word, courtesy of manner, restraint, and kindliness in speech" (OT 11).

On the question of which natural or human virtues a priest should cultivate in particular, we could answer in general terms that he should concentrate on those which are fundamental or especially relevant to the exercise of his ministry. There is a list of the human virtues which every man should cultivate outlined in a famous poem entitled *If*, by Rudyard Kipling; it is not a completely accurate list by any means, but at least it gives useful suggestions.

> If you can keep your head while all about you
> Are losing theirs and blaming it on you;
> If you can trust yourself when all men doubt you
> But make allowance for their doubting too;
> If you can wait and not be tired by waiting,
> Or being lied about, don't deal in lies
> Or being hated don't give way to hating,
> And yet don't look too good, nor talk too wise;
>
> If you can dream—and not make dreams your master;
> If you can think—and not make thoughts your aim;
> If you can meet with Triumph and Disaster
> And treat those two impostors just the same;

If you can bear to hear the truth you've spoken
Twisted by knaves to make a trap for fools,
Or watch the things you gave your life to, broken,
    And stoop and build 'em up with worn-out tools;

If you can make one heap of all your winnings
    And risk it on one turn of pitch-and-toss,
And lose, and start again at your beginnings
    And never breathe a word about your loss;
If you can force your heart and nerve and sinew
    To serve your turn long after they are gone,
And so hold on when there is nothing in you
    Except the Will which says to them: "Hold-on!"

If you can talk with crowds and keep your virtue,
    Or walk with kings—nor lose the common touch,
If neither foes nor loving friends can hurt you,
    If all men count with you, but none too much;
If you can fill the unforgiving minute
    With sixty seconds' worth of distance run,
Yours is the Earth and everything that's in it,
    And—which is more—you'll be a Man, my son!

These are obviously virtues proper to a man, qualities which
a man should cultivate: serenity, a prudent degree of confidence
in oneself, stamina, truthfulness, absence of complexes, realism
and objectivity, indifference to success or failure, self-control, tenacity, uprightness, fortitude, balance, industriousness. All of these,
and many more, apply to the priest as to any other man.

It is obvious that a priest should be serene, as our Lord was.
He ought to be a man with his head set squarely and firmly on
his shoulders, who does not get worried or excited when things
go wrong or lose his temper and react violently when the unfore-
seen happens: "Have no anxiety about anything" (Phil 4: 6). As
St. Francis de Sales said, there is nothing we should shun more
earnestly, after sin, than anxiety. A priest cannot afford to be hys-
terical or temperamental; on the contrary, as John XXIII said, he
should be able to moderate his emotions so as be in control of
himself always and in all circumstances.

He should have confidence in himself, but without being over-confident for, after all, he is human and not infallible. If he has a prudent degree of self-confidence, he will be a man of judgment; if he never relies entirely on himself, he will be able to ask for advice when the situation requires it.

He must have stamina and patience, for his work does not usually produce immediate results, and, even if it does, they are not always or necessarily visible. He needs these qualities because, like his Master who was a sign of contradiction, he can be sure that God's enemy and the enemy of souls will do everything in his power to discourage him and put him to flight, a flight into easygoing mediocrity. His fight is not only against flesh and blood, but against the ruler of this world and the power of darkness; he can expect no human rewards and no thanks from people for his work.

He must be truthful. If a priest tells lies, he can have little hope of gaining the confidence and loyalty of his parishioners or of anybody else, for anyone who trusts such a man will be deceived. If a priest is a liar, he is unreliable; so how can anyone confide in him, or trust his outlook or his word? Sincerity is perhaps the first of the human virtues that should be taught in the seminary—ensuring that future priests are sincere with God, with themselves, their superiors, and others; and that they are never afraid of the truth. "Don't be afraid of the truth, even though the truth may mean your death";[4] how much less should they fear it when the worst it could mean is a little prejudice, some misunderstanding, perhaps a bit of suffering. So they should be taught never to hide anything from the one who ought to be informed. They should be taught to be consistent, to shun pretense and deceit, to play fair, to be honest and loyal. This will help in their apostolate, for "this is one of the great moral and cultural values of our time—nowadays men passionately love authenticity in attitudes and sincerity in people, while everything that savors of falsehood, pretense, deceit or irresponsibility is automatically rejected."[5] Insincerity leads to pretense and a dual personality, even to a destruction of personality.

It is superiors and teachers who—beginning with their own example—have the duty of inculcating seminarians with this aspect of their qualities as men, namely that they must face the consequences of their own actions, without ever lying, without ever trying to evade the responsibility of what they have done. They will never really be *men* until they are sufficiently mature to abide by the results of their own decisions.

The priest cannot afford to have complexes. Yet he will have many, if he thinks too much about himself. There are far more important things in his life than that, much more urgent duties. So he must do his best to ensure that no problems occur which might give rise to worry of this negative type.

It is very important, too, that he be realistic and objective. A dreamer can seldom be a fighter, for it is easier and more entertaining to take refuge in a fictitious world of the imagination, fabricated according to one's own likeness, in which one is always the hero, than to grasp, understand, dominate or take advantage of reality. Hence dreamers always end up with little willpower or desire to act. If a priest becomes like that, he will never be much help to the Church or to others. He will be a burden and worry, even on the spiritual level. Nor can he afford to devote his life to his own thoughts or thinking, for he is supposed to be at the service of the Gospel.

If a man is inclined to be downcast, depressed, discouraged by failure, if he becomes vain, conceited, or proud when he is successful, then he shows that he is far from being mature, for he attaches too much importance to purely external things which are really irrelevant, for each one of us is what he is in God's eyes. It makes us no better than we are if people think highly of us, nor does it make us any worse if they speak ill. It is a sure sign of superficiality if we depend to this extent on people's opinions and judgments or are constantly at the mercy of success and failure. It shows one's roots are very near the surface. It is a sign of excessive levity, little solidity, and little strength, if we are so easily thrown off our balance.

As regards self-control, a priest should not allow himself to lose his temper or throw accusations about wildly. He cannot risk being classified as what a Spanish orator of the last century, Donoso Cortes, contemptuously called a race of quarrelers composed of those who, because of their troubled minds, lack the peace proper to men and instead make war with their tongues. He cannot allow himself to be over-sensitive or quick to take offense at any little thing which is not even remotely connected with him.

If a priest is not tenacious and resolute, he runs the risk of abandoning every undertaking the moment the first obstacle appears in his way. If he is irresolute, how can he even begin to understand what the Lord said about the effectiveness of prayer, or the elementary ascetical principle of beginning again each day?

The priest must also be strong and firm. Weakness, inability to suffer a setback without seeking consolation and compassion from others, unwillingness to make an effort, complaining about what he considers injustices (committed against himself, not against others), or about a lack of consideration, cowardice when faced with problems or the need for sacrifice or penance or the consequences of poverty; these and similar attitudes say little in his favor and are an obstacle in his work. As Pope John XXIII said, the Church wants strong and firm men, well formed in mind and heart, resolute and strong men who can follow the voice of the Lord without pretense or compromise, renouncing even licit enjoyments in order to live the life of heaven here on this earth.

Then we come to industriousness. Kipling's phrase is quite graphic: "fill the unforgiving minute with sixty seconds' worth of distance run." This is a law of human nature; man has been made to be active, to do things, to work. Every priest should be exhausted at the end of the day; he can have no free time, he has no right to any leisure other than what is indispensable to rest the spirit and the mind and prepare them to begin the struggle again with renewed energy. Rest does not mean being bored, trying to kill time; it consists of a change of activity. "Whoever gives himself to work for Christ, cannot expect to have a free moment, for even to rest is not to do nothing; it is to relax with activities that require less effort."[6] One type of activity, which can not only provide him with rest from his work as a shepherd of souls, but at the same time improve a facet of his education that can't be completed in the seminary, seems particularly suited for a priest, namely, activity which is aimed at improving his general culture. Obviously he should keep his knowledge of theology up to date, but he is not supposed to be just a specialist in theology, an expert on how to look after souls. He lives in the world, he deals with people, so he cannot afford to be out of touch with current ideas, problems, and trends affecting the people of his time, those living in that same world. He must either acquire a certain level of human culture—profane culture, as it used to be called—or resign himself to living in an ivory tower, unable to relate to the mentality of the people he is supposed to bring nearer to God.

It's true that sanctity can make up for everything—except, perhaps, wasting time. There can be no excuse for a priest whose working hours are not at least as long as those of a professional or manual worker with a family to support

There is one further aspect of this question which we must mention. All human beings are social animals. A man cannot achieve his end, either human or supernatural, in isolation. He is constantly dealing and interrelating with all the other people around him. This being so, God's plan has to be respected by the priest as by anyone else, on this point as on others. We have only to look at the Gospels to realize that the Lord was not a misanthrope or recluse avoiding contact with his fellow men. We cannot say he was a "socialite" or belonged to high society, for that would be untrue, but he was certainly sociable, sociable even to the point of scandalizing—naturally!—the Pharisees. He accepted the invitation to the wedding in Cana, and attended with his disciples and his mother. He accepted Simon the Leper's invitation to a meal and that of Matthew to eat with him and his somewhat disreputable friends. He was very friendly with Lazarus and he knew his family well. He decided to stay in the house of the tax-collector Zaccheus without waiting for an invitation, which he probably would never have received because Zacchaeus would not have dared to invite him.

Normal social relationships and dealings with others are not a kind of licentiousness that ought to be avoided. They are based on human nature and are essential. They are good and desired by God. The only point is that if a priest has a genuinely priestly spirit, for him they are much more than that. As a Christian, they are a means of practicing and giving expression to the virtue of charity, for he cannot forget that as often as he does anything to the least of these little ones he does it to God himself. And, as a priest, he knows that any contact with other people is a way of furthering the apostolate.

Naturally social contact must be orderly and moderate, as will be dictated in each particular case by the cardinal virtue of prudence. Henry Suso laid down the following rules: receive everyone amiably, speak to them briefly, ensure that they are consoled when they leave you, and never allow your heart to become attached. And it was St. Francis de Sales, a great saint and also the greatest living example of human perfection at the time of the Renaissance, who left us in his books and letters the main guidelines for the practice of sociability. And he was a man whose conduct and manner were not the least of the means by which he brought so many souls to God. It was he who recommended that everyone who wished to practice charity should cultivate what he called little virtues: good manners, courtesy, affability, gentleness, amiability, deference, patience with the irksome and the inopportune, kindliness and understanding.

We could also mention the importance of cleanliness in one's dress and personal hygiene as a part of our human perfection and as an exercise of charity. Canon 1369, paragraph 2, of the Code of Canon Law, for instance, contains clear allusions to good manners, hygiene, cleanliness in one's clothes, refinement and gravity. This shows how concerned our mother the Church is with details which may seem insignificant but which, in fact, are important.

Intellectual development

The most characteristic aspect of man is that which makes him God's image and likeness, namely his intelligence and his will. These are the two faculties which should be cultivated most assiduously by the priest. On the subject of intelligence, it must never be forgotten that he is an instrument of salvation, and one of his main duties is to give doctrine, to teach the

Gospel, to provide the minds of the faithful with adequate and suitable material relating to their faith. Since no one can give what he does not possess, he can hardly teach something unless he has first learned it himself.

And the object of all the intellectual training he has received in the seminary during his years of study is precisely to give him the knowledge he needs to carry out his ministry. It would be wrong to imagine that he has only to study a certain number of books and be able to answer examination questions based on them. Normally any course of studies, whether in a seminary or elsewhere, tries to give very basic information, teach certain work methods and show where further facts can be found when needed. The end of the road is not intended to be reached on those points; on the contrary, only a beginning has been made.

Naturally the subjects taught during the seminary years are concerned mainly with the ecclesiastical sciences. However, it may lead to unnecessary—and more often than not, harmful—isolation from life if too clear or too wide a separation is established between the ecclesiastical and the secular sciences or if a priest devotes himself too exclusively to the former. For really there is no human problem, there is nothing connected with life however secular it may be, that is not somehow related to God and to the order which he created.

This point is very important, because it involves a whole concept of God, the world and man, and it may easily happen — in view of the subtlety of many errors and the devil's ability to present himself as an angel of light—that the priest may adopt a wrong attitude that might prejudice his apostolic ministry, harm his own spiritual life and even play into the enemy's hands. This can happen when the ecclesiastical and the secular sciences are considered to be separate and distinct worlds.

This is an error that corresponds to the idea of a total separation of the supernatural world from the natural world, ruling out all interference or connection between them. Much of modern thought led to this error in the nineteenth century. It was condemned repeatedly by the Church, though her views were not heeded even by Catholics—or at least, most of them. The whole of the nineteenth century was characterized by the attempt to confine God to his heaven, the Church to her sanctuary, and the priest to his sacristy; and we have emanated from that century, the immediate predecessor of our own time. That view considered our world as something apart, having nothing to do with God, the Church or priests, so that they were all banished from public life and confined to the sphere that was declared fit for them. Secularism was a goal and a result; anti-clericalism was the means by which the desired object was achieved. Theology, ecclesiastical studies, were separated from life, like the world to which they referred, and they had neither relevance nor influence on life. Perhaps their feeling of being apart and separate began to be accepted even by clerics, who ended up by adapting to the dichotomy, at least from the psychological point of view.

It is also possible that this psychological impact has seeped outwards and given rise to something which, if not universal, certainly affects many priests, namely an attitude or feeling of inferiority in comparison with the scientist, or professional man trained in one or more of the profane sciences. This attitude sometimes takes the form of a certain timidity or admiration, as if apologizing for one's ignorance in regard to non-ecclesiastical matters. At other times it is shown by a certain defensive reticence, a sort of unconfessed fear of being found out. And this may lead to making virtue of necessity, leading a priest to avoid intellectual conversations on topics in which he will naturally be inferior because he has not been trained in such subjects.

Obviously, as the reader's good sense will already have told him, there is no question of acquiring non-ecclesiastical scientific information simply to compete with intellectuals on their own ground. That is not a priest's function and, if he were to try, he would be as out of place as a lay person who neglected his work in order to learn one or more of the ecclesiastical subjects in depth. Since the priest is there for the salvation of souls, the science required of him is the science of salvation, and only the Church can give him that, for she is the only true teacher in this field. It is from his study of the ecclesiastical disciplines, of the Church sciences, that he acquires the knowledge he needs to carry out his duties. If a deep spiritual life of prayer and practice of the virtues converts this knowledge into actual wisdom, then the whole of his ministry will have an unmistakable seal which derives from the truth, not just as learned, but as lived.

As far as the intellectual training of the priest is concerned, therefore—and the intellect is essential, for the Lord must be loved *ex tota mente* (Mt 22: 37)—there are two levels: the doctrinal and what we may call the cultural. The first refers to the teaching of those revealed truths preserved and taught by the Church. The second encompasses all of human and spiritual knowledge, increasing in volume as each generation adds to it, which constitutes a common heritage and greatly influences the way in which we approach, consider and resolve human problems—all those matters which God has left to the free decision of mankind.

On the question of doctrinal training, it must be made clear that the object of the years leading up to ordination and the beginning of the priest's ministry in whatever position the bishop assigns to him, that is, his years as a student in the seminary, is to lay the foundation of an edifice, not really to complete the construction in all its ramifications It could not be hoped, for instance, that in the courses taught in a seminary a candidate for the priesthood would, or even should, learn everything known about sacred scripture, beginning with Greek and Hebrew and going on to the most recent hypotheses or theories on a particular verse of a particular one of the sacred books.

The seminary's function is not to train specialists. What it should do, is to awaken an interest in pursuing theology, philosophy or exegesis on a higher level in suitable students. It should also ensure that they all finish their period of formal studies with a sufficient knowledge of books, sources and subjects as will allow them to keep up to date as time goes by, for theology is not a dead science but a living one. St. Thomas Aquinas and the Fathers of the Church are not dead ends, but open roads. Anyone who leaves the seminary with the idea that the Angelic Doctor has said the last word, rather than regarding him as a beacon showing several different ways ahead, runs the risk of losing touch with the world around him.

As a spokesman for God, the priest has to bring the word of salvation to all mankind. Therefore the first thing he has to learn is precisely that word of salvation which he is to teach. He leaves the seminary with a firm basis, a good knowledge of the essential truths of the faith, the supernaturally revealed doctrine. Doubtless he knows enough to teach the children their catechism and to explain Christian doctrine to people who know nothing about it, to administer the sacraments, and to look after the members of the faithful entrusted to his care. But he cannot rest content with that amount of knowledge, any more than a doctor can be so satisfied with what he learned at medical school as to resolve never again to read a word on the subject.

In any case, the world in which the priest has to live and work is not composed only of children and adults whose mentality is as rudimentary as that. There is not only ignorance and good will in the world; there is also a lot of error. As a good shepherd, he must take care of his flock, ensuring that the sheep have proper nourishment and that they are free from any germs that could cause illness or even death. As a good shepherd, he has to safeguard the purity of what he teaches: "If you continue in my word, you are truly my disciples, and you will know the truth, and the truth will make you free" (Jn 8: 31-32). Only Christ's word, only the revelation brought to us by him, is the whole truth; that is the only teaching the priest should impart and that is the science, the knowledge, he ought to master above any other.

Every candidate for the priesthood must take this aspect of his preparation very seriously, realizing that his objective is to be useful, to be of service. And as Blessed Josemaria Escriva said, "the best service we can do for the Church and for humanity is to give doctrine. Many of the ills afflicting the world are due to a lack of Christian doctrine even among those who wish or appear to be closely following Jesus Christ. For there are some who, instead of teaching what is right, take advantage of the ignorance of others to sow confusion."[7] Therefore serious, tenacious effort and study are essential, if we are to acquire an adequate doctrinal training, for it is not on the basis of intuitions, but of truths revealed, taught and transmitted by the Church, that the priest can truly serve his fellow men and women and be able to offer them the nourishment they need.

The Lord sowed his seed, that is the word which he had heard from his Father: "I have given them the words which thou gavest me" (Jn 17: 8); and he commanded his disciples to continue sowing until the end of time. To ensure this, he established the Church and entrusted it with the mission of teaching. The fruits of the divine doctrine, wrote Leo XIII in *Aeterni Patris Filius*, through which salvation was accomplished for mankind, would not have endured long if Christ Jesus had not instituted a permanent magisterium to instruct intellects in the faith. Since these truths are vital as far as salvation is concerned, the priest can have a fairly accurate idea of his responsibility with regard to teaching them properly and the fidelity with which he must transmit them.

"The kingdom of heaven may be compared to a man who sowed good seed in his field; but while men were sleeping, his enemy came and sowed weeds among the wheat" (Mt 13: 24-25). Perhaps if those men had been on their guard instead of asleep, the enemy would not have dared to go into that field to sow the seeds or, at worst, he might have scattered just a few seeds and gone away. In any case, as St. John Chrysostom explains, "indeed this also is part of the devil's craft, by the side of the truth always to bring in error, painting thereon many resemblances, so as easily to cheat the deceivable. Therefore He calls it not any other seed, but tares; which in appearance are somewhat like wheat."[8] In order to harm the owner of the field, the devil takes advantage of the fact that the men on whom he is relying are asleep and off their guard; then he sows these weeds, or tares, and the similarity between the seeds ensures that no one notices until the wheat begins to sprout, until the fruit begins to appear, and then it is too late.

If a priest is not alert, how can he be sure that the enemy of souls is not disseminating false teaching? And how can he know that a particular idea is wrong except by having carefully and conscientiously learned what is right?

It is true that this type of vigilance is more directly the responsibility of bishops, and God knows the enormous liability it involves. But no priest, no co-worker of the bishops, can ignore something that is so immediately relevant to salvation. Therefore they themselves must be on the alert and scrutinize all the nourishment they give their own minds in accordance with what St. Paul says: "Guard what has been entrusted to you. Avoid the godless chatter and contradictions of what is falsely called knowledge, for by professing it some have missed the mark as regards the faith" (1 Tim 6: 20).

The priest's judgment must be very clear and properly developed so that he may discern easily and almost by instinct what is in accordance with the Truth, which is Christ, and what deviates from it in any way; he must remain strong in the teaching he has received and not be dazzled by brilliant or bold theories. That situation arose as early as the first century and St. Paul felt obliged to warn the Colossians: "See to it that no one makes a prey of you by philosophy and empty deceit, according to human tradition, according to the elemental spirits of the universe, and not according to Christ" (Col 2: 8); while to the Christians at Ephesus he wrote: "Let no one deceive you with empty words" (Ephes 5: 6). By empty words here are meant all utterances that are not words of salvation, not the word of God but only the words of men; these may be more or less well spoken and composed, more or less intelligent and penetrating, but they have no guarantee but the merit of the particular men who speak them. The truths of the faith, on the other hand, the words of salvation, are not the result of philosophic research or the fruit of human intelligence—they are a *divine deposit.*

Fully aware that an atmosphere of confusion reigns in every critical period of history, a mind as broad and as open as that of Pope John XXIII felt the need to warn priests that "the *depositum fidei* cannot be interfered with. But it would not be transmitted with absolute firmness and certainty if that faithfulness to tradition, that vigilant sense of moderation and respect, that mental uprighteousness, which are an expression of integrity and courage, were to be weakened among the clergy. It is impossible to face up to the secessionist and independent spirit unfortunately propagated, frivolously but pertinaciously, by superficial learning without a philosophical basis, if vigilance against the currents of certain distractions and curiosities which *ad rem non pertinent* wanes among the younger clergy."

The intellectual training which a seminary should offer candidates for the priesthood ought to be eminently positive; it must teach truths or, rather, the Truth. Sometimes priests can fall into the subtle error of thinking themselves to be self-sufficient or, once again, allowing themselves to be influenced by that intellectual inferiority complex. They may set off enthusiastically in pursuit of any idea they find in a book or that comes from some brilliant or successful author. It is probably something sad but true that has led Pope Paul VI to ask priests to render filial submission to the Gospel, for which "it is necessary to profess fidelity to the thinking and to the norms of the Church, avoiding certain critical and reformist attitudes towards the traditional teachings of the Church, the venerable customs, the fundamental and august structures of ecclesiastical life, avoiding also a certain kind of so-called return to the sources, as is said, which attempts to justify a spirit that does not accept discipline, to destroy the Church's teaching, to adapt certain naturalist tendencies that empty souls and institutions of the genuine spirit of Christ." [9]

If priests are to prepare themselves to preach the word, they must do so in such a way that "they may always grow in their understanding of God's revealed word, may know how to grasp it through meditation, and express it through word and conduct" (OT 4). Priests who fulfill their duty have little time for intellectual excursions: the little free time their work allows them should be occupied in more basic reading. The education of the "intellectual" type of priest, who is happier reading the latest treatise than studying and deepening his knowledge of the Church's basic teaching is in danger of being based more on opinions than on doctrine, and he is bound to become superficial and frivolous like a child "tossed to and fro and carried about with every wind of doctrine by the cunning of men, by their craftiness in deceitful wiles" (Eph 4: 14).

We are not suggesting that a priest should be satisfied with knowing just a few basic facts. He must know many things; he cannot lose touch with developments in theology. He must read and be informed, study and think about what he studies. And it is in the seminary that he must be trained to take active steps to develop his intelligence, a talent he cannot leave buried, and to go on increasing his knowledge. It is there he must be taught to distinguish between a fact and a theory, between truth and opinion.

"Since doctrinal training ought not to aim at a mere communication of ideas, but at a genuine and deep formation of students" (OT 17), the priest should try, not so much to learn, as to improve, for this is how he converts what he learns into real life; otherwise everything he learns will remain barren and he will have spent his time in vain. Perhaps, therefore, if he genuinely wants to improve, he will attain that kind of inner instinct which St. Teresa has in mind when she says: "I have always been fond of the words of the Gospels and have found more recollection in them than in the most carefully planned books, especially books of which the authors were not fully approved, and which I never wanted to read."[10]

Exercising his saving ministry in the midst of the world, the priest is totally submerged in an atmosphere which is bound to have an influence on him, whether he likes it or not. He lives in his own era and he has to be responsive to it. He is a member of the human race which evolves in its thought, in its culture, its technical progress, the advances of science, all types of philosophical and political currents. Everything that happens in that world affects him; otherwise he would not be human. The climate around him, especially in the matter of ideas, tends to seep into him imperceptibly. So it happens, for example, that Catholics living in countries with a strong Protestant culture can find themselves showing certain signs of a Protestant mentality. Hence a priest should constantly try to stimulate his intelligence with nourishment which will effectively redress these influences and keep him faithful to Christ and the Church, to his priesthood and to his particular saving mission.

Commenting on the changes and developments in the ways of life and modes of thought in recent times, Pope Paul VI added: "The Church itself is being engulfed and shaken by this tidal wave of change, for however much men may be committed to the Church, they are deeply affected by the climate of the world. They run the risk of becoming confused, bewildered and alarmed, and this is a state of affairs which strikes at the very roots of the Church. It drives many people to adopt the most outlandish views. They imagine that the Church should abdicate its proper role, and adopt an entirely new and unprecedented mode of existence."[11] To safeguard herself against this danger, the Pope recommends "an increased self-awareness on the part of the Church," a better understanding of what she really is, according to Christ's will as contained in scripture and in tradition, interpreted and developed in the true teaching of the Church "under the inspiration and guidance of the Holy Spirit."

Apart from theology, which he should never neglect, a priest will derive great benefit from reading the pontifical documents and Church history.

The pontifical documents—addresses, messages, homilies and especially encyclicals—contain appropriate teaching for each particular moment according to the needs of the time. They are means by which the priest can share the same concerns as the visible head of the Church and keep in close touch with the directives laid down by the magisterium. Every priest should keep himself constantly informed on the questions of doctrine these documents contain, for they are the correct application of the unchanging word of Christ to the problems of each period. From Pope Gregory XVI onwards, and more particularly since the time of Pope Leo XIII, the sovereign pontiffs have more and more frequently adopted this method of preaching in writing so that, with the help of her priests, the words pronounced by the Church through the bishop of Rome may reach the four corners of the earth. They contain nourishing food for the mind as well as for the heart. Indeed every priest should be imbued with the teaching of the great encyclicals.

Speaking of Church history—in the words of Cicero, history is *magistra vitae* [the teacher of life], it is for nations and peoples what memory is for the individual. The people of God have their own history on earth and, in practice, this is the story of the faithfulness of Christ's spouse, the Church. It shows us how the life of Christ's spouse on earth is continually the object of contradiction in the world. It tells us of her great and glorious fight to remain faithful to Christ and to maintain her independence as against the powers of this world. We see her tireless struggles in the cause of purification and sanctity, mercy and salvation. The history of Peter's barque has been an exciting one—sailing on an immense ocean, constantly threatened but never sunk and never wavering from her course. Indeed, as Haecker says, in the final analysis, the history of the world is the history of God's grace in the world, it is the history of salvation.

The Fathers are another essential source of education for the priest, to enrich his mind and complete his training. They are an important link in the Church's tradition, very close to the sources (in comparison at least with us) and formidable defenders of the purity of the faith against numerous subtle infiltrations. They have a deep understanding of the mysteries; they explain the dogmas; they are living witnesses to the truth, despite slander and persecution, prison and exile, martyrdom and death. This particular type of reading, furthermore, leads to that other area which we conventionally call profane or secular. In fact, the Fathers moved in an environment not much more favorable than our own and their writings show a perfect insight into the mentality and culture of the people of their times, the people they wanted to reach.

It would be easy to go on and suggest that the priest ought to know the classics of world literature and the outstanding works of his own time, at least in a general way, so as to have some notion of cultural and scientific developments, or that he should be familiar with the great names in the world at any given moment and know something about the persons involved. Perhaps it will be better, however, to stay within more practical bounds.

He could help himself by spending half an hour each day reading a serious and well-informed newspaper. It might also be useful to read a review or periodical of a cultural and informative type, which would keep him abreast of the most important or most interesting topics over a wide field. Thus he would know the current state of the theory of evolution, the latest films, the problems of the Third World, the difficulties of the national and world economy and the broad characteristics of cultural trends as they develop.

It is unlikely that a priest will have the means or the time to read the classics of world literature. However, a lot can be done in the seminaries if there are good teachers who can arouse the students' interest and give them good advice, for this can be continued afterwards by recommending suitable reading matter or even the books they should have in their library. Taking a realistic view and considering the immense amount of work the priest could undertake if he were determined to do it all, normally he will have to be content with summaries and broad surveys to give him the general information that any well-educated person should possess.

It would be a shame if seminary professors, instead of devoting the best part of their time and intelligence to educating students, introducing them to new areas of interest and preparing them to carry out their mission in the world, were to give their classes without enthusiasm or effort, sticking rigidly to a plan that has gone stale after years of repetition. Sellmair quotes a terrible diatribe of Cardinal Newman's, which deals primarily with the literary aspect of education but which opens up wide possibilities for an examination of conscience and is very useful because it is so thought-provoking. The Vatican Council stresses the important role of superiors and teachers too: "For directors and teachers need to be keenly aware of how greatly the outcome of seminary formation depends on their own manner of thinking and acting" (OT 5).

The priest should, of course, be a cultured man, intellectually mature, in touch with life and capable of carrying on a conversation. It is very sad to see a priest lost for something to say because he can talk about none of the subjects that interest the people among whom he lives, apart from ecclesiastical topics. His ignorance is like a barrier separating him from life and from other people, confining him within very narrow limits. He thus widens the gap that has appeared between theology and life in modern times; he shuts himself into his own world, becomes isolated and lets life pass him by without even touching it, without influencing it, without channeling it. The people entrusted to his care will be unable to look to him for advice in their difficulties, hints for their reading, or help in their problems, for his estrangement from the world makes him useless for those purposes.

Above all these considerations, however, we must return to the fact that knowledge of the Church's teaching is important for the priest, not as a science in itself, but as a source of enlightenment for life. He would do well to ponder those words of scripture in which God says: "My people are destroyed for lack of knowledge; because you have rejected knowledge, I reject you from being a priest to me" (Hos 4: 6). God alone knows how much priests have contributed, by their negligence, to the separation between religion and life and only he knows how they can expect to give an account of their conduct.

Ascetical training

Just as the purpose of his intellectual education is to prepare the priest's mind so that he may be as perfect and able an instrument as possible in the service of his saving mission, so the object of his ascetical training is to achieve the same result by developing the other faculty proper to man, namely his will.

A division of theology which was over-formalistic and is now somewhat outdated used to distinguish three parts: dogmatic, moral and ascetical, with this last part referred to as "ascetical and mystical." As a branch of theology, this was primarily a speculative science, a subject to be studied like any other.

That is not what concerns us here, however. Etymologically *ascesis* means effort, exercise. So when we speak of ascetical training we mean practice at making an effort, the habit of making efforts. The term itself suggests activity and work, rather than speculation or repose. Here, more than anywhere else, knowledge must be transformed into life; what we know must be converted into a habit and practiced; a science must become a vital activity.

A prerequisite for any understanding of the ascetical struggle is to consider the constitution of man as he stands: a tarnished nature awaiting correction. Original sin shattered the perfect equilibrium and the harmonious condition which man enjoyed at the moment of his creation and, from then onwards, every man born of woman has had to make an effort to recover that balance and that harmony. By erasing original sin, Baptism restores man to the supernatural life and to grace but the effects still persist in his human nature: an inclination to evil, weakness of the will in following the dictates of reason, rebellion of the lower instincts. . . To be a man and to act as a man at all times takes an effort, courage and tenacity.

Through Baptism, a man becomes a Christian; as well as a natural life, then, he possesses a supernatural life which must try to transform, perfect and raise to its own level that other life from its purely human plane. Grace, however, does not act mechanically; it requires acceptance, manifested in a genuine response. Only then will it grow and develop so as to raise the person to a higher level and permeate all the actions of his life. Through the grace infused at Baptism, a Christian is a new man; he must banish the old man and overcome his resistance to the change. This new spiritual man, born of the spirit, must conquer the old, carnal man, born of the flesh. And conquest means struggle. Did our Lord not demand as the first qualification for people who wanted to follow him that they should deny themselves? Is not the cross the sign of a Christian?

There is yet another consideration over and above these. By his ordination, the priest has acquired a new character. Like his Master, he is called to carry out the work of redemption and there is no other path of salvation, no other way by which people can be saved, but the way of the cross. Like our Lord, the priest is "crucified to the world" (Gal 6: 14) and, like St. Paul, he must complete in his own flesh what is lacking in Christ's passion (Col 1: 24). If the Head suffered, can the limb hope to avoid suffering, especially limbs so closely connected to the Head as priests are? The Lord paid in full for the sins of mankind. How, then, can the priest expect to be exempt from imitating Christ by refusing to pay his contribution on behalf of his fellow-men? Is he to be greater than his master?

It must be made clear, before we go any further, that asceticism is by no means a form of hostility to nature, or a mere negation of something. Quite the contrary is the case. True, the ascetical struggle does demand penance and mortification; nevertheless, it is not something negative, but something positive, not hostility but love, not sadness and grief, but joy and freedom. It is not a negative exercise, although it often consists of saying *no*, but a positive one, because it involves refusing harmful things. In the ascetical struggle the priest says *no* to what is damaging, twisted, and distorted; and he rejects these things precisely to ensure and confirm the harmonious development of all the human, Christian, and priestly qualities which God has given him, and to achieve a proper balance between them all. He refuses and he rejects everything that would estrange him from his ministry, anything that could decrease his usefulness as an instrument, whatever might impair his priestliness, any obstacle that might hinder the perfect fulfillment of God's will.

St. Paul, who was so inured to all kinds of toil and trouble, having experienced prison and floggings, beatings and long, dangerous journeys, sleeplessness and penury, still affirmed: "I pummel my body and subdue it, lest after preaching to others I myself should be disqualified" (1 Cor 9: 27). Doubtless this is a good reason why no priest should ever slacken; he is fighting against every death-bearing germ. If he thinks that everything will turn out all right just by letting nature take its course, then he may as well believe in fairy tales, and a candidate for the priesthood is supposed to be more realistic than that.

Nobody regards an athlete as opposed to nature or inhuman just because he submits to a strict discipline of physical exercises and training, is rigidly careful about what he eats and drinks and about his sleeping and smoking, or because he abstains from countless perfectly permissible things which happen to be unfavorable to the objective he has in mind and are serious obstacles in his path to victory. St. Paul, who was closely in touch with his time and with the world in which he lived, used that same comparison: "Every athlete exercises self-control in all things. They do it to receive a perishable wreath, but we an imperishable one" (1 Cor 9: 25).

Therefore, it is not simply a question of getting control of one's will on the human level by sheer physical effort—although that in itself would not be a bad thing. It is primarily a supernatural exercise in which grace plays as important a part as in any other attempt to get closer to God. The purpose of ascetical training, then, is not only to eliminate everything opposed to God's will but to help one to climb the path towards holiness, to acquire supernatural habits, virtues, which will make one more and more like Christ our Lord.

Man's life on this earth, and the priest's life in the midst of the world, is a struggle, a contest. But he has to struggle like a man, that is intelligently; he has to run the race, but not aimlessly; he has to fight, but he must not "box as one beating the air" (1 Cor 9: 26). Mortification is not an end, but a means; it is something one does, not for its own sake, but to achieve a certain result. Reason, enlightened by grace, has to show us how and when to practice it, how to apply it properly, when to moderate and when to intensify it.

The primary object of mortification is the perfect fulfillment of God's will for, in the final analysis, this is the only thing that really matters. "Not every one who says to me 'Lord, Lord,' shall enter the kingdom of heaven, but he who does the will of my Father who is in heaven" (Mt 7: 21). Therefore the best type of mortification of all is one that makes the fulfillment of God's will easier, and we can find it in the duties proper to each individual's state in life. The most effective mortification is one that can overcome or eliminate the obstacles that hinder us from performing our duty—conquering our laziness, our love of comfort, our taste, our inertia, our whims. We must try to free our will from the bonds that restrain it from doing what God wants of it at any particular moment. We should cast aside any kind of impediment that slows down its movement towards its proper goal. In this sense, mortification becomes a weapon of freedom to break loose from the bonds keeping the will in chains. In the long run, it is the will that has to be in control, instead of allowing itself to be carried along by our love of ease and comfort.

Mortification also fulfills the function of correcting the wayward tendencies of our instincts and passions. It must be emphasized that it is not a question of repressing anything. This would really leave the task half-finished. It would be dangerous because every tension has a limit and every repression provokes a reaction that tends to liberate whatever is repressed. It is not a matter of repressing, but rather of controlling, softening, channeling. In this sense, mortification is like training for an athlete or a sportsman. It tames the instincts so as to control them and get them to run in their proper channels without going an inch beyond what the reason determines, like well-trained horses, obedient and reverential servants. "The body must be given a little less than it needs. Otherwise it will turn traitor."[12] Unless the spirit—reason and will—dominates the body, the body will dominate the spirit: "For the desires of the flesh are against the Spirit, and the desires of the Spirit are against the flesh; for these are opposed to each other, to prevent you from doing what you would" (Gal 5: 17).

It is not that we should do the opposite of whatever we want to do—for, after all, our inclinations often coincide with God's will—but as a first reaction against following our own inclinations, a reaction lasting an instant, it is good just to stop for a moment to allow the will to act with the freedom that comes from following the dictates of reason rather than to be carried along by the impulse of one's appetites.

While he is in the seminary, a candidate for the priesthood is subjected to strict discipline, to a timetable, to acts in common, not so much because of the need to maintain order and allow the institution to function properly, as to introduce him to habits that will shape his character and strengthen his will. "The discipline required by seminary life should not be regarded merely as a strong support of community life and of charity. For it is a necessary part of the whole training program designed to provide self-mastery, to foster solid maturity of personality, and to develop other traits of character which are extremely serviceable for the ordered and productive activity of the Church. Let discipline be exercised, then, in a way which will develop in the students an internal attitude by which the authority of superiors will be accepted through an act of personal conviction, that is, conscientiously (see Rom 13: 5) and for supernatural reasons" (OT 11).

However, if the student confines himself to relying on the schedule laid down for him and does everything merely as a matter of routine, making no effort of his own, as a child rests on the walking-reins held by its mother, then as soon as the reins are taken away, he will probably fall to the ground. It is an unfortunate but proven fact that when some priests leave the seminary and find themselves on their own, without the support of a routine planned for them by others, they quickly abandon all order, discipline or schedule, because these are no longer imposed from above. If there is to be order in their life, it depends on their own will. If they have not learned to impose it on themselves, if their will has not grasped those means of formation in a positive manner, but has just accepted them passively without assimilating them, if it has merely tolerated them without loving them, then the lack of habit makes it very easy to abandon them altogether.

However, even if a priest is deeply permeated with a sense of discipline, he would still do well to be very vigilant. A habit is acquired only by repeated acts; the plough has to go over hard ground again and again if it is to change it into a garden. And a habit is lost if the acts that created it are neglected. If a priest is complacent or over-confident, he may find, when least expecting it, that his soul has become hard and inflexible, that it has lost some of its abilities, that it is no longer "fit," like an athlete who neglects his physical exercise and training.

It is not a question of doing a few sporadic acts of mortification, but of *being mortified:* "And those who belong to Christ Jesus have crucified the flesh with its passions and desires" (Gal 5: 24). This involves a habitual effort to keep the senses under control: sight, hearing, and taste. It implies forcing the imagination to concentrate on whatever is being done at a particular moment, putting away all fantasies gently but firmly, banishing all distractions from the mind. It means practicing interior mortification—curbing our curiosity, vanity, self-esteem, selfishness.

One of the points which teachers should most carefully bear in mind is that future priests should be trained in freedom, and not only in freedom, but in its corollary, namely responsibility.

Man is free, certainly. But it is important that he should also *feel* free. And a man feels free when he does what he wants to do *because* he wants to do it. In this respect, the objective to be pursued is that the future priest should be taught to want what God wants of him at any particular moment, that, quite freely and because it is his own wish, he should want what he ought to want, what pleases God, what God's love for him and his love of God suggest to him. He should be able to do what he likes; if he does not like doing the things that someone who has freely decided to be a priest should want to do, then this in itself may be a clear sign that he has no vocation or purity of intention.

Those in charge of training future priests have a delicate task and one that requires great dedication. They must be able to measure out the right amount of freedom which should be allowed on the grounds of age to each of the groups in their seminary, though always, of course, demanding a certain minimum of discipline. They have to teach their students, patiently and over a period of time, to make their own way, relying on the help of grace but without undue props, to make decisions and to organize their time. They must be available always for consultation, ready to give advice, willing to listen to any suggestion, so that without any timidity or false respect the seminarians can approach them at any time. They must help them to clarify their ideas—without imposing their own—and to form wise judgments. All of this, and much more besides, is only a summary of the enormous amount of work the educators have to perform, and it is almost the work of a skilled craftsman.

Seminarians must also be taught to have a sense of responsibility. If a man is intelligent and free, then he is also responsible, that is, he knows and is willing to accept the outcome of his actions, he is not afraid to give an account of what he has done or left undone and to face up to the consequences. Otherwise, if he takes refuge in anonymity or dilutes his responsibility in the mass or the group, if he considers it preferable to be so clever and sly that he is never "caught" than to exercise personal responsibility, then it would probably be better for him to go into any other type of work rather than the priesthood. To be a priest of Christ in the service of the people of God demands a different attitude, the attitude of a man who wants to please God above all else. Such a man understands and loves discipline, irrespective of whether this or that particular detail meets with his approval.

When a priest or a student for the priesthood has adopted a supernatural outlook and is determined to be another Christ, it is amazing how much ingenuity he can develop to introduce at least a little sign of the cross into everything he does. He always succeeds in offering the Lord some little thorn that he finds on his way. He always takes advantage of any slight discomfort and marks it with the sign of the cross to make it different from the same discomfort suffered by a pagan. He does so in his personal cleanliness and the care of his clothes, in his postures—never too comfortable!—in the attention he pays to others, in the use he makes of his time, in eating and drinking, in his friendliness and courtesy when dealing with people who annoy him, in his pleasantness with the unpleasant, in his smiling acceptance of the thousand little upsets of everyday life, in the tidy way he keeps his books and papers, in punctuality, in work and in leisure, in everything. By freeing him from the weights that would keep him stuck in the mud of this world, mortification helps every Christian—including the seminarian— to rise to a spiritual level, for "if you don't deny yourself you will never be a soul of prayer."[13] To believe that God "would admit to His close friendship pleasure-loving people who are free from all trials is ridiculous" (St. Teresa).[14] And if a priest is not a "soul of prayer" what is he? If "where there is no mortification, there is no virtue,"[15] that is, if there is no supernatural habit of doing what is right, what success can a priest have if he practices little or no mortification?

However, this is not the only point. To practice asceticism, to train the will, does not mean becoming inhuman, cold, insensitive, disinterested in life. In its negative aspect, it means simply—though it is far from simple—acquiring the strength to reject everything that separates us from God, just that and nothing else. But another object of asceticism is to develop everything positive in a man, in a Christian. Was the Lord not so sensitive to friendship, for instance, as to weep at the death of his friend Lazarus? Was he not filled with tenderness for the little children? Did he not feel deep compassion for the people who were rejecting him, his own people whom he loved dearly, as he wept over Jerusalem? Was he not sad and did he not experience physical repugnance in the face of suffering in Gethsemani, when he asked the Father to remove the chalice that awaited him, if it were possible? Was he not glad to take advantage of the shade of a tree and feel the coolness of the water when he arrived one hot midday at Jacob's well in Samaria, "tired after his journey" (Jn 4: 6).

God has made things to serve man, not to gain control over him. No one can live without some minimum of happiness and pleasure. Sin corrupts everything it touches and it has corrupted even the meaning of words: nowadays "pleasure" sounds sinful. Yet there is pleasure in very many permissible things—and not only permissible, but good and positively willed by God. Evil is never in things, but in men and in their distorted wills. There is pleasure in the sun and the sea, in the cool breeze that caresses our face on a summer's evening, in a log fire that warms our numbed limbs on a winter's day, in the flowers and the trees, in music, in color and in scents, in relaxation and sport, in friendship and in reading, in laughter—though not in the laughter of those people who laugh without joy—and in the meditative silence of quiet evenings. A priest should learn to discover these pleasures, and then he will find himself quite spontaneously giving thanks to God for having made such a marvellous creation and for being so good as to place within our reach so many things that can give us pleasure without disturbing our peace, unblemished pleasures which rest the soul and the body, which increase our enjoyment all the more by bringing us closer to him.

Let us remember, once again, that the objective is to restore to creation its original function, namely to give glory to God and serve as a means for man also to give him glory. Only negative things have to be rejected: a sportsman may abstain from alcoholic drink, but he will not give up eating or sleeping.

Those who have the enormous task—and the enormous responsibility—of training students for the priesthood must pay great attention to this aspect of their education. The young men in their charge are not simply "seminarians," a strange human species—in the eyes of the outside world—composed of beings who are different from other men of their age, separated from the rest of the world and from life, supervised during vacations by the parish priest and enclosed during term-time in buildings specially designed for them. In fact, of course, they are perfectly normal people. Those coming to the end of their secondary education in minor seminaries and those studying philosophy have the same vitality, psychology, interests and problems as students pursuing other courses in other colleges. Those studying theology are like university students—or, at least, they should be. The fundamental difference, perhaps, lies in the fact that those studying for the priesthood come into contact with life when they are ordained, whereas the others never lose that contact; their physical and intellectual development is carried on while they are in touch with the environment in which they are likely to live afterwards.

Hence teachers and superiors should never lose sight of the fact that they are training *secular priests*, not religious. They must prepare them for the life that awaits them when they leave the seminary—a life of sacrifice and work in an environment that they have to transform from the inside outwards, living among people with whose problems they have to be familiar and whose circumstances they must understand, for they are the circumstances of the world in which they live; a life that is not, and should not be, organized in the same way as other peoples' lives but in a special way, the way which is proper to secular priests.

Isolation and loneliness are a real danger for the priest. This was mentioned more than once by the Second Vatican Council; the decree *Presbyterorum Ordinis* refers to it and Paul VI has returned to it repeatedly. Nevertheless, a man is not alone if he has friends, and this is something he has to learn during his years of study. He must be taught the importance of friendship and how to avoid ever being alone. During his years in the seminary he lives with companions who, in the course of time, will become priests like himself, with the same mission, the same objectives, the same vocation and similar problems. He cannot go through the seminary getting on well with the companions he likes and rejecting those he finds unfriendly. This would not be loving others but loving himself, and a selfish person always ends up being left alone.

The years spent living with other students ought to be used to cultivate a number of virtues, all of which really lead back to charity: learning how to get to know others, not making a matter of life or death out of every little difference of opinion on insignificant points, learning to give in, to help others, to be loyal (loyalty is so important and so seldom practiced), to take an interest in other peoples' problems, to cooperate so that, instead of being a collection of individuals, each one going his own way, the seminary will house a group of friends who stand together and help one another to improve and to create an atmosphere in which it is pleasant to live.

Seminarians should also learn to be alone without getting bored and not to need others to provide entertainment. Indeed, they should grow to love those periods of solitude which their work allows them. And if they learn to be sensitive, to discover the beauty of creation, to educate their taste and to avoid inventing needs, then they will be prepared, not just to tolerate solitude to the best of their ability, whenever the case arises, but to take advantage of it to develop—and to enjoy developing—their minds and then go on to enjoy the little things, the marvellous little things, that God has placed within their reach. They will then learn to find God in the midst of the tumult of everyday life and its thousand insignificant circumstances, loving and thanking him for the goodness he shows in his creatures. They will discover God in nature, where they will find rest and joy very close to recollection and peace. They should be taught the ability to be constantly surprised, just as children are who constantly discover new things and are never bored. A priest should not allow himself to get into a frame of mind where he is restless and bored, wanting things he cannot have, instead of giving thanks to God for what he has and enjoying it to the full. This attitude in itself is unbecoming of his mission and state of life as well as likely to leave him prey to all kinds of temptation. It is very important for students to learn all this; for the good of their own soul and so that they can teach what is right, they ought to assimilate and meditate on that point from *The Way* (368) which contains so much wisdom for anyone capable of discerning it: "So you are bored? Naturally, if you keep your senses awake and your soul asleep."

Apart from all these considerations, there is no doubt that the fundamental point is the importance of the spiritual director. In practice, of course, more than one priest will have this task in each seminary, for to think that one man alone could direct large groups of students at varying stages of their training is out of the question. Besides, one of the results of the Council in this regard may in fact be that spiritual direction has been made easier for seminarians. A spiritual director is not to be imposed on them, so it would seem right and reasonable, as well as being very much in keeping with the spirit of the Council's directives, that each individual should have a large degree of freedom to choose his own director. However, superiors should ensure that the students all have, in fact, spiritual directors. Otherwise it might happen that not a single one would attain a genuine spiritual life, for we cannot know something unless we learn it, and one's own mind is a poor counselor. It would be like someone who has not studied all the subjects necessary to be a doctor, trying to practice medicine on himself. Of course, forcing students to take spiritual direction from a particular priest would be to risk giving them no direction at all or, at times, to tempt their sincerity. The result would be disastrous.

Pastoral training

In the Decree on Priestly Formation we read that major seminaries "ought to provide for the development of true shepherds of souls" (*OT* 4). This development should refer, insofar as may be possible, to all aspects of the priest's apostolic ministry. While the object of human, intellectual and ascetical education is the harmonious development of the man himself, his intelligence and his will, pastoral training aims at giving him a skill, an art, namely the ability to take care of souls, teaching him how to face reality in all its aspects, how to permeate it with the spirit of the Gospel and take it to God.

The liturgy must play an important part in this aspect of priests' training if they are to "act as the ministers of him who in the liturgy continually exercises his priestly office on our behalf by the action of his Spirit" (PO 5). In order to carry out the work of redemption "Christ is always present in his Church, especially in her liturgical celebrations" in such a way that when he associates the Church with himself in the "truly great work of giving perfect praise to God and making men holy . . . the liturgy is considered as an exercise of the priestly office of Jesus Christ" (SC 7). This is so, basically, because the priest is another Christ, for if his ministry is a participation in the exercise of Christ's priesthood, then his action is fundamentally liturgy.

Every liturgical ceremony, being an act performed by Christ the priest, and by his body the Church, is a sacred action above all sacred actions; the faithful, as members of Christ, are a party to the liturgical act and therefore should "take part knowingly, actively, and fruitfully" (SC 11). The priest, then, aware that "more is required than the mere observance of the laws governing valid and licit celebration" should instruct and educate those members of the people of God entrusted to his care in the mysteries in which they are taking an active part, so that they may do so more and more conscientiously, in closer union with the Church, and so obtain greater spiritual fruit.

In view of the importance of the liturgy, "the summit toward which the activity of the Church is directed" and at the same time "the fountain from which all her power flows" (SC 10), it is not surprising that the Council should recommend certain measures to train priests in this aspect of their pastoral duties. For "unless the pastors themselves, to begin with, become thoroughly penetrated with the spirit and power of the liturgy, and become masters of it" (SC 14) they can hardly hope to educate their flock in a manner that will make their conscientious and active participation in the liturgical act sanctify them, for grace is received in proportion to the soul's capacity to accept it. "Let priests take care to cultivate an appropriate knowledge and facility in the liturgy" (PO 5)—this is essential if priests want the community entrusted to them to fulfill the duties of its common priesthood properly, by praising, giving thanks and offering the sacrifice.

There are two points regarding pastoral training—apart from preaching, which we have already mentioned—which we must consider. The first is explicitly and quite emphatically mentioned in one of the conciliar documents in reference to students in major seminaries: "Let them receive careful instruction in the art of guiding souls, so that they can lead all sons of the Church, before everything else, to a Christian life which is fully conscious and apostolic, and to a fulfillment of the duties of their state" (OT 19). If *careful instruction is* recommended in the art of spiritual direction, it clearly means that the Church attaches great importance to it, as an element in the priest's apostolate.

To guide or direct means to put someone on the right road towards a particular destination. Here it means setting the faithful on the right road in the things of the spirit, that is, in everything relating to God and to souls. Indeed, the whole of a priest's work could be called spiritual direction, for his whole purpose is to direct souls to God, their last end. This is his function as ruler of those members of the people of God entrusted to him—to rule, to direct, to show the way, not in some general sense, but by giving direction to each person individually, according to his or her specific calling, taking personal, family and environmental circumstances into account. The future priest must learn to direct the faithful according to God's plans for them and without interfering with their freedom. Clearly some training may be given in the seminary, some instruction on how to direct souls. In speaking of Confession we gave some indications on this subject. In general, many of the points worth passing on derive from the experience of the Church and of her priests. In most cases, they are effective because they have been tested in real life and are therefore realistic, which is not always true of observations deduced from theoretical principles, often the result of speculation rather than reality.

This being so, there is no reason why the philosopher or theologian in the seminary should neglect or ignore this source of wisdom. He should take advantage of the experience accumulated by the Church throughout the centuries (this is essential), but he should also add his own personal experience—not his experience as a spiritual director but the personal experience of having received, and continuing to receive, direction himself. People are always substantially the same. Only circumstances change. Supernatural familiarity with one's own soul, with its difficulties in making progress towards sanctity, its struggles and temptations, inclinations and opportunities, its anxiety and its inner peace, is one of the greatest helps towards a deep understanding and knowledge of others. Experience shows that it is difficult to direct others if one has not had spiritual direction oneself, for few things are as beneficial in dealing with others as the memory of how one was treated oneself.

Another relevant point in the training of priests is what we might call apostolic method or technique. Nowadays this question of method or technique seems to occupy a very important place in the apostolate, especially among the young and apostolically active clergy. Method means procedure. Here it means finding the most suitable procedures for reaching people whose minds, circumstances, problems and ways of life differ widely from one another and cannot all be approached in the same way. The importance of this is clear and Pope Paul VI stressed it: "It is necessary to understand the real needs, the hopes, the requirements of the world—not the world's customs or mentality—to study and consider how one can contribute to its redemption and prosperity."

Perhaps the first thing to be said about apostolic methods and techniques is that they give no automatic guarantee of success. They are not sacraments, which work *ex opere operato*, or remedies whose mere application will produce infallible results. If we want supernatural results, the means must also be supernatural: we must plough, sow and water the seed, but the fruit always comes from God. Therefore the first method that has to be learned and practiced at all times is to live a spiritual life, to pray, to make sacrifices, to be holy.

If we think about it, we'll see that, since the methods of the apostolate are ways by which we can more easily, effectively and fruitfully reach the souls of others, they can all be reduced to the exercise of the cardinal virtue of prudence. In the final analysis, this consists of choosing the most suitable and appropriate means to achieve a goal. For the priest, all questions of apostolic method, even in the specialized apostolates, are matters of prudence, for a particular technique cannot be chosen without first finding all the facts and carefully considering the possibilities of success offered by the various procedures. Obviously, too, the end to which the methods are intended to lead must be kept in mind. Too much concentration on the methods themselves may cause us to waste our time in thinking about or erecting scaffolding, while forgetting that what we really ought to be doing is building the house, which is the purpose of the scaffolding.

All apostolic techniques must have one thing in common, one indispensable basis, if they are to be effective instruments; they must be authentic. This authenticity comes from the intrinsic nature of the apostolate itself, which consists of helping souls and bringing them nearer to God. Any method that aims at the success of its inventor or user, rather than at the welfare of souls, is false, as is any procedure that divides people into groups, cliques, circles or associations, rather than integrating everyone into the people of God, the universal Church. For there is no point in gathering people around us, when they should be gathered around Christ. Purity of intention, forgetfulness of self, generous renunciation of all personal success are signs that one is genuinely working with one's eyes fixed on God and for his glory.

In this area, as in all the priest's apostolic work, and indeed in his very Christianity, charity, love, should permeate everything he does. The thing that all methods and all techniques should have in common, if we genuinely want to help souls, is that they should be saturated with love. There is a well-known story about St. John Bosco relating to this. He was once asked a long list of questions about the tactics he used to reform the neglected youngsters of Turin. Don Bosco listened patiently to all the questions and then answered: "Very simple; I loved them." Undoubtedly, this is the best method, in fact an indispensable method, for any technique that is not the result of love of souls, love of people, any procedure not deriving from a passionate desire to save them, will be false down to its roots. The Church is not looking for human success; she has no interest in it. She wants souls, she wants to save her children, to gather in her maternal embrace all those who live far from her without prospect of peace, without joy and without hope.

As a general rule, the first method a priest should use is to train a few lay people from his parish in the spiritual life and inspire them with apostolic zeal, choosing those who can best attract others by the talents God has given them. He should then set them on fire with zeal for souls, and teach them to work for the Church by doing discreet and effective apostolate among their own friends, beginning with the most able of them, even though these may be the most difficult. This is the method of doing apostolate through friendship, it is the "apostolate of discretion and confidence"[16] which gave the Church such excellent results at the time of the early Christians. Thus by associating the faithful in their apostolic work—without "clericalizing" them— priests will more perfectly and effectively fulfill their duty as shepherds, a duty which "is not confined to the care of the faithful as individuals, but is also properly extended to the formation of a genuine Christian community" (PO 6).

4

Sources of Strength

I N VIEW OF THE MISSION entrusted to the priest and in view also of the place and the conditions in which he has to fulfill that mission, he needs certain qualities without which he will scarcely be able to make progress or to help his fellow-men. As we have seen, the world puts continuous pressure on the man of God and this inevitably tends to dislodge God from his soul and to set itself up in his place. If the world succeeds in this, it weakens his priestly nature and then he becomes like salt without its taste, like a quenched torch, like a city on top of a hill but in ruins. He is a broken and vanquished man, bearing tragedy in his soul.

Besides these considerations, the message of salvation which the priest is supposed to preach to mankind is in radical opposition to the basic principles of this world. It begins by affirming that the world is provisional, fleeting, temporary; it sets before us for our imitation the example of Christ, crucified and humiliated, not a victorious hero of the pagan type; it preaches poverty and humility to people for whom greed is the only incentive of all their activity, riches and triumph the goal of their desires; it preaches chastity to men of flesh who seek every opportunity to satisfy their instinct and go to the extreme of seeking theoretical or "scientific" justifications for all kinds of deviation; it teaches obedience and meekness in a world in which cult of the ego is almost a religion; it calls for charity and love on a battlefield of selfish struggles.

The priest must therefore possess a number of virtues, or strengths, which will allow him, on the one hand, to withstand the pressure of the world and, on the other, to introduce the teaching of Christ into people's hearts so that it is this teaching, and not the spirit of this world, that permeates their lives. I am certainly not suggesting that the virtues I will go on to mention are the only ones that exist, much less that they are the most important. One might even question whether these virtues are any more specific to the priesthood than others might be.

As regards the first of these points, there are doubtless many other virtues which are necessary and certainly more important, theologically speaking; we have only to think of the theological virtues of faith, hope and charity or the cardinal virtues of prudence, justice, fortitude and temperance, to see this. I could also mention humility, without which no other virtue can properly exist. The reason why I choose poverty and love of the cross, faith and obedience, order and chastity, is that these are logically and tactically related to the priest's character and mission.

If every creature, by the very fact of being such, is dependent on God, the priest has an added, and very powerful, reason for depending on him to a greater extent and more intensely than any other being in creation. By his ordination, the priest has become a minister of God. He is, then, a minister, that is, a servant of God, not only in the general sense, but in a very specific sense, for he deliberately and voluntarily devotes his life and energy, his faculties and his activities, to this service. He makes it his purpose in life and the purpose of his life. The relationship in which he places himself as a servant of God is engraved on his soul through the character imprinted on it by the sacrament of Orders, in such a way that he will never again be a mere man, or even just an ordinary Christian; without ceasing to be both of those things, he is something else as well, something more and something different.

Both his priesthood and the mission entrusted to him by virtue of his ordination disqualify him from serving any other master, for if "no one can serve two masters" (Mt 6: 24), the priest can do so even less than anybody else. No creature can dominate him to the point of making him his servant or his slave. He has no right to break his voluntary and loving subjection to God and transfer his allegiance—or let himself be tied—to any creature; if he does, he is jeopardizing the deepest roots of his very being.

The priest has three virtues at his disposal, three sources of strength, which will enable him to maintain his freedom from other creatures and guarantee his faithfulness in the divine service to which he has committed himself. By the power which he derives from his poverty, he protects himself from the attraction exercised over him by creatures outside himself. He can make use of such creatures, but without losing his independence in relation to the things he possesses or may possess. Chastity gives him the strength to keep his own flesh in subjection, frees him from the demands of his sexual instinct and allows him to control it or rather, to tame it, thus making of his body an instrument in the service of a more noble end and maintaining it in the holiness, cleanliness and dignity due to a "temple of the living God" (2 Cor 6: 16). Finally, obedience is the virtue that imposes order on his freedom, correcting the deformity with which original sin has blemished the will, and restoring it to the way of righteousness. Obedience gives him the strength to adapt his will to the will of God, explicitly communicated to him by the indications of the superiors representing God or manifested to him indirectly through other creatures: his duties, circumstances, and the like.

Order itself is not, strictly speaking, a virtue, but it is a condition without which virtue is almost impossible. "Virtue without order? Strange virtue!"[1] It is also a means the priest can and should use to organize his activities according to their importance in relation to the divine will. It allows him to control his time; in modern terminology, we could say that it is one of the most important factors in his productivity.

Faith provides the impulse that stimulates him, the light which clarifies the goals to be pursued, and shows the ways to reach them, the sinew that keeps him in position at all times and despite everything. Love of the cross, finally, is the vaccine that protects him against failure, guarantees his serenity and ensures that he will not swerve or weaken; it is his armor.

We have mentioned the cracks through which the spirit of this world may penetrate into the soul and deaden the priest: lust of the flesh, lust of the eyes and pride. The virtues considered here are those which he can use, not only to keep himself from being infected by these evils, but to counteract them in the souls of the people he is attempting to save.

The cornerstone

The first condition required of anyone who wishes to enter the kingdom of heaven is faith, for without faith it is impossible to please God (Heb 11: 5-6). Because of the particular nature of his vocation and his ministry, the priest, above all other things, must be a man of faith. There is probably nothing more hideous in the world, nothing more monstrous or tragic than a priest without faith; anyone who has read *L'imposture* by Georges Bernanos will doubtless have shuddered at the thought of the central character, a priest who has no belief and is condemned to be an imposter for life, bearing an unbearable burden of inner desolation and despair, dry and sterile like a shoot cut off from the parent vine.

Faith, "the assurance of things hoped for, the conviction of things not seen" (Heb 11: 1), is not a sweet consoling sentiment that makes our eyes shine with an excited sparkle, making us feel a warm thrill in the struggle to rescue souls from the world and deliver them to God. Occasionally it may have some effect on the feelings and arouse these or other similar emotions, but basically it has nothing to do with sentiment or emotion. Other things may produce these results. Faith is rather more serious and certainly much deeper than this. Neither light-headedness nor temerity nor high-sounding words nor fiery slogans have anything to do with it. Faith has a simplicity, a warmth, a firmness which distinguishes it clearly from all superficial imitations.

There are various degrees and shades of faith. There is a living faith, which produces good works, and there is a faith that produces no works and is dead, like a tree that yields no fruit. "What does it profit, my brethren, if a man says that he has faith but has not works? Can his faith save him?" (James 2: 14). If life has to manifest itself in some way and if every living thing expresses itself according to the nature of the vital principle animating it, then it seems obvious that supernatural works are the sign of a living faith and also an indication that the faith is really alive. Faith without good works is dead; it may be faith, but it is dead. And nothing dead can save, for salvation is—precisely—eternal life.

Faith is an assent to revealed truths, given by the intelligence when moved by the will, based on the authority of God, who reveals them; but the will has to be impelled by grace in moving the understanding to assent, if the act of faith is to be meritorious, for faith will not be a virtue if this intellectual habit is not moved to action by the impulse of charity on the will. A dead faith is faith which does not act, does not produce acts proper to the virtue of faith, does not express itself in supernatural works. In a priest faith which is dead is a grave liability, for this talent of incalculable price was not given to him to be buried: "You believe that God is one: you do well. Even the demons believe — and shudder" (James 2: 19). The object of faith is no mere theory or system of truths, but Truth itself, which is Christ and, being Christ, is life (Jn 14: 6). Faith is not something to be thought about, but to be lived, as St. Paul says to the Romans: *Justus autem meus ex fide vivit* (Rom 1: 17). If every Christian has to live by faith, every priest ought to make it the principle of all his actions, the motivating force behind all his work as a priest; he should allow himself to be so shaped by it that the very least and most insignificant of his acts or utterances will have that undefinable characteristic by which he can be identified as a man who believes in Jesus Christ.

In the whole of the gospel, there is probably no point which our Lord emphasized so insistently as this question of faith. One day the Jews asked him: "What must we do to be doing the works of God?" Jesus answered them, "This is the work of God, that you believe in him whom he has sent (Jn 6: 28-29). Indeed, in the final analysis, this is the decisive factor: to believe in Jesus Christ, for "truly, truly I say to you, he who believes has eternal life" (Jn 6: 47) while, on the other hand, "he who rejects me and does not receive my sayings has a judge; the word that I have spoken will be his Judge on the last day" (Jn 12: 48).

In order to appreciate the importance of the virtue of faith for the priest, we may perhaps consider two particular moments in the history of the Church.

Apart from St. Paul, whose human personality was quite exceptional, the first Christians were not men of means, culture, wealth, influence, or outstanding personality; they were average people, mainly of humble origin and with no powerful friends. Yet those men, without any of the human resources necessary to be successful in the world, with no other weapon than their faith in Jesus Christ, boldly set out to fulfill their Master's command: "'Go into all the world and preach the gospel to the whole of creation'" (Mk 16: 15)

They taught all men their obligation to obey the commandments of Christ, commandments radically contradicting the whole system of life, all the beliefs and customs of their pagan world. They went to the most corrupt cities—Rome, Corinth, Ephesus, Alexandria—and these were men with absolutely nothing in their favor but their faith in Jesus Christ. Yet they revolutionized the ancient world, they renewed and transformed it completely. They gave it their own beliefs, their customs, their manners, their social ways, their culture. They achieved all this, not by their personality, not by any methods or techniques, not by subtlety or intelligence or by eloquence, but only by their faith in Christ.

What is the situation today? There are millions of Catholics and hundreds of thousands of priests in the world. We have elaborate means at our disposal: money, influence, techniques, methods, powerful friends, people of outstanding personality and prestige; we have the support of a long and glorious tradition of saints, martyrs and doctors of the Church. Nevertheless, society—which once became Christian—no longer follows Jesus Christ. Vast numbers of intelligent minds are corrupted by philosophic materialism, naturalism or sheer indifference. The wills of many human beings are deflected and led astray by apparently uncontainable waves of neopaganism. Morals are undermined by licentiousness, provoked by the rejection of any objective standard or norm. How are we to explain these results when the means at our disposal are so incomparably superior to those which the first Christians had nineteen centuries ago?

Perhaps the answer is that those first disciples of our Lord lacked everything, but they had faith in Jesus Christ, whereas today, on the other hand, we lack nothing except that faith in Christ, which was the only thing they had.

They took things as they were and we refuse to do this. They knew that "whatever is born of God overcomes the world;

and this is the victory that overcomes the world, our faith. Who is it that overcomes the world but he who believes that Jesus is the Son of God?" (1 Jn 5: 45). We think, perhaps, that we have to take the battle to the world on its own ground, fight it with its own weapons and be as astute as the children of the world. We seem convinced that the key to success lies in being able to attract people by waving whatever banner happens to seem most seductive at any particular moment, so as to show that we are not old-fashioned or out of touch with reality. In fact this means that—quite unconsciously, of course—we seek our success by earthly methods which not only are short-lived and ephemeral, but even lack any real value at the moment when they are most flourishing. We thus move our center of gravity from the supernatural level to the human and the transitory. We are deeply confused if, instead of *making use* of human means we actually place our *trust* in them. We must *use* such means, obviously, for otherwise we might even be tempting God, just as a farmer has to sow and reap if he wants a harvest, but the truth is, and will always be, that it is God who gives the fruit. The priest must undoubtedly make use of every human resource at his disposal, all the advances of modern technology, all his own intelligence, but he must do this *knowing* that these things are mere vehicles, nothing but instruments, and can never be the cause of a supernatural effect.

If a priest's faith in Jesus Christ does not, above all else, make him adapt his life to the gospel or, in more concrete terms, lead him to seek holiness with all that that implies and above all other things, then his faith, if not dead, is sick and very weak. When Jesus pointed out the immense fields of crops to his disciples, the vast extent of work to be done, telling them that the harvest was great but the laborers were few, the solution he proposed was this: "Pray therefore the Lord of the harvest to send out laborers into his harvest"(Mt 9: 38). *Pray therefore*—can a priest even imagine that there could be fruit without prayer? Is prayer not the primary consequence, as well as the first sign, of one's faith being genuinely alive?

When the father of the sick boy went looking for Jesus in the belief that his word would cure his son, Jesus could not be found. His disciples tried to take their Master's place, and they did what they could to heal the child. However, the only result of their good intentions was utter failure, and the man's initial faith crumbled, mainly perhaps because of disappointment at seeing the sad attempts of the disciples to do what he had hoped the Lord himself would do. When Jesus returned and asked what was happening, the man ended his account with this passionate plea: "If you can do anything, have pity on us and help us." Jesus laid down one condition: "All things are possible to him who believes." The man then made a supreme act of will and replied: "I believe; help my unbelief!" (Mk 9: 14-27). At that moment he was doing all that was required of him; Jesus saw the sincerity, humility and resignation of his attitude, and worked the miracle. When they were alone again, the disciples asked him why they had failed, and he answered them quite categorically: "Because of your little faith. For truly, I say to you, if you have faith as a grain of mustard seed, you will say to this mountain, 'Move hence to yonder place,' and it will move; and nothing will be impossible to you"(Mt 17: 20).

Nothing will be impossible to you! The gospel was written for each and every one of us, and therefore the priest will be making no mistake if he regards these words as referring to him individually. Nothing will be impossible to him because his faith in Jesus Christ makes him invincible; for his faith makes him trust in God, not in himself, and God, who is all-powerful, has not allowed his power to be curtailed. The number of passages in the gospel that refer to faith is really remarkable; we have only to keep in mind that its words were not set down twenty centuries ago to be understood in the context of that time alone. On the contrary, they are as relevant in our time, always and every day, as valid for us today and now as they were for the disciples. the word of God is eternal, like himself; Jesus Christ lives and still speaks to us today, to each and every one of us, through the Gospel which he left to his Church.

The priest will find nothing impossible if he lives by faith—if his faith is even like that grain of mustard seed! It is clearly stated that "all things are possible to him who believes." His unbelief will be helped, that is, his faith will be increased, in the first place, by praying for it. "Increase our faith" (Lk 17: 5), the disciples asked the Lord. And if *they* did not find it humiliating to ask for an increase in faith, surely there's no reason why any priest should consider himself satisfactory on this point—or indeed on any other.

In the second place, faith increases through practice. In our ordinary lives, the practice of the virtue of faith takes the form of what is often called "supernatural outlook." This means getting into the habit of seeing everything, even the most ordinary things, the little events of each day, in the light of the plan of salvation which God has worked out for us, in the light of the redemption. It means going about our daily work as if watching the Lord out of the corner of our eye to ensure that what we are doing is really his will and to see if that is exactly how he wants us to do it. It means cultivating the habit of discovering God through his creatures, sensing his presence behind what the world might call chance or accident, being conscious of his footsteps everywhere. In brief, practicing the faith means getting into the habit of being constantly aware of the fact that we are instruments, collaborators as it were, executing a plan conceived by him.

If every priest genuinely lived by faith, the miracle—and the results—of the Curé of Ars could well be repeated in each of them. Here was an insignificant man, faced with countless obstacles in his way, working in an adverse atmosphere, deprived of almost all human means but with a faith in Jesus Christ so great that he transformed everything with which he came into contact—people, surroundings, ways of life. It is faith that gives strength and efficacy to a priest, for he is not working for himself or trusting in his own power. It is faith that gives him the courage to face up to any obstacle and the daring to embark on any undertaking: "However, in your name I will let down the net"(Lk 5: 5). On the other hand, scripture warns us of the dangers that come from an excessively human outlook on things: "Woe to timid hearts and to slack hands. . . . Woe to the faint heart, for it has no trust! Therefore it will not be sheltered"(Eccl 2: 12-13).

Independence from the world

There is no need to be an expert on Church history to see that she has fought long and hard to preserve her independence in relation to the powers of this world; this is essential if she is to fulfill her function.

The same is true of the priest, a man of the Church sent by her to infuse the spirit of the gospel into all creation, "to restore all things in Christ" (Eph 1: 10). He, too, must remain independent of the world. He can, and must, be dependent upon the Church that has sent him, but on no other power or force outside of himself. To maintain this independence he has, if he wishes to make use of it, one great source of strength, a *virtus*, in itself capable of giving him control over all things, so that no bait set by the world to trap him can succeed through anything outside himself. Poverty—including inner detachment—is his strength and protection against the things of this world. Poverty gives him a detachment that allows him to use created things to whatever extent the glory of God and the service of souls may require, but no more. It ensures that he neither covets what he lacks nor becomes attached to what he has. God is his treasure, in him he trusts and has confidence; all other things are added unto him, they are mere accidents.

Like all virtues, poverty consists of finding the golden mean between two extremes, from which it must remain equidistant. Obviously the genuine virtue of poverty is very far from greed or covetousness, but it is just as distant from slovenliness and misery. These are not virtues; neither a priest nor anyone else should love or seek them. If, however, misery should ever befall him, then he should love it, not for its own sake, but because it has been permitted by God and brings humiliation, anxiety and the cross. It is not in itself a source of strength or help. The Lord was poor but he was not a beggar. He would have been unable to devote himself fully to his mission if he had had to spend all his time and energy finding even the minimum amount of food and clothes necessary to live: "created goods are altogether necessary for the personal development of a man" (PO 17).

Obviously slovenliness or dirt, shabbiness or untidiness, waste—unnecessary and thoughtless spending even of small sums—or carelessness in using things that don't belong to us, have even less to do with the virtue to poverty.

All the goods of this world, everything on this earth, has been placed there by God for our use to the extent to which we need them, but always with a view to our final destiny Strictly speaking, everything belongs to God; we are only "agents"who will have to give an account of the use we make of things which are not ours. The parable of the talents (Mt 25: 14-30) has a direct application to earthly goods also.

One good reason why the human heart should never become attached to the precarious things of this world, as St. Paul explained to Timothy, is that "we brought nothing into the world, and we cannot take anything out of the world"(1 Tim 6: 7). Another good argument in favor of remaining as free as we can of this world's fetters was given by St. Gregory the Great: "Detach yourself from creatures until you are stripped of them. For, says Pope St. Gregory the devil has nothing of his own in this world, and naked he comes to battle. If you go clothed to fight him, you will soon be pulled to the ground: for he will have something to catch you by."[2] And it is St. Paul again who warns us against the dangers we face if we lack the spirit of poverty: "But those who desire to be rich fall into temptation, into a snare, into many senseless and hurtful desires that plunge men into ruin and destruction"(1 Tim 6: 9). One of the characteristics of riches is that they give rise to new needs, desires and lusts. "Don't forget it: he has most who needs least. Don't create needs for yourself"[3].

However, it is not the material fact of having or not having that determines the spirit of poverty. A person who has nothing may be covetous of what he does not possess or miserly with whatever little he has. As regards actual property, wealth or money, few priests can be accused of being rich. The priesthood is not a way of life that leads to great wealth or allows great fortunes—or even small ones—to be amassed. Since it is not work done in return for a salary, but a ministry which the priest has to make his only occupation and to which he has to devote all his energy and all his time, the Church provides him with the indispensable minimum for his livelihood. If it is unable to do so, the charity of the faithful should make up the difference by their alms. This is the purpose of the donations made by parishioners at Baptisms, weddings and funerals and of the stipends given when Mass is offered for a particular intention. The priest himself, if he is practicing the spirit of poverty as he should, will clarify the real purpose of these contributions and he will avoid any scandal which they might cause to uneducated persons.

Few things can do as much visible harm to the Church as a priest—any priest—who appears to be greedy or covetous, whether in fact he is or is not. It is not always enough to *be* good: there are many times when we must also *be seen* to be good, even though this may involve renouncing things to which in strict justice we have a perfect right. What a priest must never do, however, is to use or take advantage of his priesthood to obtain worldly benefits, honors or goods: "You received without pay, give without pay"(Mt 10: 8). St. Paul was undoubtedly following his Master's instruction when he laid down that "those who proclaim the Gospel should get their living by the gospel"(1 Cor 9: 14). Yet he himself was often in need and refused to be a burden on anybody or to expect anyone to pay for his upkeep (2 Cor 11: 9), even though this meant he had to earn his living by the work of his hands and accept aid from other sources. He was concerned not to cause scandal or give the appearance that he was preaching the gospel to earn money. "By never attaching their hearts to riches, priests will always avoid any greediness and carefully abstain from any appearance of merchandising"(PO 17).

The virtue of poverty is essentially freedom, detachment, absence of any greed or any addiction to money or the things that money can buy: "if we have food and clothing, with these we shall be content"(1 Tim 6: 8). It means freedom of spirit, having few needs, being happy with what we have, as St. Paul explained to the Philippians: "I have learned, in whatever state I am, to be content: I know how to be abased, and I know how to abound; in any and all circumstances I have learned the secret of facing plenty and hunger, abundance and want. I can do all things in him who strengthens me"(Phil 4: 11–13).

As far as its manifestations are concerned, lt must be remembered that the spirit of poverty is not always practiced in the same way, though the essentials—and even their expression—remain constant in all cases. Obviously a secular priest cannot practice poverty in the same way as a religious. He lives in very specific circumstances and these determine in each particular case the degree to which he should properly make use of things, not only things relating to his personal use but also anything he uses' as an instrument in his apostolate, whether it be a car—I repeat: as an instrument of his apostolate—or a pen. Especially nowadays, when there is world-wide concern with standards of living, progress in the underdeveloped countries and productivity, it is easy to overestimate the importance of human means or to regard one type of value—namely, the economic—as at the top of the scale, when in fact it should be lower down. This idea seems to have been in the mind of Pope Paul VI when he spoke of the prominence which the spirit of poverty receives in the gospel and says that "yet it is greatly jeopardized by the modern trend to set so much store by wealth."[4]

On this question of poverty, it is very difficult to get down to particular details as far as the secular priest is concerned. Nevertheless perhaps it would be in order to mention some of the symptoms which might help him examine his own conscience, in much the same way as, when speaking of lukewarmness, we might consider the symptoms in order to diagnose the disease and then the most suitable remedy could be applied.

We could begin by referring to the care we should take of the things we possess. Obviously if something is treated well, it not only remains in better condition but it will also last longer. If a priest is careless and if, through neglect—it would not be inaccurate to say: through lack of mortification—he allows his clothes, books, furniture and anything else around him, or anything he uses, to become torn or broken, without caring in the least because he knows that he can simply replace them when they are gone, then he has no spirit of poverty. If someone is really poor, he does not act in that way. On the contrary, he takes care of his poor things, he lavishes attention on them to make them look new and make them last longer. He repairs everything the moment it begins to break or wear, lest it get beyond repair. Sometimes the appearance of a priest's house (and indeed his personal appearance) or the parish offices, far from showing signs of honest poverty—things in themselves inexpensive, but clean and tidy—instead shows signs of neglect, carelessness and laziness. This is not poverty, we should note, because it often involves greater expense later.

We could also mention, in a general way, the whole question of expenditures. To spend money on useless things or on unnecessary whims, to spend immoderately or on the impulse of a moment without considering the why's and wherefore's, is a clear sign that there is no spirit of poverty. A priest should have all the essentials, everything appropriate to his dignity as a priest and whatever he needs to make his house habitable and his personal appearance clean and respectable. He ought to have whatever is required for his work—books for example—and he must even remember that the things that cost least money are not necessarily the most economical. He must also realize, however, that gravity is an apostolic virtue, that there are certain little vanities a priest should not satisfy, that it is not right to develop cravings for useless trifles, to make use of things which are unbecoming to his state in life or to frequent places of entertainment where, apart from spending money, however innocent such places may be in themselves, his presence may cause scandal. Here, of course, poverty is not the only consideration. If someone is really poor he has no money to satisfy his whims, to buy costly items or to indulge in expensive hobbies. He never spends unthinkingly, but examines the quality of various items, compares prices, visits various shops, and all of this after first seriously considering whether he cannot, in fact, do without the article in question. Here the thought of the countless people who are suffering real need, who lack even the necessities of life and who could benefit greatly if he gave in alms the money he thought of spending, may help him decide whether it is necessary, or at least advisable, to do so.

Poverty itself is not the virtue, said St. Bernard, but rather the love of poverty. And "you don't love poverty if you don't love what poverty brings with it" (*The Way*, 637). No priest must really be surprised if at times he is even short of basic necessities; indeed, he should be glad when this happens for he then resembles his Master, who had "nowhere to lay his head"(Mt 8: 20). With her own special elegance, but also with all her common sense and all the light showered on her by God, St. Teresa wrote the following: "Poverty is good and contains within itself all the good things in the world. It is a great sovereignty—what I mean is that he who cares nothing for the good things of the world has dominion over them all. What do kings and lords matter to me if I have no desire to possess their money, or to please them, if by so doing I should cause the least displeasure to God? And what do their honors mean to me if I have realized that the chief honor of a poor man consists of his being truly poor?. . . With true poverty there goes a different kind of honor to which nobody can take objection. I mean that, if poverty is embraced for God's sake alone, no one has to be pleased save God."[5]

It is the spirit of poverty that guarantees the priest's independence and sovereign freedom, for there is no one so feared by the powerful as those over whom they have no means of control. Since he has nothing to lose and attaches importance to nothing whatever except to doing God's will, he can scarcely be diverted from his path or from his work. Furthermore, he has a security backing him up, namely the word of God, reminding him: "Therefore do not be anxious, saying, What shall we eat?' or 'What shall we drink?' or 'What shall we wear?' For the Gentiles seek all these things; and your heavenly Father knows that you need them all. But seek first his kingdom and his righteousness, and all these things shall be yours as well. Therefore do not be anxious about tomorrow"(Mt 6: 31-34).

The words addressed by the Apostle to the Colossians are also relevant here: "I say this in order that no one may delude you with beguiling speech"(Col 2: 4).

Making good use of time

Each and every passage in the gospel gives us more than sufficient material for meditation. Some passages, however, either because they have been much commented on over the centuries or because their meaning is more obvious even at first reading, lend themselves to more immediate application than others.

One of these texts, placed by St. Matthew at the end of the Sermon on the Mount, is as follows: "Not every one who says to me, 'Lord, Lord,' shall enter the kingdom of heaven, but he who does the will of my Father who is in heaven. On that day many will say to me, 'Lord, Lord, did we not prophesy in your name, and do many mighty works in your name?' And then will I declare to them, 'I never knew you; depart from me, you evildoers'" (Mt 7: 21-23).

It seems quite clear that the most important thing of all is God's will, for whether we have fulfilled it will decide nothing less than our entry into the kingdom of heaven—our salvation, in other words. It is so important that many actions which are intrinsically good, or even excellent (such as, for instance, prophesying, working miracles or casting out devils from people possessed—can we think of anything more excellent?), may become evil if, by doing them, we go against the will of God. This would mean that, in choosing between God's will and our own, we have chosen our own and placed it before God's: this would be a disorder. In fact, every sin is a disorder, for it diverts us from our goal, and every disorder is evil, for it distorts the direction which any action must take to reach its final end. Hence, as far as the life of a priest is concerned, order is of prime importance.

It is not a mania or an obsession. It may become one, of course, like anything else, if taken to extremes or treated as an end instead of a means. When practiced correctly, however, it is a great resource, almost an irreplaceable instrument, for the spiritual life, for using our time to the best advantage, and consequently for making our apostolate more effective. St. Augustine, who combined long and intensive experience with an exceptional intelligence, said: "Safeguard order and order will safeguard you." If we distribute everything we have to do according to its relative importance and organize our time properly, we shall not only be safeguarded from many temptations but also more productive on the supernatural and human levels.

Because of the importance which, as has been said, we should attach to the fulfillment of God's will throughout each day by adapting our own will voluntarily, freely and lovingly to his, we must be careful not to seek ourselves, to ensure that it is not love of comfort, our own whims or likes and dislikes, human respect or vanity that inspire us to do whatever we have to do. And if we are to do the will of God above all else, the fundamental thing is undoubtedly to know what that will is, to know what God wants of us at every moment. Once we know all the things we should do to please God, we can distribute them in order of their importance throughout the day. In other words, we must make a plan or schedule, for "without a plan of life you will never have order."[6]

Obviously we are not suggesting that our whole life be divided up into airtight compartments; the plan is made for the priest, he is not made for the plan. It is meant as a help, not a straitjacket. A plan is no less necessary for a priest than it is for an architect, who has to draw up plans before beginning to build a house. It would be just as disastrous for the priest to flounder on aimlessly, simply following the impulse of each particular moment throughout the day, as it would be for the architect to build unthinkingly, improvising as he went along.

To continue the comparison: just as an architect draws his plans so as to include strong outside walls, strong enough to bear the weight of the whole building, the priest also in drafting his plan of life, should pay special attention to the strength of some fixed points or pillars, which will help to guarantee the solidity of the order he has worked out. The first of these, and perhaps the most important, is a fixed time for getting up each morning. This is the starting-point for the day's work. If it varies continually, the rest will vary too and then, instead of something solid to which the rest of the edifice can be fixed, he will find that the pillar of support will be as fluid as liquid and any attempt at order will become impossible: "If you don't get up at a fixed time you will never carry out your plan of life."[7]

Since sleep is indispensable for restoring lost energy and a minimum number of hours are necessary to keep the organism healthy and efficient, the time for going to bed can be calculated in relation to the hour fixed for getting up. In theory this is easy, but in practice it requires mortification, especially for those people who always feel lazy just when it is time to go to bed and just when it is time to get up. If we take a third fixed point, determined by another natural requirement, namely the mid-day meal, then we can distribute the tasks we have to perform in order of importance throughout the two halves of each day, and it will then be easy to organize anything else so as to oc-cupy the spare moments.

In order of importance, the first things are the obligations which are specific to the priest's function and ministry, namely the holy Mass, the Breviary, administration of the sacraments, visiting the sick and catechesis. Immediately after these things, and almost equal in importance, comes his spiritual life, remembering that he must *never* be short of time to take proper care of his own soul. The running of the parish, the registers (which should be kept up to date), study, reading, mental relaxation (I think classical music is highly recommendable to the priest, not only because it is very relaxing in the agitated world of today, but also because it inspires recollection and silence), friendship and contact with other priests as well as with lay people, the immense amount of apostolic work he has to do (discussions, meetings, talks, etc) more than fill the day, so that he will always find himself short of time and will al-ways have to leave something for the following day.

In a way, his plan of life will protect the priest from his own "brilliant ideas," which are often—not to say always—a prod-uct of the human mind and usually an obstacle both to his spiri-tual life and to the success of his activities. The danger that threatens the priest and from which order may give him protec-tion is very graphically pointed out by Thomas Merton: "One of the first things to learn if you want to be a contemplative is how to mind your own business. Nothing is more suspicious, in a man who seems holy, than an impatient desire to reform other men. A serious obstacle to recollection is the mania for directing those you have not been appointed to direct, reforming those you have not been asked to reform, correcting those over whom you have no jurisdiction. How can you do these things and keep your mind at rest?"[8]

Certainly when we are doing what we should be doing and putting great effort into it, using our five senses, recollection be-comes more easy and the work more effective, among other rea-sons, because our energies are less diversified. This avoids temptations which would very probably assail us if we diverged from the plan we have worked out, and experience confirms that it keeps us more consciously in the presence of God. For just as it would be wrong even to work miracles, if the Lord wants us to perform some humble or obscure, routine chore, so also we can be sure that we are doing what he wants of us if we stick to the tasks planned and approved; nor is there any better way of remaining in God's presence.

Order is like a path along which the priest must walk, a path marked out and defined clearly enough to be really a path while at the same time sufficiently wide to allow that minimum amount of mobility we all need. Therefore on the one hand a plan of life should tie up all loose ends and leave only the narrowest of margins for impulses and whims, while on the other hand it should be flexible enough to make room for all those things that may—and so often do—arise, if their importance justifies leaving aside what was planned in order to give them priority because they are a clear sign of what God wants us to do. This freedom—which is not fickleness—will give the priest the agility to avoid settling into a staid routine which could become a disastrous way of using order and degenerate into a comfortable rut. For this would mean making use of a weapon, intended to help him serve God, the Church and souls more effectively, as a shield to protect himself from the calls of grace, the inspirations of the Holy Spirit and the demands of God.

Order is also a method for stabilizing the golden mean, which it does by means of the plan of life. In effect, it protects us both from wasting our time by doing nothing and from being uselessly overactive. If a neglectful priest, not knowing what to do with his time—when in fact the harvest in the Lord's field is so great—is a sorry spectacle and a deplorable example, the priest who spends his day hurrying about from one thing to another and proving the truth of the saying "the more haste, the less speed" is no less pitiful. Overwhelmed by so much all-consuming activity, he always gives the impression of being behind schedule in whatever he is doing (and indeed it is not only an impression), of not even having time to think. He is like a bad swimmer who uses up most of his energy splashing and waving his arms about, when he would achieve more with less effort if he controlled his movements and went straight to his goal.

A time for everything and everything in good time; without hurry but without pause, as Goethe said of the movement of the stars. Time is short and the work is immense, so no priest can really hope to do everything—which is another reason why he should try to eliminate the less important things in favor of the essentials. Perhaps we should mention at this point, though we shall be going into more detail later, that the source of the priest's strength and success lies, not in his activity but in his prayer and sacrifice. It lies not in moving about like a cat on hot bricks, but in working serenely, as befits a man doing what he should be doing, namely the will of God, minute after minute, not in an externally active life, but in a recollected and profound inner life of even more intense activity. Such an inner life however, is impossible without order, and order is impossible without a plan of life in which prayer occupies a place as fixed and essential as sleep and food, as obligatory as the most necessary daily tasks.

There is one other facet of order which we should mention, namely the external aspect: "Let your outward conduct reflect the peace and order of your soul."[9] A person's interior inevitably shows on the outside. Disorder in outward things, whether in one's personal appearance or in one's books, papers or the drawers of a wardrobe, is usually a sign of internal disarray.

"Safeguard order and order will safeguard you." There is very little time in the day for sin or even for temptation, if a priest is orderly and makes an effort to keep to his plan of life. Before getting inside him, the enemy has to break down, one by one, all the lines of defense raised by order around the sanctuary of his soul. And if holiness is based on union with God through the fulfillment of his beloved will, is there any method more effective than this for helping to achieve it?

The spirit of freedom

A priest may be indifferent to everything outside himself, he may keep his body pure and uncontaminated, and yet he may be a slave, a slave of his own self. In other words, he may be as proud as a demon. What a terrible temptation this third one is, the "pride of life," when the ego raises itself up as a universal norm, as a criterion of truth.

If there is anyone who ought to be genuinely free, it is without the slightest doubt the priest: freedom is at the very root of the decision which led to his ordination. Only human beings can be free because only they are endowed with reason; there is no true freedom in irrational beings. Freedom is an indispensable condition if there is to be any merit, any holiness, any love, but obviously it will be in direct proportion to the clarity and the accuracy of one's knowledge and in inverse proportion to one's ignorance of the truth.

Man's real situation being as it is, freedom like everything else shows the detrimental signs of original sin. It needs to be protected from its own inherited imperfection; and the force that defends it from its own congenital weakness is, in fact, obedience. No one should be surprised to hear this. Far from being an attack on one's liberty, aiming to limit or destroy it, obedience is actually the condition it needs in order to develop fully. It would be illogical to think, for example, that because a torrent is channeled, its strength disappears. On the contrary, this is a way of directing that strength most intensely and most beneficially to where it is most needed; indeed, it is a way of ensuring that it will be constructive rather than destructive.

However, the priest has more supernatural and more important reasons than these.

The Church is the mystical body of which Christ is the Head, and the priest is a member of this body, a member with a special role. Though all members must be united with the Head and be one with him, in the priest's case this union must be exceptionally close, for it is not for nothing that he is a living instrument for Christ's redeeming action. Now, it is always the will that brings about any kind of union, and this means that the priest will be united with Christ in so far as his will is united with the will of God: and this is precisely the object of obedience.

Speaking of the mystical body of Christ, Fr. Eugene Boylan wrote: "Obedience is obviously the law of its life. Every single act, even the slightest, done contrary to the will of God, cannot be shared by Christ, it is not part of the life of His Body, and therefore it has no real value."[10] Since Christ is the Head of the mystical body, which is the Church, it is obvious that he must govern all the members, in big things as in small. If any one of them acts independently of the Head, it is equally obvious that he is not being governed by the Head. If he refuses to be ruled, he harms the entire body, since he is no longer living for the whole organism, but for himself; he is not seeking the common good of the people of God, but only what seems good to and for himself alone. Indeed, when he is acting for himself and not in accordance with the Head, then he is living separately from the Head. The will which should be in control, namely God's, and the will which should be controlled, namely the priest's, are not united, but divergent. Since the Lord clearly laid down that 'without me you can do nothing' (Jn 15: 5), if a priest is not interested in obedience, he will probably do, at best, merely human work that will have nothing to do with salvation; for if he is not obedient he cannot be united with Christ and therefore it will not be Christ who is acting in and through him. He will end up quite alone and completely unproductive.

"He humbled himself and became obedient unto death, even death on a cross" (Phil 2: 8). A disciple cannot expect to be greater than his Master; the priest must be obedient unto death and, if necessary, death on a cross. He will never be left without grace, so on that account there will be no problem. The problems arise on the human side, even when the humans are priests, because that mark left by original sin in the soul, that germ of rebelliousness, which is pride, never totally disappears. As St. Teresa says, "We are in no way masters of our own wills, and cannot employ them purely and sincerely in the service of God, until we submit them to reason; and the true way for us so to submit them is that of obedience. This cannot be done by means of reasoning; for our nature and our love of self can argue so effectively that reasoning would never get us anywhere. Very often what seems to us the best of reasons for not doing a thing if we have no desire to do it seems ridiculous when we want to do it."[11]

This tells us that the basis of obedience is humility, that is—to use St. Teresa's word—truth. Humility is what makes a priest willing to obey always and everywhere. Jesus described himself as being "gentle and humble in heart" (Mt 11: 29), and he prefaced this description with the highly significant phrase: "Learn from me." He was indeed gentle and humble of heart and over a very long period of time his entire activity consisted of being "subject to them" (Luke 2: 51); his constant occupation was "to do the will of him who sent me" (Jn 4: 34). Likewise, if a priest is gentle and humble of heart he will truly be a collaborator, a co-worker, with the hierarchy and, like the Lord, his activity will consist of doing the will of him who sent him, namely God's will as shown through the Church and the bishop.

A priest is unlikely to be obedient, however, unless he has both a supernatural outlook on things and the humility necessary to get to know himself. If his outlook is too human, he runs the risk of seeing the hierarchy, not as successors of the apostles carrying on their original mission, but as slow-moving wheels in a complicated system of administration, and he then strips the bishops of their true nature and reduces them to the category of mere men. If he lacks humility, he may fall into the temptation of placing too much reliance on his own points of view and believing them more accurate, deeper and better than those of his superiors, with all the attendant dangers of criticizing, gossiping and even contradicting them which may be involved in such an attitude. This can disrupt all possible unity and make every effort sterile, like a soldier acting according to his own ideas and ignoring the rules or the commands he is given. This is deplorable, for "there is no authority except from God, and those that exist have been instituted by God. Therefore he who resists the authorities resists what God has appointed" (Rom 13: 1-2).

On the question of docility and solidarity with the hierarchy, it would appear to be an undeniable fact that nowadays priests are influenced by trends and tendencies which are too exclusively human and seem to be tearing the Church apart, rather than contributing to its unity. It is not insignificant that a man as understanding as Pope John XXIII should have felt obliged to insist upon the virtue of obedience, calling it "that capital virtue, today so ignored" and referring to "the energy with which our predecessors denounced the grave dangers of the spirit of independence among the clergy."

Now that we talk so much to the faithful about the Council, perhaps it would be right that we ourselves should also consider its documents seriously and without any preconceived ideas, so as to try and assimilate their spirit.

"Since the priestly ministry is the ministry of the Church herself, it can be discharged only by hierarchical communion with the whole body" (PO 15). Here, for instance, is a passage that concerns us directly; it also shows that our ministry is the ministry of the Church herself, and therefore it must either be performed in union with the hierarchy or it cannot be performed at all. In considering this passage, a phrase used by our Lord comes immediately to mind: "he who does not gather with me scatters" (Lk 11: 23). If the priest is really a co-worker and a sharer in the sacred order which the bishop possesses in its fullness, then it can logically be expected that he should in fact cooperate and share. He should not regard himself as the leader or dictate to the bishop as to how he should govern that section of the people of God entrusted to his care. If the occasion arises, he ought to have sufficient confidence and courage to say humbly and clearly whatever he thinks needs to be said; but when he has done so, he should leave God and his grace to do the rest. There are certain attitudes which might be normal among people dealing with purely secular matters but which would be out of place within the Church, especially on the part of priests, and it would be quite wrong to adopt such attitudes.

Priests are supernaturally united with their bishop by the sacrament and the ministry. Between them there is union and unity of mission, within which each of them fulfills his own particular function, while sharing in the common responsibility, in whatever position God, through his Church, has chosen for him. This is how obedience arises and this is also how priests' freedom should be exercised: "they accept and carry out in a spirit of faith whatever is commanded or recommended by the Sovereign Pontiff, their own bishop, or other superiors. . . . For in this way they will preserve and strengthen the necessary unity with their brothers in the ministry, most of all with those whom the Lord has appointed the visible rulers of His Church" (PO 15).

Nowadays, when the call for freedom is so topical and on everybody's lips, the priest should be very careful not to allow himself to be unduly influenced by overly human or, what is worse, overly superficial ways of interpreting that word. While the world lays such tremendous emphasis on one particular meaning of the term "freedom," the priest must stress the term "obedience" in his own life and give it even more importance than the world attaches to its freedom. There are many reasons for this, but the main one is that without obedience there can be no freedom, because obedience is what makes us do the will of God. This, in turn, unites us with him for, when we obey, it is his Spirit that moves us: "Where the Spirit of the Lord is, there is freedom" (2 Cor 3: 17). Obedience is an essential condition if he is to fulfill himself to the highest degree in freedom, not in just any freedom, however, but in the only freedom truly deserving the name: *in libertatem gloriae filiorum Dei* (Rom 8: 21).

A priest must never lose sight of what he is. And, precisely for that reason, neither can he forget that one of the greatest services theologians have done to mankind is to clarify certain concepts in such a way that any ambiguity or possibility of confusion has been reduced to a minimum, if not totally eliminated. The word "freedom" is highly ambiguous in common speech; it has too many different shades of meaning to be acceptable without some qualification whenever anybody uses it for a specific purpose. It has been used, and is being used, as a slogan in the cause of all sorts of interests, ideals, policies and objectives, some violently opposing the others, and in each case we ought to ask what in fact is being concealed or what meaning is really being given to that sacred word

If obedience is the opposite of freedom, then Jesus Christ was not free, for he came to do the will of him who sent him and he prayed that his own will should not be done but only the will of his Father. In fact, anyone—whether a priest or not—who reads the Gospel can easily find passages emphasizing this, and not a single word disproving it.

There is no contradiction between freedom and obedience, no identity between disobedience and freedom. What makes people disobey God by doing the opposite of his will is not freedom, but rather its imperfection, the damage done to their freedom by original sin. A free man is one who obeys God, not who disobeys, for "everyone who commits sin is a slave to sin" (Jn 8: 34). When Michael Schmaus tells us that freedom attains the highest degree of its development when the human ego is surrendered to God, he is not just making a banal statement to be quoted from time to time, for there is no will more free than God's will, nor has there ever been anyone on earth so free or who lived with such sovereign liberty as the Son of Man. Yet it was he who said: "I seek not my own will but the will of him who sent me" (Jn 5: 30); and if there is anyone who should teach the world that lesson, it is the priest, another Christ, sent to preach the Gospel, the truth which will make men free.

Today, as in all times of crisis, this is especially relevant. When obedience is practiced voluntarily and not under duress, it is a declaration of freedom, and it acquires particular greatness when it is exercised in a hostile environment. It is in those circumstances that the courage of the people who practice it comes into evidence, precisely because there are so many singularly plausible ways of avoiding it (intellectual convictions, sociological conditions, faithfulness to one's own personality or to one's deepest sentiments, etc.). In spite of everything they keep a firm hold on their faith and remain united to the authority, the legitimate authority which is the ordinary line of communication for the will of God, without stopping to make their own opposing opinions the deciding factor in the attitudes they are going to adopt. Here lies the terrible responsibility before God of those in charge; they will have to render a detailed account of the use they make of the authority vested in them. The priest, on the other hand, has only to know that what he is told to do is not offensive to God, detrimental to his own soul, or harmful to the souls of others.

"Every kingdom divided against itself will be destroyed, and every city or house divided against itself will not stand" (Mt 12: 25). Just as division is a symptom of death, unity is an essential of life; if the limbs are separated from a body, they inevitably die and the whole organism is seriously harmed. So it is with the Church. Every act of obedience to our mother the Church is an act of love of God, and it increases the cohesion, the unity, of all the members of the people of God, the mystical body of Christ. On the other hand, every act of disobedience is a step outwards, a move towards separation. St. Cyprian attached so much importance to the unity of the mystical body as to say that we cannot have God as our Father unless we have the Church as our mother and that anyone who lays up treasure outside the Church undermines the Church of Christ. He asks how, since the Father, the Son and the Holy Spirit are but one, that unity derived from the divine oneness could be fragmented by anyone in the Church; and he says that if a person does not observe this unity, he does not observe the law of God, he does not preserve life or salvation. Especially because of his particular position in the Church, the priest has a more serious obligation than anyone else to practice this virtue because he is supposed to be an element of unity in the Church, which he cannot be unless he learns to obey.

Learning to obey: this is often the problem. Obedience is something that has to be learned, otherwise it can't be practiced. The priest's primary attitude and disposition, provided he has the minimum foundation of humility, should be one of charity, and charity demands that the superior's duty of governing should be made easier, for it is often more difficult than it seems. One of the most refined ways of being charitable towards a superior is to be at his disposal at all times for whatever purpose—within his area of jurisdiction, of course. For, as St. Thomas says, "Charity . . . cannot exist without obedience. . . . This is so because friendship makes friends one in what they will and in what they reject."[12] And this is so, independently of the superior's abilities, good qualities or personality: "But, is it only for his personal qualities that you obey? Or do you in your selfishness interpret St. Paul's 'Obey your superiors' with an addition of your own. . . . 'always provided they have virtues to my own taste'?"[13]

We must learn to obey and to obey properly. This means—especially in a priest's case—that we must be prompt, must never allow laziness to take a hand, never put things off until tomorrow or even until later (for procrastination is the thief of time), never let things build up on top of each other, day after day, just because we like doing some things more than others. "With that slowness, with that passivity, with that reluctance to obey, what damage you do to the apostolate and what satisfaction you give the enemy!"[14]

Obedience must be all-embracing, for since God's will for us is continuous there is not a minute in the day when he has not some specific thing in mind for us. The priest has to realize that there cannot be any moments in his life over which God has no power or rights; his whole life and all its ramifications must be subjected to obedience. The priest must do all in his power to adapt his will to the will of God, and he must learn to see this in every instruction from his superior.

It must be repeated that the priest is a co-worker with the bishop, not a freelance, independent worker acting in his own name or answerable to himself alone. His supernatural success depends to a great extent on how united he is with his bishop. It is true that if he is well instructed he will obey better, for he will never feel uncertain or disconcerted, but in the final analysis obedience is not essentially affected by that. In due course the bishop will have to give an account before God of how he has directed his co-workers, but it is never for the priest to judge him. When obedience is based on one's personal judgement as to whether the instructions are wise or not, then it has no virtue, merit, or even (we might almost say) anything approaching a priestly attitude.

The priest's obedience must be refined: consequently it must certainly be silent. There can be little refinement if we express our dislike of doing whatever we are instructed to do. On the other hand, there is no insincerity or hypocrisy in smiling while doing something we dislike or which forces us to change our own plans. This is not hypocrisy but good manners (if we look at things on a purely human level) and charity (from the supernatural point of view). As well as being in bad taste, protesting, complaining, showing our reluctance, giving any form of expression to our unwillingness to do something we had not planned to do are all poor ways of obeying, and will not only lead to nothing useful but will take from the merit of obeying and make it even more difficult and unpleasant for us. Man is an intelligent and free being. Consequently obedience, like any other human act, must also be intelligent and free. A priest cannot perform God's will, especially that part of it which comes to him through his bishop, as if he were merely a mechanical puppet. He must obey intelligently and make his own intellectual contribution in every case, so as to do things as efficiently and perfectly as possible, at the same time attempting to adapt his own thinking to that of his superior. And he must do so with all the freedom he possesses, which means that he must be enterprising—he is a co-worker with the bishop, not a robot. He must follow instructions, but in doing so he must use all his initiative and all the resources that his zeal, his ability and the particular circumstances suggest to him. He must cooperate with the bishop by proposing ideas, finding new openings for the apostolate and using all the means God has placed at his disposal, but asking whenever he is in doubt.

However, no priest will find it easy to incorporate this particular virtue into his life unless he has a very supernatural outlook and great love of God. When three crosses had to be carried to Golgotha, one of the prisoners had to be dragged, resisting, protesting, complaining. Only pure force could overcome his rebellious spirit, which in any case remained unbroken inside him. Another went unwillingly, cheerlessly, unhappily and without accepting what was to come, but at least he was resigned; however, he did not go in freedom, for if he could have avoided going, he would have done so. Only Jesus could have avoided going, and yet he went voluntarily and freely, inspired by the love of his Father . . . and his love for us. He obeyed freely and deliberately; he overcame the resistance of his human nature—we must remember his prayer in Gethsemane; he consented fully and was fully aware of all that was involved; he was determined and accepted it all: *obediens usque ad mortem.* This is how he taught us to obey—without force or threats, without any human respect or any feeling of compulsion, but acting with total freedom and moved by love. Our obedience must also be joyful, as we know from the apostle's instruction: "Whatever your task, work heartily, as serving the Lord and not men" (Col 2: 23).

The fruits of obedience are enormous. First of all, comes peace (except in the case of a proud man obeying under compulsion; but here we are referring to the type of obedience taught us by the Lord). Certainly no one who does the will of God can be anxious or uneasy. Obedience, furthermore, is the force, the virtue, that establishes unity and makes it possible for the Church, a single body with a single Head, to be also "one heart and one mind." As Blessed Josemaria Escriva put it: "It is obvious that anything living, though it may consist of many different parts, is unified. . . . If the hand, the body or the foot is given its freedom, it corrupts inexorably; it rots because it loses the bond that unites it to the rest of the body, the link that gives it life and liberty."[15] Priests are, and must always be, instruments of unity; they themselves must be united and gathered, together with their bishop, around Christ's vicar. By surrendering their own right to judge and making their own mind conform to the mind of the bishop, with a strong spirit of initiative, with the humility necessary to consult and ask for advice, with the courage to express their points of view humbly and objectively and with a heart full of charity, their work and their success will be immense. Otherwise, they will only harm and confuse people, hinder the apostolate, cause sterility and division, separate the members from the body and give bad example. And any "freedom" that produces results such as these is very dubious.

Effective apostolate

When God wished to choose the most appropriate means of saving mankind, the instrument he selected—for whatever reason—was the cross. And there is no other way by which we can be saved, except by the cross of our Lord Jesus Christ. Hence from the very beginnings of the apostolate, from the moment the apostles started to fulfill their mission, the cross has occupied an essential part in the Church's teaching and preaching.

Pain and suffering, contradiction and persecution, misunderstanding and anxiety, every kind of evil, including death, are all the result of sin. With sin they came into the world, as if the first sin had opened the door behind which all of them had been locked up and hiding, waiting for a chance to escape and be free. No one can delude himself into thinking that this vale of tears may be changed into an earthly paradise where everything will turn out exactly as we wish. Every intelligent person must accept facts, and it is a fact that life in this world, from Adam and Eve onwards, has been very far from the ideal of perfect happiness, and as long as he is on this earth, man will have as travelling companions sorrow, illness, contradiction, and finally death.

"Behold, I make all things new" (Rev 21: 5). By Christ all things were made and by him also all things were renewed and restored when he overcame the ruler of this world through his passion and death. "Where sin increased, grace abounded all the more" (Rom 5: 20), and ever since Jesus lived on this earth, pain and death, persecution and suffering, sadness and sorrow, have ceased to be negative elements. They have lost, so to speak, their "badness" for, by his cross, Jesus Christ has converted the consequences of sin into instruments of salvation, into purification and expiation for sin.

This is why preaching the cross, which "is folly to those who are perishing but to us who are being saved it is the power of God" (1 Cor 1: 18), has occupied a central place in the Church's teaching from the very beginning. Certainly this teaching, like the cross itself, has been "a stumbling block to Jews and folly to Gentiles," rejected by some and despised by others. Surely basic human prudence would have shown that some other method more acceptable to all sides, something less harsh and less likely to provoke hostile reactions, would have been more advisable? Yet when St. Paul reminds the Christians at Corinth of the start of his own evangelization, he confesses quite innocently and simply: "For I decided to know nothing among you except Jesus Christ and him crucified" (1 Cor 2: 2).

When we read the Acts of the Apostles, we cannot but be surprised at the hard life those first Christians had to live. It is almost as if God had abandoned them to their fate, never intervening to save them from trouble or to make their duties the least bit easier. St. Paul was received favorably in very few places; wherever a Christian community was founded, wherever the gospel was preached in a city, it was paid for in blood, pain and humiliation: lashes of the whip, beatings, prison, riot. The apostle has left us an account of his life as a herald of Christ, which should be carefully and deeply considered by any priest who needs to be cured of the danger of becoming over-idealistic: "For I think that God has exhibited us apostles as last of all, like men sentenced to death; because we have become a spectacle to the world, to angels and to men. We are fools for Christ's sake, but you are wise in Christ. We are weak, but you are strong. You are held in honor, but we in disrepute. To the present hour we hunger and thirst, we are ill-clad and buffeted and homeless, and we labor, working with our own hands. When reviled, we bless; when persecuted, we endure; when slandered, we try to conciliate; we have become, and are now, as the refuse of the world, the off-scouring of all things" (1 Cor 4: 9-13).

St. Paul, of course, was no novice as far as this kind of treatment was concerned, for when the Lord had sent Ananias to cure him of his blindness, he had told him: "I will show him how much he must suffer for the sake of my name" (Acts 9: 16). Therefore no priest can be surprised to find contradictions and persecutions, misunderstandings and sufferings strewn along his way. It would be foolish to think that redemption can be achieved without a cross or that supernatural fruit can be obtained simply by using methods, techniques, eloquence, arguments or surveys.

However, there is more to be said than this. We are living at a time and in an atmosphere where it has become almost a goal, if not standard practice, to put man himself on a pedestal. Some people still dream of a baptized form of humanism, of Christian naturalism, and they still find it possible to advocate Christian humanism, at least as a desirable ideal. But if we take the cross away, we are left with something different, something that is not Christian at all, for if we ignore the mystery of the cross we are suppressing from Christianity both the sign by which it is recognized and a characteristic which is intrinsically essential. "Let us never seek Christ without the cross," wrote St. John of the Cross, and Suhard adds that we shall thus avoid finding the cross without Christ, which so depresses our contemporaries.

The enormous progress of technology has helped to give mankind an even greater—if such a thing is possible!—feeling of power, of strength and of independence. Perhaps this is why the worst sin at the present time is that the advances of science and technology often make it more difficult, instead of easier, to go to God, for they tend to make us think of things in themselves, totally separated and independent of their Creator.

The saints earnestly wished to suffer for the sake of Jesus Christ and in his name, perhaps because, like St. Paul, they wanted to complete in their own flesh "what is lacking in Christ's afflictions for the sake of his body, that is, the Church" (Col 1: 24), but the world, today as always, has rejected the cross, which is totally foreign to its way of thinking. Scientists carry out research into new cures for disease, ways of prolonging our days on this earth, methods of alleviating pain; technologists present us with wonderful discoveries to make life more pleasant and comfortable. This is all good, God wishes it and approves of it, for he told us to "subdue" the earth (Gen 1: 28), and anyone who uses his intelligence for the benefit of mankind is performing an act of charity towards his fellow-men—if he supernaturalizes it. However, there is a danger that the soul may become attached to the comforts of this world and regard the ideal of an easy life, protected from all discomfort, as its goal, living for itself instead of living for God, and therefore we need to preach the cross today more than ever before unless we want souls to be nourished by a caricature of Christianity and empty teaching.

The priest should be able to say with the apostle: "I have been crucified with Christ: it is no longer I who live, but Christ who lives in me" (Gal 2: 20). If we look at things from a merely human point of view, as the world looks at them, then there is nothing in the whole of history to compare with Christ's great failure: his entire life, his miracles, his preaching, his rebellion against dead formalities, his pretensions to be the Saviour and the Messiah, all led finally to death on a gallows, with a common criminal on either side, betrayed by one of his own followers, denied by another, abandoned by the rest, challenged by the Jews at that supreme instant to prove the truth of his statements, judged and condemned by his own people, executed by the authority of Rome. Yet so many people had benefited from his boundless goodness and from his miracles! And what of the crowds that had followed him? Then it all ended with that terrible, frightful, cry: "My God, my God, why hast thou forsaken me?" (Mk 15: 34).

Humanly speaking, a failure: a colossal, blatant failure. Yet when all seemed to be lost, all was in fact saved. The cross signals the end of man's enmity with God, the removal of barriers and the beginning of a new era involving a renewed friendship, a new relationship. This is the victory over sin, over death, over the power of darkness, over the ruler of this world; from then on, through Jesus Christ and through his passion and death, "in everything God works for good with those who love him" (Rom 8: 28): in sorrow, exhaustion, sickness, dishonor, prison, failure . . . in everything!

The priest, another Christ, has to be nailed to a cross, but it must be the cross of Christ, and no other. For there are indeed many crosses which are not Christ's but our own, crosses which do not come from him but from our own stupidity and stubbornness, consequences of our own personal undertakings, in which God's will has no place and which he has no reason to support. We can, of course, sanctify this type of cross, but only if our humility first opens the eyes of our soul so that we can acknowledge our mistakes and accept, as payment of a debt, the consequences which we have brought upon ourselves. Not all troubles are crosses, but only those that derive from our service of God. Nor can we speak of "the will of God" if in fact it has been our own will—perhaps even in opposition to God's will—that has directed our footsteps along a path where obstacles were inevitable and to be expected. There is a subtle but clear difference between Christ's saving cross and the fruitless crosses carried by those others who accompanied him on Calvary, which they had been making for themselves through a life of crimes committed one after another. Yet these were also crosses.

"My son, if you come forward to serve the Lord, prepare yourself for temptation. . . . For gold is tested in the fire, and acceptable men in the furnace of humiliation" (Eccles 2: 1 and 5). Such is life! The priest must remember this, if he is not to be depressed when things go badly. He must look out for the cross, heavy or light, not only in the sense of denying himself, but also in the sense of expecting that some day or other he will come face to face with one of the forms the cross of Christ can take: tribulation or failure, persecution or derision from others—remember how some people scoffed at the Lord and dressed him up in a red rag as a purple robe, and how they played games by forcing him to guess which of them had struck him!—slander or sorrow, misunderstanding or long series of those silly difficulties that can interfere with good work being done in Christ's name for the good of souls.

When the cross does come, he should bear it not just with resignation but with great inner joy, even if his whole fragile human nature rebels. For this is one of the good things that we have attained through the cross of Jesus Christ: this serene, lively joy where there was only sadness and gloom previously, this willing and hopeful acceptance in place of the most rebellious hopelessness that was formerly in control. On this point as on all others, if there is anyone who should preach by his example, it is the priest, for if he wishes to win souls for God he must be willing to pay the price, and the price can be none other than the price paid by Christ, namely the cross. "Just as Christ carried out the work of redemption in poverty and under oppression, so the Church is called to follow the same path in communicating to men the fruits of salvation" (LG 8). And the priest, a man of the Church, is called to follow exactly the same path.

The priest's love

"The unmarried man is anxious about the affairs of the Lord how to please the Lord; but the married man is anxious about worldly affairs, how to please his wife, and his interests are divided" (1 Cor 7: 32-33). Doubtless this is the natural reason for celibacy, the state voluntarily and knowingly embraced by priests in the Catholic Church. There may be other reasons too, of course, such as the greater ease of attaining the kingdom of heaven. Above all, however, the purpose of celibacy is to leave the priest free and flexible, fully devoted to the mission entrusted to him by the Church in the name of Christ, a mission of such great and vital importance for mankind—after all, it is our salvation that is at stake—that he cannot prejudice, encumber or disrupt it on account of any other duties which, once undertaken, and precisely because they would be quite legitimate in themselves, he could not neglect.

It was the Church's gradual extension, from her beginnings with that first Christian community in Jerusalem, that demanded of priests a more and more exclusive and all absorbing devotion to the care of souls, to looking after the flock entrusted to them by the Church. In the early days, those chosen for ordination were pious men of wise judgement and proven doctrine, even though they might be married, but then the freedom of action required for proselytism—preaching the word of salvation—and for looking after the Christian communities already in existence began to require celibacy. This involved, and still involves, heroic sacrifices, one of the finest acts of charity towards souls, a most expressive and magnificent way of practicing that self-denial which the Lord demanded of his closest followers. "How we should admire purity in the priesthood! It is its treasure. No tyrant will ever be able to wrest this crown from the Church."[16]

The priest, then, undertakes to remain chaste and he does so in such a deliberate and definite way that his commitment is expressed in a decision for life. As a man, he has an obligation—as have all men, and not simply those who believe in Christ—to be chaste, but as a priest he also renounces that type of human love to which his nature as a man impels him, the right to set up a home and to perpetuate himself physically by having children. He is not, therefore, simply giving up something that is evil, disordinate or so vile that it reduces human beings to the level of animals. His sacrifice also includes marriage, with everything that it implies: a sacrament—therefore, a holy thing—willed by God so that the human race should be perpetuated and the number of the children of God should thereby increase.

It would certainly be altogether wrong to regard the perfect chastity, the celibacy practiced by the priests in the Church merely as a dry, negative abstention. Just as chastity is not simply continence, neither is celibacy just bachelorhood generously accepted in order to be able to devote oneself more fully to a great enterprise. Obviously it is not chosen out of natural inclination, love of an easy life, as a *modus vivendi* or as a response to a challenge; much less is it a solution for people who are shy, disillusioned or unsuccessful. We cannot all offer ourselves to God in the priesthood, "but only those to whom it is given" (Mt 19: 10), and therefore perfect chastity is meaningful only in the light of love, as a human response to a divine calling. It is thus a supernatural vocation; it is the way in which we react with total love to the all-embracing demands of God's love

The kind of love which inspires a man—a priest—to give himself completely and absolutely to God, surrendering his body and his soul, his whole life and every moment of his life, his heart and all the feelings of which it is capable, is not, and cannot be, a mere substitute for human love. It is not something intended to fill a sad gap or space left by the involuntary sacrifice of a woman's love. There is no involuntary sacrifice, no hollow to be filled, but a free, generous renunciation of a great, noble, pure, legitimate human love, in favor of an even more sublime, intense and immaculate love, a supernatural love of Christ Jesus, a love which so fills the heart that it leaves no room for any other, except in and through him, a love which involves refinement, extreme respect and gratitude. For we must think, says Msgr. Escriva, "of the fact that even our body becomes divine, of that tongue which brings God to us, of those hands which touch him, of that power to work miracles by distributing grace."[17]

Celibacy is equivalent to loving; it has been called a service orientated love; it is love of God and of all that God loves. Consequently it is also an expression of love for souls; those who, with the help of divine grace, detach themselves from all creatures (including their own bodies) in order to rise on high and give themselves completely to Love itself, devote their entire lives to the service of others.

There is nothing in celibacy that goes against human nature: on the contrary, in a sense it makes it more dignified. First of all, "unlike food, which is necessary for every individual, procreation is necessary only for the species, and individuals can dispense with it."[18] The duty of propagating life has been imposed on the human race, not on any particular individual. Of course, no one can evade the duty of preserving his life, but he can certainly abstain from following his natural tendency towards marriage in order to fulfill a higher supernatural vocation, provided it has been "given" to him. Apart from this, there is in human nature itself the possibility of a union which cannot be achieved in marriage. Fr. Romano Guardini has expressed this very accurately: "Is it perhaps so, after all, that love cannot harness its entire force to any human need because no human is big enough to receive it; that it is impossible to embrace an earthly lover with perfect intimacy, because essentially he or she is always distant? Perhaps precisely through the never completely satisfactory experience of human love, one begins to sense the presence of another love, unrealizable on a merely earthly plane, to whom we not only can but must surrender our most intimate being—the love revealed by revelation."[19]

Priestly chastity is therefore an expression—and perhaps the highest expression—of love, because it is the priest's love for the souls redeemed by Christ that makes him remain unbound to any human being. It is also an expression of love in another sense. Schmaus explains that when the Church speaks of the supremacy of virginal over married life, she refers to the *form* of life, not to the *person* living it; the order in which the Church places the various forms of life has as its norm the fullness of the hereafter. The world is advancing towards a stage where the present forms will disappear and be replaced by a glorious and imperishable form, presignified already in the risen body of Christ. The married way of life, Schmaus goes on, belongs to those transitory modes of existence and will pass with them. Virginal life, which in advance and by analogy represents the perfect form of life of the world to come, is a continual reminder that the present form in this world is passing and that an immutable and imperishable form will come, and anyone who chooses the virginal form of life does a supernatural favor to naturally forgetful men and women by reminding them of the future, and warning them not to lose themselves in the perishable. Schmaus concludes that virginity thus becomes a realization of love.[20] It is not insignificant that the Vatican Council advises priests to "keep in mind the great mysteries which are signified and fulfilled" in celibacy (PO 16).

Celibacy may become incomprehensible, even to priests, if its basis, its meaning and its purpose are not kept clearly in mind. If the priesthood is a ministry instituted by Christ for the service of his mystical body, which is the Church, as Pope Paul VI reminds us,[21] then the priest as such is meaningless outside the context of the service for which he has been constituted. The more fully his meditation and prayer allow him to grasp the mystery of the Church—Christ's sacrament to perpetuate the redemption and extend it to the end of time—the more deeply rooted will he become in the Church. The further he advances into the mystery of Christ and his Church, the more firmly will he sink his roots into the nourishing soil which is to sustain, feed and strengthen him.

Without this depth and this firmness, he will come nearer and nearer to the surface and gradually he will be uprooted. He may even reach a situation in life whose falsehood may become evident to the faithful, to their grave detriment. Such a situation would be very sad for the priest himself, for the Church and for everybody else. It may arise if, because of his shallowness in the mystery of Christ (in whose priesthood he shares) and the superficiality of the roots he has sunk in it, he comes to regard his state of life, that is, his celibacy, as inappropriate, superfluous or meaningless, as a purely artificial position deriving from canonical rules whose meaning, necessity or appropriateness he fails to understand. In those circumstances his ministry begins to seem to him just like a means of earning a living, a job to be done without necessarily being vitally *committed* to it, an occupation distinct and separate from a ministry.

On the other hand, a proper consideration of the mysteries which "are signified and fulfilled" in complete surrender to God, in order to be at the service of the redemption, makes it easier not only to understand celibacy but to accept it joyfully, not as a burden borne for love of God and of souls, but as a fullness, the most free and the most complete fulfillment of one's own personality.

Some people may consider this last point as rather exaggerated. However, the Church's long experience in this matter—we have only to remember people like St. Augustine, St. Francis of Assisi, St. Teresa, St. John of the Cross, St. Francis de Sales, St. Paul and many others—is contradicted only by unsubstantiated, and in some cases merely offensive, statements, or rather suppositions. To say that marriage would allow priests to bear more complete witness to the Christian life is equivalent to saying that if they are celibate, and precisely because of their celibacy, they can bear only an incomplete witness, and this statement is as superficial as it is gratuitous. To say that their celibacy makes their situation physically and psychologically unnatural is to accuse them of being a monstrous species of deformed individuals. To think that getting married can protect a man, whether a priest or not, from being unfaithful or unchaste is to show total ignorance of reality and to live in a land of childish fantasy.

To understand celibacy and to live it properly, we must continually consider the mystery of Christ and his Church more and more deeply. For "the link between celibacy and priesthood is not something artificial or ephemeral. Although it is not part of the fundamental constitution of the Church, the celibacy of priests is not a 'superstructure' which has no basis, nor is it a hang-over from some particular historical period. It is a result of the action of the Holy Spirit and therefore a lively sign of the development of the seed which is growing into a fruitful tree (see Mt 13: 31-32). Before the theologians deduced its christological, ecclesiastical and eschatological appropriateness, the *sensus fidei* of the people of God had begun to intuit the deep spiritual and pastoral connection between celibacy and priesthood. Thus, the supernatural instinct of the prophetic community anointed by the Holy One (see 1 Jn 2: 20) anticipated the successive acts of the magisterium which first recommended celibacy to all the clergy and eventually established, in the Latin church, a legal obligation whereby all who were ordained had to be celibate" (Alvaro del Portillo).[22]

However, the priest must realize that neither his celibacy nor his consecration makes him cease to be a man. He retains his natural inclinations, his instincts and the lust aroused in all human nature by original sin. A priest's purity is a great treasure "but we have this treasure in earthen vessels" (2 Cor 4: 7); we must take the utmost care, for the slightest breath could tarnish this mirror in which the divine image is reflected. And to preserve our chastity there is nothing worse than to think we are safe and free from danger, for that makes our downfall even more likely, perhaps "to show that the transcendent power belongs to God and not to us," as St. Paul says.

So delicate is this virtue that we must be constantly on the alert, for the flesh is an enemy we carry around with us, an enemy living under our own roof: "So then let us not sleep, as others do, but let us keep awake and be sober" (1 Thess 5: 6). To this advice we could add that we must use every means possible to do so. If we are not careful to safeguard every door through which temptation may come and take possession of our soul, then certainly our priestly purity will become a problem. But we must not regard this alertness as any kind of negative repression, for as Pope John XXIII said, the necessary asceticism of chastity, far from enclosing the priest in sterile selfishness, makes him more open-hearted (Sacerdotii Nostri Primordia).

Normally there need be no problem involved in remaining pure, at least in the usual meaning of that word, either for a priest or for anyone else. First of all, the question itself should never occupy a foremost place; a man who works hard should be so busy that he has little time for temptations which, as we all know, just lie in wait for any idle moment. If a priest is fully involved in his work and occupied with the task of helping the souls of the men, women and children in his parish, whom he knows personally and about whom he knows everything or almost everything there is to be known, there will be very little risk of serious danger. If he also uses the appropriate means, not just to avoid falling, in a negative way, but to become more and more closely united with God, to become a saint with all that sanctity implies; if he lives a spiritual life, strengthened every day by prayer, holy Communion, mortification and the practice of humility—which, among its other desirable results, teaches him to ask God's help at the least sign of danger; if he also uses the human means at his disposal and takes whatever steps his common sense dictates; then it will be extraordinarily difficult for his purity to suffer in the slightest. On the contrary, every day will make it more perfect, more refined and more intense.

In order to evade the cruder type of temptation, the type that comes from disorderly tendencies of the instinct, he must guard his senses and control his body; as St. Augustine says: "Why do you follow your own flesh? Turn round, and let your flesh follow you" (Confessions). The fact is that "it is the spirit that gives life, the flesh is of no avail" (Jn 6: 63) and even respect for our body itself should impel us to discipline it in order to confine it within its proper limits and reduce its demands to precise requirements. Any temptation against chastity, however strong and violent, can have little chance of prevailing if we take a cold shower in winter, or a good fast walk or a run on a hot summer's day, for then the body will demand no more than is strictly necessary to recover from such treatment and return to normality. Restraint and moderation at all times, prayer, mortification and work are the ordinary procedures to keep the body in control. However, if the occasion requires it, no procedure, however extraordinary, can be regarded as too extreme, so long as it is effective: "To defend his purity, St. Francis of Assisi rolled in the snow, St. Benedict threw himself into a thornbush, St. Bernard plunged into an icy pond. . . . You . . . what have you done?"[23] As far as the senses are concerned, they can be trained—though never perfectly trained—to concentrate on what they are doing and to avoid everything else. If the senses are guarded, the heart will surely be protected.

The custody of the heart is most important, for the danger threatening us from that angle is more pernicious and has more fatal consequences than any other. A fall occasioned by the heart is never the result of a momentary weakness, but the climax of a long conscious process. The priest has the initial disadvantage of being alone, which may sometimes make him yearn for a type of human affection to which he renounced his right when he consecrated himself to God. Because of this, the temptation creeps into the heart by another route: through pure friendship with persons of the opposite sex, without any evil intentions and solely on a spiritual level. Ordinary friendship with persons of the other sex, however, is always difficult because it either leads to love (if fostered by frequent contact, for that encourages affection) or it dies out completely, (if such contact does not take place). In any case, there is always the risk of the natural attraction between persons of different sexes. Hence any tendency to dream or think of other ideals, any nostalgia or longing for what his own life "might have been" in different circumstances, any hint of self-pity because of having no home of a kind enjoyed by others, or any indication of the beginnings of an attachment to a particular person should be offset immediately by some act, performed with complete deliberation and slowly, involving the whole strength of his will, by which he renews his dedication to God—because he is the greater good, because he alone is God, and because, if every human being should faithfully fulfill what he has undertaken, the priest should do so more unerringly than anyone else.

When dealing with custody of the heart, we must stress the risk to the priest's mission and to his human development if his feelings are not properly controlled and kept within just limits and if his heart is allowed to rule his head. If he thinks with his heart, he becomes blind, because not the heart but the mind should govern his actions. Every priest should be a man of heart, a man with a big heart, but he must not be a sentimentalist or led by his feelings. There is always a certain amount of imagination or 'idealization' in the sentiment, which falsifies and hides reality from us. Sentimentalism makes it difficult for the heart to remain detached; and as all sentiment is fickle, anything erected on that basis is doomed from the beginning to crumble as soon as the emotional state on which it was based starts to change. The instability from which all sentimental people suffer makes the priest too soft and too weak a support to be of help to anybody. Apart from this, he is in danger of ending up by craving affection from any creature, for a sentimentalist is incapable of loving but always wants to be loved; he can never genuinely give himself to God. We can easily imagine the havoc a man like that could cause in souls.

On this question of the heart, there are some passages from St. Teresa on which any priest could profitably reflect. Speaking of charity she says: "This, as I have said, is love without any degree whatsoever of self-interest; all that this soul wishes and desires is to see the soul it loves enriched with blessings from Heaven. This is love, quite unlike our ill-starred earthly affections—to say nothing of illicit affections, from which may God keep us free."[24] If love seeks its own satisfaction and not the spiritual welfare of the person loved, this is a wretched love— not evil, of course, but wretched—because it is not love but self-love. Therefore, St. Teresa says she often thinks it is blindness to desire to be loved except by people who can help us to attain goods which are in themselves perfect.[25]

These are not vain words; if we think about them, we shall see that they are much more meaningful than a cursory reading might suggest. St. Teresa had vast experience, and in another place she wrote: "I had a very serious fault, which led me into great trouble. It was that, if I began to realize that a person liked me, and I took to him myself, I would grow so fond of him that my memory would feel compelled to revert to him and I would always be thinking of him. Without intentionally giving any offense to God, I would delight in seeing him and think about him and his good qualities. This was such a harmful thing that it was ruining my soul. But when once I had seen the great beauty of the Lord, I saw no one who by comparison with Him seemed acceptable to me or on whom my thought wished to dwell."[26] It is true, of course, that normally the priest will not have "seen," as St. Teresa did, "the great beauty of the Lord," but neither is this essential. It is quite sufficient to *know* of it, as he undoubtedly does. He has not had the experience, but his knowledge is quite sufficient, especially since it is guaranteed by revelation and confirmed by the experience of others.

There is an old piece of ascetical advice that "between holy man and holy maid, a wall of solid stone be laid." Perhaps this need not be taken literally, but it is sufficiently expressive and clear to be a good guide for the priest in his relationships with members of the opposite sex: he should carry out his apostolate with women through the confessional or by preaching—if there is a group—but never directly. There is a short story by Somerset Maugham entitled *Rain* which is very useful and instructive to read, because it illustrates this point. If there is any problem or matter of a different kind that requires a meeting outside the confessional, then it is advisable to leave the door open, unless the room has a glass door. This is a question of refinement and will avoid even the slightest hint of scandal. Unnecessary meetings should also be avoided and those which are necessary should not be too personal; a priest should be courteous, well-mannered, friendly and polite to everybody, but especially to women. Spiritual direction by correspondence is not really to be recommended, both because it is of very little use and because of the unnecessary degree of intimacy set up between two persons in such circumstances.

It is very important for a priest to be perfectly faithful to his celibacy, his loving commitment to God, and the more he loves it, the more faithful will he be. On no account can he regard it as an onerous burden that makes him wish deep—or perhaps not so deep—in his heart, that the Church would abolish or at least relax this rule of ecclesiastical discipline. If this is how he practices his chastity, "against the grain" as it were, then there is a real danger of repressions and compensations, or even of neuroses. It is true that we sometimes speak of the "weight" of chastity borne by the priest, but this is like speaking of the weight of a dove's wings, a necessary and useful weight, for without wings the bird could not fly. As St. Augustine says, if there is love there is no labor and, if there is, it becomes a labor of love, something additional to be loved.

Our devotion to the blessed Virgin, a confident and loving devotion as befits a son who loves his mother, is such a powerful help that it can make what is difficult easy. For many centuries, indeed from the very beginning, the Church has recommended devotion to the Virgin Mary as one of the most effective means of ensuring perfect purity of soul and body—even her name evokes her virginity. Had Jacinta the little girl at Fatima, absorbed some of our Lady's wisdom, for on her death-bed she said that priests must be pure, very pure?[27]

5

Spirituality

WHENEVER WE SPEAK OF THE "SPIRITUAL LIFE," we refer to "supernatural life," and this means the life of grace. When a person is in the state of grace he is living a supernatural life, and in this sense he has a spiritual life, which is deeper than the natural life he lives as a mere human being. From the supernatural point of view, anyone who lacks a life of grace is a corpse, for he has no life. Since the natural is transient while the supernatural remains, this is death indeed; it is death for all eternity.

However, life is not something that can sustain itself without outside help. In the natural sphere, life sustains itself by nourishment and food and, when necessary, with the help of medicines to combat germs which try to take over living organisms or kill them. And the supernatural life can't sustain itself without outside help either. Just like physical life, the supernatural life also needs nourishment to preserve itself and develop; just like physical life, it is also threatened by countless germs and viruses, and sometimes it needs specific and effective remedies to combat a particular disease which is especially dangerous. A priest, and indeed any Christian, is living a spiritual life, not simply when he is in the state of grace, but when he is carrying out some spiritual activity intended to provide his soul with proper daily nourishment and is actively concerned to advance in the practice of the virtues and in the performance of good works: that is, when he is constantly responding to grace and making a genuine effort to cooperate with it.

This effort is all the more important in a priest, since his position in the world is so difficult and delicate and the mission he has to perform is so vital and transcendental. He is a solitary figure fighting to keep a torch alight in an atmosphere capable of quenching every supernatural spark. If the pressure of gas in a room is higher than the pressure in the surrounding atmosphere, then if the outside atmosphere and the inside of the room come into contact, the gas in the room because of its greater pressure, will expand outwards and change the pressure of the atmosphere. On the other hand, if the gas outside is of higher pressure and we open a window to allow free movement, then the gas will rush into the room and impregnate it with its substance.

Likewise, if the pressure of a priest's spiritual life is high, higher than that of the atmosphere surrounding him, then he will undoubtedly influence the environment deeply and decisively through his normal contact with the world around him. But woe to him if his spiritual life is low-pressured, unhealthy, superficial or weak, for the atmosphere around him will invade him, influence him, make him more worldly, diminish his supernatural outlook on life, change him into a bureaucrat and make of his vocation a mere job, of what should be holy a matter of routine, of the man of God a man of the world, of his freedom a trap, of his detachment from created things a gnawing desire for those very things. If a priest neglects his spiritual life, he runs a grave risk; he becomes almost helpless in the face of the noisy onslaught of the world's attractions pulling at him as a magnet attracts a nail. His spiritual life, therefore, is a question of life or death—for himself and for others. If he is not living a spiritual life, he is like a corpse or, at best (if he is at least in the state of grace though not engaged in that deliberate spiritual activity of seeking and struggling to do God's will at every moment) he is like a paralytic. What part, then, can he play in the front line of battle when facing an implacable enemy? He can only be a dead weight, a liability, a hindrance to the Church in whose service he has enlisted as a volunteer.

The means he must use to preserve and gradually increase the life of grace and to keep up a high inner pressure, are not substantially different from those available to any other member of the faithful. The Gospel makes no distinctions, for just as the life of grace is one, so also is the nourishment necessary and appropriate to preserve and increase it.

Taking the sacred text as our guide and our basis, we can see that, when it comes to saying just what that necessary nourishment is, the minimum essentials are laid down in a phrase from the Acts of the Apostles. In describing the life of those disciples who composed the first Christian community in Jerusalem, the Acts say "they devoted themselves to the apostles' teaching and fellowship, to the breaking of bread and to the prayers" (Acts 2: 42).

Reading the Gospel

Following the order we find in the Acts, let's consider first of all the apostles' teaching. Strictly speaking, at no time did the apostles ever have a doctrine of their own. They were not people of the type we might—especially since the Renaissance—call "thinkers," men with powerful brains capable of working out great theories and systems. As far as we know, they were nearly all rather simple men, of humble origins, with little education and —to judge by the Gospel—little understanding of the supernatural world, rather slow perhaps to grasp the meaning of everything Jesus said. Certainly not a single one of them had any teaching of his own. To put it plainly, none of them had anything worth saying.

They confined themselves—and perhaps this is not the least of their claims to greatness—to bearing witness to what they themselves had seen and heard. They were primarily honest men faithfully repeating the Gospel, the teachings of Jesus, acting on the explicit instructions they had received from him. In all simplicity, they told everything they had seen and heard and they spread the good news of salvation. Then the time came when this teaching was set down in writing, under divine influence, first by Matthew, then by Mark, who took up Peter's preaching, later by Luke and finally, by John (whose Gospel may have been written as late as the end of the first century). And here we have, basically, the apostles' teachings, to which we must add the letters and other documents they wrote under the inspiration of the Holy Spirit to instruct the faithful.

It would seem to be a matter of simple common sense that if we want to follow and persevere in a certain teaching, the first essential is to know it, as the old scholastic adage puts it "knowledge must precede volition." So if we want to persevere in the teaching of the apostles, that is, in the Gospel, the first requirement is to know what it is. And it would seem logical that the best, simplest and most obvious way of knowing the Gospel is to read it.

Hence every priest's daily schedule should always include reading the New Testament. Perhaps it would be more accurate to say that he should study it, but in view of the usual meaning of that word, we shall merely say that he should read it. After all, it is not primarily an intellectual exercise, but a pious act. Intellectual curiosity or mere speculation should be neither the motive nor the purpose of the priest's acquiring a deeper and broader knowledge of the Gospel, but an inner impulse to love God, a straightforward attempt to know him in order to love him. Therefore we should read the New Testament like little children, in a spirit of submission, mentally disposed to accept the teaching it offers us. "Let us therefore hear the Gospel," wrote St. Augustine, "just as if we were listening to the Lord himself present: nor let us say, O happy they who were able to see him! because there were many of them who saw, and also killed him; and there are many among us who have not seen him, and yet have believed. For the precious truth that sounded forth from the mouth of the Lord was written for our sakes, and preserved for our sakes, and recited for our sakes."[1]

How can we love someone unless we actually know him? And if the way, the only way, that leads us to God is Christ, how can we love God unless we know Christ? Obviously every Christian—and even more especially, every priest—has to know who Jesus Christ is. The priest has studied theology and at some time or other he has read the treatise *De Verbo Incarnato*, but yet there is something in the Gospel itself, as far as knowledge of our Lord and his teaching is concerned, that all the theological treatises in the world can never give us. A certain vitality and freshness, a spontaneity, shades of meaning, an atmosphere and inspiration can never be replaced and no amount of study or ingenuity, however profound, can ever allow us to get to know Christ better than the simple account written so objectively and so impassively for us by those disciples who knew him, talked to him and loved him.

Besides this, the New Testament is the new law and therefore the basis of all our theology, its primary and most fundamental source. Certainly the Old Testament is also the word of God and the priest should be familiar with it and reflect on it, but there are good reasons for paying special attention to the Gospel. In the Old Testament we see that "in many and various ways God spoke of old to our fathers by the prophets; but in these last days he has spoken to us by a Son whom he appointed the heir of all things, through whom also he created the world" (1 Heb 1: 2). And, as St. Augustine says, everything the Law and the prophets announced to us as in the future, the New Testament gives and shows to us fully accomplished.

Jesus Christ is God and man because, though God, he became flesh in the spotless womb of the Virgin Mary and dwelt among us; he is our only model because he assumed our nature and, being a man, we can all imitate him. The Gospel gives us the opportunity to contemplate his life; therefore if we read the Gospel, it leads us to contemplative rather than to discursive, knowledge. The important thing for us is to contemplate our Lord just as his disciples saw him, to see his reactions, his behavior, the perfect union between his divine and his human nature, to listen to everything he says, to see him full of compassion at times, angry at other times, understanding with sinners, hard on the Pharisees who falsified religion, and very patient with those disciples who were so obtuse at times. If we go a little further, we might recall St. Ambrose's comment that the Gospel is the manifestation of the mystery of God, which is Christ, but which until then had been hidden in God himself. Christ is indeed the only way, he is the mystery of God, and the Gospel unveils him for us, it is the only way by which we can reach him.

There is a phrase in the Athanasian Creed that refers to our Lord as *"perfectus Deus, perfectus homo"* ("perfect God and perfect man"). Priests may sometimes tend to forget Christ's humanity. It would be worth giving some thought to St. Teresa's comment that one of the reasons why many souls make little progress in their spiritual life is precisely that they have little devotion to our Lord's most sacred *humanity*. It will be very difficult indeed to have such devotion, unless we constantly deepen our acquaintance with him, and there can be no doubt whatsoever that one of the easiest and most practical ways of doing this, whatever one's personal situation, is to read the Gospel. For instance, historians know that no study of Philip II of Spain, however much research goes into its preparation, can tell us as much about him as the book written about 1630 by Baltasar Porreno entitled *Deeds and Sayings*. Likewise, no theological treatise can give us such intimate knowledge of our Lord, such personal and direct information about him, as the Gospel. St. Jerome rightly said that not to know Scripture is not to know Christ.

As to *how* we should read the New Testament, no rule can, or indeed should, be laid down, for it depends on each individual, his circumstances and his devotion. However, since our aim is to get to know the Gospel so as to be able to contemplate the life of Jesus, the simplest thing would seem to be to start at the beginning and read a bit each day until we reach the end; then we can start again at the beginning.

There is no danger of exhausting the material, for it is not natural reasoning—at least, not only natural reasoning—that helps us to discover and assimilate the teaching contained in the New Testament. Neither should we feel discouraged if the apparent monotony of reading the same things over and over again, without any new ideas occurring to us, tempts us to give up this devotion, for it is a devotion that yields excellent results. It's quite impossible to exhaust this book. Twenty centuries have passed since it was written; many scholars, eminent for their science and their sanctity, have written commentaries on it; many more have preached on it constantly and continually. Theological systems have been constructed on the basis of its contents; each word, each phrase, each passage has been analyzed. Yet we are as far from exhausting it now as we were at the beginning. The word of God is unfathomable, it is deeper than the most penetrating human mind. We can always—absolutely always—go a little further in our understanding of revelation, by means of humility, faith and grace, because, as St. Jerome said, it contains as many mysteries as words, and each mystery of faith constitutes in itself a lifetime's work. Certainly the text of the New Testament is short and it can be read quickly, but its contents are immense—few words but great words, as St. Jerome said.

The second point we mentioned—that is, the apparent monotony—is equally irrelevant if it is read humbly, in a spirit of faith and with the help of grace. "Without me you can do nothing"— by themselves, human means are useless and incapable of producing supernatural results. We might read a passage from the Gospel countless times without seeing any point in it. Then one day, for no apparent reason, we could read the same passage and be amazed to discover a lesson, an important meaning, as if the words stood up and shouted their message at us. When this happens—and everyone who makes a habit of reading the New Testament has had experience of it—it is not because on that day, at that particular moment, we are exceptionally lucid or intelligent, but because the Holy Spirit has opened up our mind to show us something we never saw before, and to let us see things which until then had remained hidden from our sight. This could happen any day at any time, but it may be that the Holy Spirit associates that particular grace with our reading that very passage for the fifteenth time, and only after our love of God's word has remained constant after fourteen—apparently—sterile readings of the chapter or the verse does he respond to our efforts.

God knows that this sustenance which we can provide for our soul every single day, to keep it living and healthy, is easy to take; it requires only three or four minutes a day. Can we, in all honesty, ever have any excuse for depriving the soul of this basic nourishment?

Devotion to the Eucharist

The "breaking of bread" and reception of Christ's body was an essential part of life in the early Church. The members of the faithful gathered together, sang God's praises, gave him thanks and received from the hand of the priest the food necessary for their supernatural life. Jesus himself had clarified this when he said: "I came that they may have life, and have it abundantly" (Jn 10: 10) and "I am the bread of life" (Jn 6: 48). No one can hope to live without nourishment to sustain and renew his life.

In practice, of course, frequent and indeed daily reception of the Eucharist is no problem for the priest. God's wishes on the subject of how often his children should approach the altar were made explicit and quite clear by St. Pius X, the pope who encouraged the faithful to go to Jesus in the sacrament as frequently as possible. It is true that no one is worthy, but there is no question of worthiness involved. No one is, or ever will be, worthy to be united to God in the way in which we are united to him when we receive the Blessed Sacrament—or in any other way for that matter. In relation to God, none of us is worthy of anything. Here we could appropriately quote the words with which Bernanos concludes his *Diary of a Country Priest:* "All is grace." Jesus did not decide to remain with us in the tabernacle because we were in any way worthy of him, but because, knowing our weakness and wretchedness as he did, he wanted to be of help to us, to be our strength and our nourishment; he wanted to give us life.

It is not easy to find words to express properly and adequately or to applaud appropriately all that the Eucharist means, both in its divine aspect, in its origin (such an intense love for men that it made the Son of God humble himself to the extent of disappearing under the appearance of bread and wine) and in its results for human beings—we become living tabernacles, monstrances, carrying the living Christ within us. *Mysterium Fidei!* A great mystery which we can attain only through faith, but which is more real than any of the natural occurrences known by science or by the everyday evidence of our senses.

The priest's ministry brings him into direct daily contact with the most tremendous mysteries. Because of his very function, the supernatural world constitutes the climate in which he habitually has to move and act. The Mass, the breviary, administration of the sacraments, preaching, all remind him repeatedly throughout the day, with scarcely a moment's interruption, that the only thing that really is, the only thing really necessary, the only thing that really matters or has any importance is the supernatural reality which does not pass, but remains for ever.

In the eyes of lay people, indeed in the eyes of everyone, a priest is in the Lord's confidence, he is his friend. And this is as it should be. But is each individual priest without exception a personal friend of the Lord's, a man in whom he can trust, on whom he can rely without the slightest fear that he may break down and fail him? A priest is a human being, like everyone else. Therefore he must never have too much confidence in himself, in his own strength or even in his good intentions. As a man, nothing human is alien to him—not even a tendency to get into a routine or a rut. When actions are repeated, they give rise to habits, but there is an important distinction between a supernatural habit of doing what is right—which is a virtue—and merely "getting used" to something. If a priest is not on his guard, he may become accustomed even to the most sacred things and get into a routine, an almost mechanical and absentminded way of doing things—things whose very nature demands the greatest attention and all the refinement of which he is capable.

In everything relating to the Eucharist, he should be inwardly alert, particularly careful about his inner purity, but paying special attention even to his outward appearance. "Truly, truly, I say to you, unless you eat the flesh of the Son of man and drink his blood, you have no life in you" (Jn 6: 53). A priest without life is dead, and if he is dead he is worthless. Reception of the Eucharist is a matter of life, and as in all vital matters, we must put our whole soul into it. It is true that the Eucharist, like all the sacraments, works *ex opere operato*, by its own intrinsic power. Since priests receive every day, not just life, but the very Author of life himself, doesn't it seem strange that they show so few signs of this vitality? Day after day, they receive nothing less than the Lord himself, the source of all holiness, indeed holiness itself; is it not surprising, then, that every single priest is not truly a saint?

The fact that he is not can't be attributed to any deficiency on the part of the sacrament itself. The reason why the grace of the sacrament affects us so slightly lies rather in the fact that our own personal disposition so greatly reduces our capacity to receive that grace. If we place a thimble under the Niagara Falls, it will collect only the few drops of water that it can hold. If a priest fails to make constant progress in perfection and holiness, in love of God and of his fellow men, in humility and self-sacrifice; it is never because of any deficiency in the Holy Spirit's action on his soul, but always because his own capacity to accept grace is still very low. He has not yet emptied his heart of himself and it is so full of human things that there's very little room for grace.

Nevertheless, the fact that many Christians—and priests, or at least some priests, must be counted among them—are spiritually so unrefined and negligent should neither discourage us nor estrange us from the Eucharist (falling into the mistake made by the Jansenists, who thought this was a way of showing reverence to it). "Have you forgotten what Jesus said? It is not those who are well, but those who are sick, who need the physician" (*The Way*, 536). What we must do, therefore, is to prepare our soul spiritually so that it will continually increase its capacity for grace, its hunger for Christ, its thirst for Life, its need to be united to our Lord. And, as always, the will has to be motivated by knowledge, while grace must give impulse and light to both the will and the knowledge.

The priest is certainly well aware of the greatness of this sacrament and of its effects. However, he must know and also think about what he receives. Knowledge is of little use if it is easily forgotten, if it is not actively in the forefront of his consciousness but only lies dormant or anaesthetized, alive but buried under a heap of rubble, swamped by the many events, memories, worries, problems and bits of gossip emanating from the life that goes on around him. How can it hope to have any strength, oppressed as it is by the dead weight of so many things?

The priest should think about the Eucharist every day before approaching the altar, so that he may be deeply conscious and aware of the greatness of this sacrament, the sacrament of love; that is how he will foster a hunger for the Lord in his soul, an intense desire to be united to the source of all purity, all fortitude, love and holiness. For it is not easy to love something deeply if it is only perceived faintly.

"That they may discharge their ministry with fidelity, they should prize daily conversation with Christ the Lord in visits of personal devotion to the most Holy Eucharist" (PO 18). Sometimes, during moments of difficulty, when the soul is invaded by anxiety or depression, when apparently insoluble problems or situations weigh on us heavily, we may think how easy it would have been to solve this if we had been living at the time of Christ. We may think, or perhaps just imagine, that we would have approached him with great confidence and asked his help—that help which he dispensed so easily and so generously to everyone who was suffering. But when we receive Christ in holy Communion, our union with him is indescribably closer than any relationship we could have had with him at any time during his mortal life. In St. Teresa's words: "As the wondrous effects produced by this most holy bread in those who worthily receive it are very well known, I will not describe all the things that could be related about this person I mentioned, though I have been enabled to learn about them and I know that they are not fabrications. The Lord had given this person such a lively faith that, when she heard people say they wished they had lived when Christ walked on this earth, she would smile to herself, for she knew that we have him as truly with us in the most holy Sacrament as people had him then, and wonder what more they could possibly want."[2]

This is absolutely true. For our sake, inspired by his compassionate love for us, knowing how weak we are and how we all need his help (priests as well as, if not more than, anyone else), he decided to hide even his human appearance and to remain enclosed in the tabernacle so as to be perpetually at our disposal and at our service. Can there be any greater humiliation than this? "The humility of Jesus: in Bethlehem, in Nazareth, on Calvary. But more humiliation and more self-abasement still in the Sacred Host: more than in the stable, more than in Nazareth, more than on the Cross."[3]

He is truly a hidden God (Is 45: 15). In human eyes, there is just a round white host that seems inert and passive; in reality, though perceptible only through faith and love, there is a magnetic force that attracts everyone, calling urgently, and inspiring each of us individually in the depths of each one's personality.

"Just as Christ on the Cross 'loved *me* and delivered himself up for *me*' (Gal 2: 20), so, here too he loves *me* and comes to *me* in the Blessed Sacrament. When he finds himself united to me in Communion, he is by no means surprised to learn that I am a sinner. He knew that before, and he loved me as I am. He comes to me because he is still the friend and the refuge and the savior of sinners. For my part I should do my best to respond to his love, even though I may be unworthy of it. And the best way to respond is to believe in its inexpressible reality and act according to my belief."[4]

To act according to his belief: that is exactly how the priest will increase his capacity to receive Christ. Since the effect of the Eucharist on each individual soul depends, so to speak, on its capacity to be filled with Christ, thus to the extent that a person becomes emptied of his own self, he will acquire an ever-increasing capacity to be filled with Christ. Therefore, it is the realization of what he is about to do that makes a priest prepare his soul to receive the Eucharist with acts of love, desires for union, attempts to overcome his own will, in order to offer them all to his Lord—giving them as the gift of a poor cripple whose poverty scarcely permits him to give anything other than tokens of love and good will, humble expressions of his earnest wish to please. If any priest thinks such exercises are childish or unimportant, he is showing that he has very little love, for, even on a human level, love is normally expressed by good manners, little gifts, small details which show how attentive we are to the person we love.

Therefore the priest's behavior towards the people entrusted to his care, whoever they may be, is also a way of preparing for Communion. As St. John Chrysostom put it: "Do you want to honor Christ's body? Then, do not neglect it when you see it covered in rags. After honoring it in the church dressed in silken garments, don't leave him outside dying with cold because he has not enough clothes. For Christ himself says, 'This is my body' and it is he who also says, 'You saw me hungry and you gave me nothing to eat: what you have denied to the least of these little ones you have denied to me.' The Body of Christ in the Eucharist, asks for pure souls, not expensive clothes. But Christ in the person of a poor man asks us to help him in every way. . . . Give him, therefore, the honor he himself has asked for. Once again it's true: God wants not golden chalices but golden souls."[5]

It is what is on the inside that matters. But "you will know them by their fruits" (Matt 7: 20), and we cannot escape from the fact that everything we do is cloaked in external behavior; even what we do within ourselves, unless we are very skillful at keeping up a pretense, must show through in one way or another. If a priest is not known by his fruits—by his piety, recollection, awareness of the presence of God and charity—he has plenty of material for meditation simply in thinking about the fact that he shows no signs of living a spiritual life and that he has little capacity for grace. If he does not regard the reception of the Eucharist—the *Sacramentum pietatis,* the "summit of the spiritual life and all the sacraments are ordered to it"[6]—as the most important action of his day, the point towards which his thoughts and deeds, his ministry and his life, all converge, then he shows that he really attaches very little importance to the mystery of the body and blood of Christ, even though he may theoretically know everything to be known about its immeasurable greatness.

If there were only one tabernacle in the whole world, and if each of us could receive Jesus Christ in the sacrament only once in a lifetime, surely we would look forward to that event with great enthusiasm and prepare for it with special attention and reverence. Would not our whole life revolve around that inexpressibly profound fact, that we had received God himself made man? Yet we receive the same Lord and experience the same event every day and how little we appreciate it! "Easy come, easy go" might be the deplorable description of our attitude. Perhaps it is because it's so easy for us to receive the Lord, because he comes to us so simply, so generously, that we feel, psychologically at least, little inclined to attach great importance to his coming. He comes to us so humbly! He is God; yet he allows himself to be received unworthily, sacrilegiously, and he never lashes out at anyone who commits such a crime; he puts up with discourtesy and neglect, bad manners and hurried greetings, solitude and profanation, impoliteness and abandonment. How little we care about him, how seldom we thank him for lovingly insisting on transforming our poor human nature; how very badly we treat him!

Prayer

So much has been written about prayer, from the Gospel era to our own day, that any attempt to add something new would seem to be vain.

It would seem to be, but in fact it is by no means vain. The very fact that there are so many excellent books on the subject shows how important it is and, besides, each generation needs to be taught anew. Indeed it is never vain to speak of prayer, even to priests, and this is truer than ever as the twentieth century comes to a close, precisely because the pace of life, so fast and frightening, so anxious about work and productivity, so technical . . . and so very superficial, can threaten the priest's stability and sense of balance by launching him into a whirlwind of activity, as if the success of his ministry depended on that alone.

A priest who neglects his prayer is like a plant without roots; eventually he will either dry up completely or, like the barren fig tree in the Gospel, produce some leaves but none of the fruits of holiness. Of all the bonds that unite us to God, prayer is the most easily accessible to everyone and the most permanent; it establishes contact between him and us throughout the day, amid the numerous problems and worries of daily life. It is equivalent to friendly contact and conversation between two people. Is there much chance of friendship between two persons if they do not even speak to one another? Can a friendship develop and advance, can it bring two people together, if there is no personal contact between them? Without prayer, there can be no friendship, no understanding, between man and God.

As we follow our Lord in the Gospel, we have only to notice how strongly he emphasized this subject again and again, grasping whatever opportunities he could to show us what great importance he attached to this matter. We have only to notice how he expressed himself in order to see how insistent he was that his disciples—and we, centuries later—should learn this lesson.

It would probably be inappropriate in a book like this to presume that we could teach priests what prayer is or define the importance it should have in their lives. But perhaps we could remind them of some points they know so well that they may have forgotten them. Perhaps we could help them to renew their awareness of elementary principles and simple truths which have always been so taken for granted that they may have been a little neglected, if not totally abandoned, or encourage them to take another look at the Master's teachings which are so clear, so direct, and so decisive. Perhaps it would not be a waste of time to attempt these things—it might even be useful, especially if we remember the risk priests run of becoming immune to serious thought on these subjects due to the great familiarity with them which they have to show in their dealings with the faithful. After all, there's no worse ignorance than that of someone who thinks he knows everything.

At the request of his disciples, our Lord taught them to pray (Lk 11: 1-13), and it would seem that what he actually taught them was not so much a formula as a method. He showed them how they should address God, our Father, what they ought to say and what they ought to ask of him. He showed them with what great confidence they should approach him to tell him their worries, like that annoying man who went to ask his friend for bread at midnight. If we read that passage from St. Luke slowly and carefully, realizing that those words were spoken by our Lord and that he spoke them for us, it will undoubtedly be very difficult not to be persuaded of the importance of prayer and the simplicity with which we should pray to God. When we really say the Our Father—not just repeating the words—we are speaking to God exactly as a child speaks to its father.

This is what prayer is: talking to God. It is not thinking about him, but talking to him. Thinking about God, or meditation, as it is usually called, is an excellent thing and it would be impossible to overemphasize its importance. It is very difficult to speak meaningfully to someone unless we are somehow or other thinking of that person. Nevertheless, thought or reflection is an act which in no way obliges the person concerned to "come out" of himself, whereas the moment he begins to speak, communication is established with the person being spoken to. Prayer means establishing contact with God, speaking to him. When we do this we are no longer static but moving towards him. This means telling him things, however insignificant. After all, when a small child speaks to its father, it's unlikely to expound brilliant scientific theories or new formulas for success in business.

Here are a few brief lines written by Blessed Josemaria Escriva, which have proved helpful to many people, including priests: "You don't know how to pray? Put yourself in the presence of God, and as soon as you have said, 'Lord, I don't know how to pray!' you can be sure you've already begun." "You wrote to me: 'To pray is to talk with God. But about what?' About what? About him, and yourself: joys, sorrows, successes and failures, great ambitions, daily worries—even your weaknesses! And acts of thanksgiving and petitions—and love and reparation. In short, to get to know him and to get to know yourself—'to get acquainted!'"7

That is the fundamental thing—to get acquainted. If we want to be united with someone, we have to love them, for love is the force that unites. But we cannot love someone without knowing them; and how can we know someone unless there is some contact between us? There is no other effective way to achieve this union except prayer, and it's impossible to overemphasize how essential it is.

Here perhaps we could mention a trustworthy illustration of this point, even if its main value lies merely in the fact that it involves personal experience. It comes to us from St. Teresa who went through it quite intensely and, we might almost say, sadly. In judging it, we must remember that, besides actually undergoing the experience, when she came to write it down she had all the enlightenment that her closeness to God gave her. And we must not forget that the Church numbers her among those writers regarded as authorities because of their sound teaching. She wrote: "Another reason is to show what great blessings God grants to a soul when he prepares it to love the practice of prayer, though it may not be as well prepared already as it should be; and how, if that soul perseveres, notwithstanding the sins, temptations and falls of a thousand kinds into which the devil leads it, the Lord, I am certain, will bring it to the harbor of salvation."[8] St. Teresa places tremendous emphasis on prayer throughout all her writings and never misses an opportunity to mention it.

There is also another passage from her *Life* which deserves mention here, one even more explicit and clear, if that is possible, than the lines just quoted. It is rather long, but the teaching it contains and the elegance of the writing itself makes it worth repeating. "This is one of the reasons why, though being what I am, I was encouraged to obey my superiors by writing this and giving an account of my wretched life and of the favors which the Lord has granted me, albeit I have not served him but offended him. I only wish I were a person of great authority so that my words might be believed; I beseech the Lord that his Majesty may be pleased to grant me this. I repeat that no one who has begun to practice prayer should be discouraged and say: 'If I am going to fall again, it will be better for me not to go on practicing prayer.' I think it will be [tragic] if such a person gives up prayer and does not amend his evil life; but, if he does not give it up, he may have confidence that prayer will bring him into the haven of light. This was a matter about which the devil kept plaguing me, and I suffered so much through thinking myself lacking in humility for continuing prayer when I was so wicked, that, as I have said, for a year and a half I gave it up—or at any rate for a year; I am not quite sure about the six months. This would have been nothing less than plunging into hell—nor was it: there was no need for any devils to send me there. Oh, God help me, how terribly blind I was! How well the devil succeeds in his purpose when he pursues us like this! The deceiver knows that if a soul perseveres in practicing prayer it will be lost to him, and that, by the goodness of God, all the relapses into which he can lead it will only help it to make greater strides onward to His service. And this is a matter of some concern to the devil."[9]

These lines contain not the slightest exaggeration either regarding the efficacy of mental prayer or in referring to the devil's great concern that no one should practice such prayer. Both points are quite obvious. Prayer means speaking to God or, in other words, "friendly intercourse, and frequent solitary converse with Him who we know loves us."[10] Sin, on the other hand, is enmity with God. Therefore since contradictory attitudes to somebody cannot exist at the same time in one and the same person, it is impossible to be God's enemy (by sinning) and at the same time have friendly intercourse with him (by praying). Both attitudes cannot exist side by side for long, because either the sin or the prayer is bound to be abandoned. If prayer continues, if the soul is determined to keep it up whatever the cost, then sin will inevitably be eliminated. God repays our good will, our faithfulness to prayer, either by giving us the strength necessary to break away from anything that separates us from him, or else by breaking down the barrier himself. Prayer is therefore a guarantee of faithfulness, an assurance of spiritual progress, and, we might almost say, a pledge of salvation. "Blessed be God, who does not reject my prayer!" says the psalmist (Ps 66). On the supernatural level, to persevere in communication with God is something of obvious significance.

(It must never be forgotten that the purpose of prayer is not that the Lord should do our will, but that we should be so united with him as to have the strength and the light to accomplish his. If prayer is *determined* by temporal needs, Fr. Peters tells us, it can easily lose its religious merit and its Christian character and become a pagan act.[11])

In theory, prayer is the easiest thing in the world. God is always present, he always sees us and he hears us. We can speak to him at any time, in any place, in any circumstances. All we have to do is to say "Lord," and he will turn towards us to listen to us and hear whatever we have to say to him. There is no need to have a lot of theological knowledge or even subjects of conversation. There is no one, or rather there are very few people, who can pray better than a child, and a child just turns to our Lord simply and innocently and says whatever enters his head.

In spite of this, there are in fact very few Christians who practice mental prayer. So we have to ask ourselves: if prayer is so feasible, so simple, so easy that a child can do it and so certain of producing results, how is it that so few people take it seriously and persevere in it?

One reason may be that given by Newman. He says something to the effect that some people are incapable of any kind of thought and would be incapable of reflecting for an hour in silence, that it would be a great punishment for many others if they were obliged to think about themselves, while many more are happy to live in a whirlwind, in any kind of excitement that distracts their mind and saves them from having to think about themselves.[12] If a priest is one of these people, it may be that the excitement and distractions of the world have filled his mind and heart so that he is incapable of any intimate relationship with God. So much deafening noise makes it very difficult for him to hear God's voice, which is scarcely audible outside an atmosphere of recollection and inner concentration.

A secular priest must be a contemplative; he must live and act always in the presence of his Lord. Being a man of God, as he is, he must be able to see God in his creation, in nature, in people and in events; he must see God behind everything—willing, permitting, and watching always to extract some good from everything, whatever it is. So at least some recollection is essential. He cannot live in solitude, away from all noise and distractions, like a monk; on the contrary, he is required to live totally surrounded by whatever circumstances are normal in the surroundings in which ordinary people live and work. Yet, for that very reason, he must try at all costs to keep some period free every day to be alone in the presence of God—some time for solitude and silence, away from all external distractions, to allow him to maintain inward recollection throughout his working day.

It is true that the most important thing is inner silence and solitude, but it is no less true that sometimes they can be abused. There is a lot of truth in Thomas Merton's dismal picture of some pseudo-apostles: "There are men dedicated to God whose lives are full of restlessness and who have no real desire to be alone. They admit that exterior solitude is good, in theory, but they insist that it is far better to preserve interior solitude while living in the world. In practice, their lives are devoured by activities and strangled with attachments. Interior solitude is impossible for them. They fear it. They do everything they can to escape it. What is worse, they try to draw everyone else into activities as ceaseless and as devouring as their own. They are great promoters of useless work. They love to organize meetings and banquets and conferences and lectures. They print circulars, write letters, talk for hours on the telephone in order that they may gather a hundred people together in a large room where they will all fill the air with smoke and make a great deal of noise and roar at one another and clap their hands and stagger home at last, patting one another on the back with the assurance that they have all done great things to spread the Kingdom of God."[13]

Any activity ceases to be good when it takes control of a priest and makes it impossible for him to live a spiritual life. Our Lord was God and never ceased to contemplate his Father; yet he frequently retreated into the desert to be alone—and not because he had nothing else to do: "But so much the more the report went abroad concerning him; and great multitudes gathered to hear and to be healed of their infirmities. But he withdrew to the wilderness and prayed" (Lk 5: 15-16). How, then, can we imagine that without prayer, without some prayer at least, we can keep our activity from destroying our intimate relationship with God, that closeness which requires silence and recollection if it is to exist and without which spiritual life is totally impossible?

It is also noteworthy that when St. Teresa speaks about prayer she often mentions the devil. The devil exists; he is not a myth or a character invented to frighten disobedient children. He is a real being and a very active being. He knows very well what he stands to lose if someone prays. He knows that if a soul prays perseveringly, it is lost to him. He is supremely interested in every priest, for he knows that if he can incapacitate a minister of the Lord, many souls will be left absolutely helpless, and then he will have won a great victory. He cares nothing as to whether the priest is always active, doing countless things, spending every day or even his whole life moving around from one place to another, organizing events, holding meetings, launching new enterprises, starting new apostolates—provided he does not pray. (This is human nature: we are quite capable of busying ourselves with a thousand trivial things while we ignore the most important thing of all). But the devil also knows that it is very difficult for a conversation to degenerate into mere habit, mere routine, if a genuine effort is made each time it starts; that in any relationship between two people the one with the stronger personality influences the other; that the more frequent the meetings the more the friendship, the confidence, and the mutual understanding develops. Therefore he invents as many obstacles as he can, in his own subtle and efficient way, to ensure that the habit of prayer is not kept up day after day, for otherwise the priest will not only escape his clutches forever, but will also take a large number of souls with him on his way to God, giving them spiritual nourishment, light, courage, warmth, and strength.

Prayer is undoubtedly a matter of life or death. It is important enough to be treated with the greatest seriousness; otherwise no one can complain, for we shall have only ourselves to blame for whatever may happen. The result may be, for instance, that a priest will have insufficient strength to overcome his lukewarmness and that his general condition—his spiritual condition—will be very weak. He may become like a man who continually falls to the ground because of weakness due to lack of nourishment. Common sense would seem to dictate that the most urgent thing for such a man to do, if he wants to be able to stand without falling, is to take plenty of proper food to give him back his strength. In like manner, there is a way to avoid being spiritually weak, and that is to nourish the soul. Prayer is the soul's nourishment, for what man cannot do God can do quite easily. We have only to depend on him and ask him for the strength we need. Prayer is as important for the life of the spirit as food is for our physical development; therefore it must be practiced daily.

However, it is not sufficient to know all this; we have to convert it into life. It's not enough to have good ideas about prayer and how important it is—what really matters is that we actually pray, and that we do so every day. There is plenty of experience to show what happens when good resolutions take the form of vague desires to do something worthwhile. The essential thing is to be specific and, above all, to make a start. If we are to ensure that we pray every day, a certain fixed time must be set aside to be exclusively devoted to speaking to God, to being with him. We must be fully determined that this daily appointment will not be at the mercy of whims or moods. It cannot depend on our having nothing else to do. It is advisable and only right that we reserve this period above all else, whatever the obstacles that may arise. We may find we have no time to meet a friend or to watch a television program, we may have to be late for a meeting or for something else, but the time we have set aside for prayer should never be curtailed or missed, even if we have to omit almost everything else.

If possible—and it is usually possible—the period devoted to prayer should be at the same time every day, at a fixed hour, so as to fit in well with the general plan of our day's work. When the time comes, we should leave whatever we are doing and go to pray. It is totally irrelevant whether we feel like it at that particular moment or not, whether we go to pray enthusiastically or not. Only one thing matters, namely to spend the allotted period of time trying to tell our Lord about our great difficulties and our little successes, our worries and our joys, asking him to help us, or, monotonously but sincerely, repeating some simple phrase, as the Lord himself did in Gethsemane (Mt 26: 44). If this seems boring, we just have to realize that if what we want is entertainment, then it would be better to go to the circus than to the tabernacle. At the very worst, we shall feel as if we were on the rack, wanting to get away but remaining there, doing our best to explain to the Lord what is happening to us, trying to avoid distractions. Even at the very worst, he will know that we are there because we want to please him, for there is no purely human motive that can compensate us for those minutes, passing so slowly that they seem more like hours. In fact, this may well be the best prayer for, as Thomas Merton says, "It is much better to desire God without being able to think clearly of him, than to have marvelous thoughts about him without desiring to enter this union with his will." In the final analysis, perhaps this perseverance in the suffering and helplessness we encounter in our search for God may be the best expression of how much we really do love him.

The amount of time a particular priest ought to spend in mental prayer each day should be worked out in consultation with that brother in the priesthood who has agreed to be his spiritual director, but it must always take account of the circumstances of his life and work. In any case, an hour will be sufficient, especially if he takes the precaution of dividing it into two half-hour periods. It would be advisable to spend the first period in the morning, before celebrating holy Mass, and the other in the evening, reasonably early, when there is least likelihood of being disturbed. In view of the increasing complexity of the priest's life, it would be difficult to devote a full hour uninterruptedly to mental prayer, whereas if he divides it into two halves, it will give his plan of life more flexibility, as well as renewing his direct contact with God and being strengthened twice instead of once. Besides this, it is easier to concentrate for two periods of half an hour each than to do so continuously for sixty minutes.

However, this is not the only type of prayer a priest has to practice; in fact, he has a duty to practice another type, namely his daily reading of the breviary. This is a highly important way of praying, not only because it is laid down for every priest as a matter of discipline and under pain of grave sin, but because it is an official prayer of the Church. The priest represents the Church, Christ's bride, when he speaks to God using the words of the breviary; the Church herself *uses* him as an instrument to praise God.

The priestly function of giving praise to God, a function introduced by Christ, the Priest of the new and everlasting covenant, when he assumed our human nature, must be continued until the end of time by his body, the Church. The purpose of the Office is to glorify God at the various times of the day and night. "Therefore, when this wonderful song of praise is worthily rendered by priests and others who are deputed for this purpose by Church ordinance, or by the faithful praying together with the priest in an approved form, then it is truly the voice of the bride addressing her bridegroom; it is the very prayer which Christ himself, together with his body, addresses to the Father" (SC 84).

Since there is actually a duty to read the breviary every day, it is a means of sanctification that may either yield visible results or, instead, become an unpleasant chore to be dispatched as quickly as possible, doing the indispensable minimum just to comply with the rules, but without the slightest attempt to comply with them properly. In other words, the letter of the law may be fulfilled without any respect for its spirit.

Somebody once remarked that the gradual deterioration of one's priestly spirit is first noticeable outwardly in a total or partial loss of the high regard we should all have for the breviary. Instead of considering it first and foremost as the Church's way of giving praise to God the Creator, the Redeemer and Provider; instead of regarding himself as a spokesman for his brothers in Christ so as, on their behalf and in the name of the Church, to give God the honor which he has a right to expect from his creatures, and thanks for the loving care he has taken of them; instead of seeing the psalms as composed of words inspired by God himself to allow us to address him in an appropriate manner, since we are so wretched and our language is so inadequate; if a priest's spirit is worldly, he will see the breviary as of no practical purpose whatsoever, taking up a lot of time which, he thinks, could be devoted to more urgent and productive work.

Instead of treating the breviary as a prayer, he then reads it, recites it, or just somehow gets through it. Since his main concern is simply to save time and he cannot do this by actually omitting any passages, he does so by hurrying through it all, and the words come pouring out on top of one another, jumbled together, carelessly and meaninglessly muttered. Instead of praying, carrying on a sustained conversation with due attention and respect for the majesty of a good God who cares for us all, it becomes a distracted, artificial recitation, performed reluctantly. There is a point we might appropriately recall here: "Consider what you are saying, to whom it is being said and by whom. For that hurried talk, without time for reflection, is just empty noise. And with St. Teresa, I will tell you that, however much you work your lips, I do not call it prayer" (*The Way*, 85). The result of such an attitude to the breviary will not be holiness but, perhaps, lukewarmness.

It is quite possible that, as an ever watchful mother, the Church made the breviary an obligation so as to ensure that secular priests would not abandon recollection and prayer totally, at a time when nearly all prayer had taken refuge in the monasteries. In any case, as mediators, priests must represent their fellow men before God, they must support the Church's saving function; and therefore they must give praise and thanks, ask pardon, and make offerings; and they must express the attitude that creatures should adopt before their Creator. The divine Office is precisely the way in which glorification of God, to whom all honor and glory are due, is accomplished by the priest officially delegated by the Church, in the name of the community which he represents at that moment, as well as in Christ's name; for with him, in him and through him, all prayer is offered to the Father. Just as Jesus Christ took upon himself the miseries of all mankind, so also when the priest, as *ipse Christus,* is praying for the community, he takes upon himself the duty of speaking for all the redeemed. For the priest who is capable of availing of it, the knowledge that, on the very same day, in various places all over the world, other priests with that identical spirit and that identical intention, using the same words, are also offering to God the praise of the liturgical prayer is an enormous source of strength, love, and confidence in God, and it gives him a deep feeling of sharing in the common sonship of the Father and in the brotherhood of the many brothers of Christ, the first-born.

The priest must have a spirit of prayer if he sincerely wants to fulfill his duty to give praise to God, and that spirit will be the result of mental prayer. The Church is always realistic and has simplified the breviary. But, as Pope Paul stated at the time that this was done: "If we now simplify some expressions in our public worship and try to make it more comprehensible for the faithful and closer to present day language, we certainly do not intend to diminish the importance of prayer or rank it after other duties of the sacred ministry or of pastoral activity."[14]

Nowadays, when life in the world all around the priest shows so many signs of breaking down and becoming disjointed, the man of God should be more determined than ever to have some recollection and solitude, some inner quiet so as to achieve the only thing necessary, if his prayer—whether private or official, personal or liturgical—is to be like a giant reservoir damming up large quantities of pure water to be released in due course in the form of energy that provides power, and irrigation that brings growth to millions of souls that are paralyzed, dry and barren. Prayer is so important and decisive that without it the priest cannot be a useful instrument in the Lord's hands, for there is one essential and immutable characteristic of his priesthood which cannot be attained without prayer, namely that perfect union which should exist "between priestly mission and consecration, or in other words, between a personal life of piety and the exercise of the ministerial priesthood, between the priest's filial relationship with God and his pastoral and fraternal relations with men. I do not believe in the ministerial success of any priest who is not a man of prayer."[15]

Friendship

The priest devotes his life to others. He is a shepherd who has to look after the flock entrusted to him and take great care of them. But his concern must not end with that flock; it should extend to all mankind, for he has been called to perform a universal mission. He must try to ensure that they all get proper nourishment for their souls, so that their lives can develop; he must help them in moments of difficulty, encourage them at all times, raise them up when they fall, seek them if they are lost or have gone astray.

What about the priest himself? Everybody needs the priest, but does he need anybody? Can he reach his goal alone, with his faults, his limited amount of knowledge, the weaknesses he shares with all mankind? Is he alone to be deprived of help from others; is he alone to be abandoned and live his life without any shepherd to care for him?

This is a problem that the priest has had to face throughout the centuries. He is not a cold, impersonal creature, devoid of human feelings. On the contrary, he is deeply human—he must be, if he is to fulfill his function. And it is impossible to be a human being without knowing and experiencing, to a greater or a lesser extent, the feelings common to all men, to all who share this human nature of ours. The priest, like everyone else, feels fear and joy, peace and unrest, euphoria and depression. He can feel terribly lonely and need someone to whom he can simply talk. He is by nature a sociable person, and therefore he can never develop fully if he remains alone.

Furthermore, of course, the vocation he has received from God, and the fulfillment of the mission entrusted to him by the Church, do not allow him to alleviate his loneliness in the same way as other men, by setting up a home and sharing his life with other people related to him in a very special way. Neither can he share his worries, his most intimate sentiments or his most excruciating problems, matters referring to his relationships with God or his pastoral life, with people in a different sphere of life, with lay people. He cannot go to weep on their shoulders or expect them to rejoice with him, because they are not appropriate for this type of relationship. A priest has no right to look for sympathy; he cannot pour out his troubles to the first person he meets. There is an area in every individual, the deepest and most delicate area of all, to which only God should have access; otherwise there is a risk of losing all sense of intimacy and the most basic characteristics of one's personality.

So if the priest is not to be alone, and if his relationships with lay people can be useful to him and appropriate only to a limited extent, there is only one way open to him, namely to be on friendly terms with his brothers in the priesthood.

At this point perhaps we could say a little about this subject. It may cause some surprise to find "friendship" listed among the means a priest should use to sustain his spiritual life of faithfulness to Christ and to his Church, a means of keeping up a high spiritual pressure and of transforming the atmosphere in which he lives so that it conforms to the Gospel. Yet it is a fact that friendship is an aid in living a spiritual life. Friendship—not its substitutes—when properly understood, is exactly how priests should practice the charity of Christ among themselves. It is exactly how they should fulfill the "new commandment." It is a living expression of that *fraternitas sacramentalis* to which the Council refers (PO 8).

Everyone needs some relationship with others, not just to exchange opinions, to comment on trivial events or to chat about current affairs. The need to communicate goes deeper than that, for things happen deep down in everyone's soul.

Some things are pleasant and cry out for cheerful expression of the joy they bring with them. Remember, for instance, how the woman who swept her house carefully to find the coin she had lost then ran to her neighbors to share her joy with them (Lk 15: 9). Other things are sad or distressing, and then too the soul needs to pour out its sorrow, for no one can live with too much weight in his heart; peace, at least some peace, is essential if life is to be worth living. When the prodigal son "came to himself" (Lk 15: 17) and realized the injustice he had committed against his father, he felt the need to relieve his soul of that weight by talking about his guilt. And even Judas himself was obsessed with his treachery; alone and with his callous soul troubled by remorse, he felt impelled to pour out his troubles by going to the Jewish leaders and saying: "I have sinned in betraying innocent blood" (Mt 27: 4).

Is there anyone who can get by without the help of someone else? Is there anyone in the world who is really self-sufficient? Every soul, however holy, needs an outlet, and obviously when it is not so holy, the need is all the greater. But not all outlets alleviate; some do not absorb the troubles being poured out, while others simply reflect them or bounce them back again. The prodigal son and Judas met very different reactions in their attempts to pour out their inner anguish—the one was totally freed from it, while the other was thrown into deepest despair because he projected his remorse onto a hard surface that repelled it at once: "What is that to us? See to it yourself" (Mt 27: 4).

If we try to confide in someone and our confidence is rejected, not only does a door close on us but a wound opens. And often it is we ourselves who are to blame for choosing to confide in someone who is unsuitable for the purpose, instead of someone qualified to understand and able to give advice. Some inner conflicts may give rise to states of neurosis, obsessive ideas or personality breakdowns which may go so far as to need psychiatric treatment. Then many repressions come to light which need never have become so extreme if they had been clearly shown to the right person at the proper time.

Viewed in this context as in so many others, the priest's position is unique, which makes extreme tact essential when it comes to this type of confidence, affecting the most intimate corners of his personality. If friendship of any kind requires not only mutual understanding and good relations between the persons concerned but also a certain equality, it is unlikely that someone with no beliefs could understand the terrible conflict going on inside someone else struggling in darkness to preserve his faith, however well they may understand one another from a human point of view. Neither is it likely, however, that a believer could achieve such an understanding as to be of help or to offer support, if he is not on sufficiently intimate terms as to be really—and not just theoretically—interested in the problem.

If a priest is truly exercising his priesthood, he'll find it impossible to communicate his deepest self to anyone but a fellow priest; in general—we can't speak in absolute terms—he'll be able to open up his soul only to another priest, for all his serious or vital problems will necessarily be related to his character as a priest or his pastoral function. A purely human matter can be easily resolved by anyone who is prudent, has experience or is properly qualified, but when the problem refers to the most intimate corner of a man's character, affecting that deepest of all areas where human nature comes into contact with God, then only a priest is qualified to listen to another priest's confidences with some hope of being able to help him, for he is the person appointed by God for that very purpose; he has received the proper training; and he has had the experience (perhaps personal experience) necessary to help and advise, to understand and restore peace to his colleague.

We have seen that love, charity, is the real and effective basis of all the priest's pastoral work with souls. "Charity" is a word which has been used so often that it has become almost a cliche in everyday language, an empty sound meaning almost nothing. Charity concerts, charity performances, acts of charity, to be charitable—in ordinary speech, the word no longer has all the immense connotations given to it by St. John when he says *Deus caritas est*. God is love. Charity does not simply mean not harming one another; it is not a negative thing. Neither is it a kind of indifferent politeness or superficial comradeship. It is something different and deeper; it is more refined and more delicate, more intimate and more noble.

Friendship with other priests, mutual communication on problems arising out of one's pastoral ministry, and, obviously, full examination of one's spiritual life; these are undoubtedly the sincerest and the most evangelical ways for priests to practice the charity of Christ, the love of Christ—*congregavit nos in unum Christi amor.* Friendship means unity between friends. The Lord commanded us to love one another "as I have loved you" (Jn 13: 34) and to be one as the Father and he were one. He said: "As the Father has loved me, so have I loved you. . . . Greater love has no man than this, that a man lay down his life for his friends. You are my friends . . . . No longer do I call you servants, for the servant does not know what his master is doing; but I have called you friends, for all that I have heard from my Father I have made known to you" (Jn 15: 9, 1315).

It is here, on the question of opening one's heart to another human being, on the question of sincere friendship, both supernatural and human, that a dialogue between the different generations of priests should take place. And such a dialogue ought to bear fruit to enrich both the priests and the Church in general. Those who have grown old caring for souls, who have spent their entire lives performing apparently routine tasks, day after day and year after year, without ever doing anything brilliant, and those who, after years of experience can no longer be shocked by anything, are in a position to pass on to the younger generation some of their pastoral experience, to temper their youthful enthusiasm which is sometimes more emotional than deep, to moderate their boldness with the prudence they themselves acquired, perhaps through many failures. When the young pour out all their thoughts to the old, with the confidence of a son talking to his father, they are also doing the older priest a great service; for they may well infuse some of their own enthusiasm into them, revive ideals which they also may have had in past days (now quenched perhaps by the apparent fruitlessness of their efforts), and rejuvenate their minds with new ideas coming to light within the Church. The older priests, in turn, may communicate to the younger ones some of their own serenity and some of the wisdom they learned not in books but from their contact with souls. They may help them in their undertakings and collaborate in discussing them so as to make their way easier. In this way helping to hand on the torch, so to speak. The younger ones can make the others feel quite proud to see that their work is being continued by men full of enthusiasm and willingness to serve and to continue the struggle, as their predecessors did, of caring for souls and extending the kingdom of God.

Friendship is the bond that allows one priest to open up his soul to another and encourages him to discuss his problems and difficulties—all that spiritual activity going on in his soul which he cannot always understand or interpret properly himself because he has neither the perspective nor the grace of state to be his own spiritual director. It may happen, as our Lord said to Nicodemus, that "the wind blows where it wills, and you hear the sound of it, but you do not know whence it comes or whither it goes" (Jn 3: 8). Although in theory any priest can open up his soul to any other, in practice he may find a lot of resistance inside himself; he may have great difficulty in unburdening his worries, unless he finds another priest whom he can sincerely regard as a friend. It is true that if we have a supernatural outlook on things and people, this should be sufficient for us; but it is equally true that we are human, and friendship gives us greater confidence.

A brother aided by his brother is like a strong city (Prov 18: 19). In the economy of the redemption, God has willed that men should be brought to him by other men, perhaps to inspire them with a sense of solidarity, with a kind of trust and a more deep rooted feeling of being united than merely human motives would produce, perhaps also to show us that no one is self-sufficient and that we all need each other. A brother aided by his brother is like a strong city: he will not fall, for he is well supported. Yet, do we not sometimes give the impression that we are not too anxious to help one another, that we find it hard to be real friends and have little genuine interest in each other? Logically it should be quite normal for priests to be closely united, to help one another to be better and more effective in our apostolic ministry, to be of one mind and one will. Yet, in practice, how many of us have the humility and love of God to accept spiritual help from another priest? "Woe to him who is alone when he falls," says the scripture, "and has not another to lift him up" (Eccles 4: 10).

We need someone to help and support us, to lift us up; we must not remain unknown to one another. There should be another priest—at least one—who is familiar with our spiritual life, with that part of us where the most radical truth of each one of us is rooted. Otherwise, we run the risk of remaining absolutely alone, this time in the most awful sense of the word, enclosed in a selfishness that isolates us from all others.

Some priests seem to have a kind of allergy to spiritual direction nowadays. The very expression makes them shudder. Are they perhaps afraid of losing their freedom? Yet we know that the more closely we are identified with Christ, the purer is our freedom, and if the communication of our interior life is a way of knowing and accepting the will of God more fully, spiritual guidance is the best help we can get to exercise our freedom properly.

Do they think it may damage their personality? If they do then, with all due respect to such people, we must say that their prejudice is not to be taken seriously. No priest with even a moderate degree of pastoral training can ever share this particular prejudice. Do the faithful who receive spiritual direction from them suffer from damaged personalities? Does not the Council ask all priests of the Church to direct their brothers towards God and to help them discover his ways and his will in the little things of every day? Do we seriously think that without intermediaries we can get to know God's will, understand our own wretchedness or avoid the subtle obstacles the enemy lays in our path, which is often in a wood we cannot see through because of the many trees?

No, if we think seriously about the matter, we realize that we cannot do without help, advice or support. We are our own worst counselors, rocked to and fro by the changing tides of our own selves and by all the winds of our intuitions, personal impressions and opinions picked up from reading books. "That they may be able to verify the unity of their lives in concrete situations too, they should subject all their undertakings to the test of God's will, which requires that projects should conform to the laws of the Church's evangelical mission. For loyalty toward Christ can never be divorced from loyalty toward his Church" (PO 14). We have no right to expect special enlightenment if we are unwilling to use the means at our disposal, for normally the will of God is made known to us through ordinary channels. Let us not forget the Lord's words: "He who hears you hears me" (Lk 10: 16). St. Paul himself had no hesitation in humbly placing himself at the disposal of Ananias to be told what God wanted him to do. God certainly had no need of any intermediary any more than he needed one for St. Paul's conversion; nevertheless, instead of communicating his will personally, he made use of a man. This is his normal procedure, and that is why there are priests, whose function includes helping their brothers in the priesthood.

It may be that underlying all our reluctance to be known by a brother priest there may simply be an element of fear, fear that he may get to know us as we really are, fear of losing our "prestige" in the eyes of others, fear of holiness itself, fear of presenting a poor picture if all our faults are seen, fear of going deeply into our own selves and seeing the false image we have built up, fear of losing our "independence"—we who have surrendered ourselves totally! —fear of losing our life even though we know that it means we shall gain it.

Or is it pride? Do we consider ourselves so great that we cannot accept help from people we regard as inferior to us? Or are we too immature to admit our own faults and limitations, to acknowledge our errors and our weaknesses, to resign ourselves to our own worthlessness?

This is quite unreasonable; something rings false in these attitudes. As priests, our tendencies must be the opposite of these. We must be completely and unreservedly open with that particular brother of ours to whom we have entrusted the task of listening to us and advising us. We must be open, instead of closing in upon ourselves; we must throw our soul wide open and let the Holy Spirit's fresh, life-giving air ventilate every corner. It is to be assumed that we want to be holy, to serve God to the best of our ability; it is to be assumed that we wish to be good instruments but that we know how defective we are. Why, then, should we be reluctant to let someone, a brother of ours, get to know us fully? Why this strange unwillingness on our part to regard another priest as an instrument of the Holy Spirit to direct our soul towards holiness?

Perhaps at the root of this kind of resistance which we sometimes feel to accepting a genuine, honest and sincere friendship between priests, there lies a rather frightening diabolical temptation to isolate ourselves, to keep really out of touch, absolutely enclosed in our own insufficiency or perhaps accompanied only by the dumb devil.

"Anyone who cannot see the apostolic effectiveness of friendship is forgetting Jesus Christ—'No longer do I call you servants . . . but I have called you friends'—and his friendship with the apostles, with the disciples, and with the family at Bethany."[16] Let us remember the Lord, for he was certainly capable of friendship. He was very friendly with Lazarus but was never as close to him as he was to his disciples. They were in different spheres. With his disciples, especially with his closest friends, Peter, James and John, there was no barrier, no secret, nothing in which they did not share. They were witnesses of his transformation on Tabor and he took them with him to Gethsemane so that they would not be deceived by seeing only one side of the coin or have a partial view of him which would not have been the whole truth. He wanted them to see his humiliation also, to see him trembling, anxious, upset, broken.

As St. John of the Cross said, where there is no love, give love and you will get love in return. If there is no friendship, give friendship and you will get friendship in return. If we each begin to give ourselves a little, to open up and to confide in our brother, another priest, to put something where there is nothing, we shall be very surprised at the results. We shall never again be alone, but like a strong city. And our mother the Church will be very happy to see how those sons of hers—in whom she has so much confidence that she entrusts the care of others to them—are united in loving, helping and supporting each other.

Spiritual reading

Anyone who has looked through some of the many excellent books on how to meditate will have learned that reading and thinking about a passage are like rungs on the ladder that leads the soul to contact with its Creator. Reading and meditating on a text provide that climate of recollection and faith, of concentration, of personal and profound conviction of a God who is present, who sees us, who hears us, who desires our good and is hoping for some movement on our part before he can take us into his confidence and shower us with graces—a climate which is indispensable if we are to pray.

Reading, then, takes on a special importance in relation to prayer, for it supplies the mind with ideas about God and the supernatural world which affect the will in such a way that they encourage it to move towards God as it should—as a creature moves towards his Creator, a sinner towards his Saviour, a son towards his Father.

Since man has been created in God's image and likeness, his intelligence is one of his specific characteristics. God wants man to love him also "with all his mind," with his intelligence. Since the food of the intelligence is truth, and the Truth is Christ, it is he who must fill the priest's mind with thoughts and ideas, ideas which normally are acquired by using ordinary means, though sometimes the Holy Spirit himself deposits them in the minds of simple people who have a great love for God and are very holy. But we must not expect that the Holy Spirit will infuse wisdom into a negligent priest who is not sufficiently interested in learning about sacred matters. And certainly if he does not study or read, but lives on the memory (which becomes hazier and more imprecise as time goes by) of what he learned in the seminary, as if he then knew all there was to be known and no one could teach him anything further after that, then he is undoubtedly negligent.

In view of the priest's real situation in the world, and especially in today's world, with so much work on his shoulders and such a vast field in which to exercise his ministry, and in view also of the conditions required for study (solitude, silence, freedom from worries, plenty of time), it would be rather idealistic to ask a priest to devote time to studying the sacred sciences. On the purely theoretical level, study should undoubtedly be one of the essential occupations in any priest's plan of life, but on the realistic level we have only to look at the enormous amount of apostolic work that has to be carried out by so very many priests—whether in charge of a parish or not—to see that a few hours' study each day in such conditions would be nothing less than utopia. Because of their position, some—seminary teachers, for example—have a duty to make time for study, but the vast majority have no such duty.

Can we therefore conclude that they are exempt from having a deep knowledge and understanding of Christ's message? Can we accept the idea that the vast majority of priests have to resign themselves to learning no more and to being content with slowing down as much as possible the process of forgetting what they learned as students?

This would be quite wrong. The ministry itself, to which their specific vocation has called them, demands that their knowledge of the truths of our salvation should always be adequate to the capacity of those people whom they have to lead to God. The circumstances may leave no time for serious academic study in peace and quiet, but there are no circumstances whatever which can excuse priests from serious reading in peace and quiet, for reading requires neither the time, the concentration nor the means needed for study. To read, we need only a book, a few minutes and a suitable place, that is, somewhere that meets the minimum requirements that will allow us to read—and these conditions are within reach of the poorest, most overworked and most exhausted of priests. Is there a single one whose circumstances will not allow him to devote fifteen or twenty minutes daily to spiritual reading? Each individual should find the most convenient time: in the morning, perhaps after Mass and before visiting the sick, doing parish business, and receiving visitors, or later in the morning, or in the evening before going to bed, when he has finished his day's work.

Since he is totally submerged in the battle, in the midst of a world becoming more and more pagan, surrounded by a completely secularized atmosphere, he can hardly hope to escape its influence, to avoid being infected by it all, unless he takes some kind of counter-measures which will constantly—as constantly as the environment influences him—remind him of the supernatural world which is his real environment. Spiritual reading is so important that Eugene Boylan does not hesitate to say that "this practice ranks equally in importance with mental prayer and the other exercises of devotion, and in fact it is so closely connected with these other exercises, especially the essential one of mental prayer, that without it—unless one finds some substitute—there is no possibility of advancing in the spiritual life."[17]

We must make it clear that when we speak of spiritual reading, we are recommending, not another intellectual exercise (although doubtless it is one) but primarily a pious practice. If it is to help us advance in the spiritual life, it must fulfill certain conditions, the first being that it must be well chosen. (The order in which we mention these conditions is not necessarily the order of their importance.)

Only those authors faithful to the Magisterium of the Church should, of course, be chosen for spiritual reading. It is obvious, however, that the same books are not suitable for everyone. A rather lukewarm priest cannot profitably use the same reading as another who lives an intensely spiritual life. And even among priests with an equally deep spiritual life, one who is going through a period of darkness and dryness, with many temptations, will not benefit from the same book as one who is perfectly calm and serene. Some will need books that give more emphasis to recollection, while others will need to be stimulated into apostolic activity. Certainly the teaching, the principles and the basis of the spiritual life are invariable, but they need to be applied differently to the specific conditions of each particular individual—unity does not mean uniformity. Hence every priest should get advice from his spiritual director, who has the grace of state and can suggest the most suitable book for that particular moment in the individual's life.

Then another condition, which is necessary if the spiritual reading is to be fruitful, becomes rather easy, namely to have a supernatural outlook. When a suggestion is made to us by our spiritual director as to the book we ought to read, we know that it is God our Lord who, through that priest our brother, is telling us where to seek what we most need at that particular moment. The attitude or outlook with which we then perform that act of piety will make the reading itself meritorious. We are actually seeking Christ, for we are looking for his response to our needs. We are seeking an indication of God's will so as to assimilate everything he has to teach us. On this point, was it St. Augustine who said that, whereas we speak to God in our prayer, it is he who speaks to us in our reading? Obviously this is particularly true of Sacred Scripture, but it can quite accurately be extended to any other spiritual reading too. It is this spirit of faith, the source of our supernatural outlook, that makes us thank God whose infinite goodness and mercy at some time in the past has made someone feel inclined to take a pen and write that particular book which now, at a later moment in time, is needed by a certain soul. Reading a book has often brought peace and serenity to troubled souls, courage and optimism to the depressed, enthusiasm to the exhausted and clarity to the confused.

Finally, humility. We must repeat once again that our purpose is not to learn, but primarily to improve. With the same receptive attitude and the same simplicity and good faith as a child at school listening to the teacher's explanations, ready to learn every lesson, the priest should be willing to take in whatever the Lord wants to tell him through his reading. Consequently it is here, in choosing books for spiritual reading, that he must heed that warning given by St. Teresa about such books, namely that they should be "fully approved." Rather than the latest publications or original essays, he should choose solid doctrine, books that have proved they can yield results, with the firm guarantee of the Church's approval.

Thus, in return for very little effort, for a few minutes each day, the priest will advance in wisdom as time goes by. Some basic books will have left their mark on his mind in the form of ideas, without causing him any undue effort or trouble. Without hurry but yet without interruption, his mind will have been nurtured with a daily ration of proper sustenance, assimilated by the supernatural organism which retains whatever is necessary, useful or suitable for the soul. Like an enormous reservoir, the intelligence accumulates truths, and later on, in prayer, it converts these truths into life. At an opportune moment, the priest "brings out of his treasure what is new and what is old" (Mt 13: 52), with which he in turn will be able to nourish other souls. There is no danger of becoming intellectually rigid, of allowing what he has read to dry up for lack of watering in depth and breadth, of getting into a routine of reading dead letters. Neither will there be any danger that the supernatural may be "humanized" by the continual impact of stories, events and comments in the newspapers, radio, television, theater, magazines, novels, essays, reviews etc. which tend to concentrate our interest and attention on the things of this world. Boylan writes: "the general effect of our modern environment is not merely negative; it has even a positive tendency to lead us away from God. This it does not so much by being against God, as by leaving Him out. We live in fact in a pagan civilization. The remnants of Christian ideals that are still found in common opinion, and which still express themselves in common practice, are divorced from their dogmatic foundation of real fact and true faith—they are based mainly on sentiment—and like all branches cut off from their original stock, they are withered and warped, and often twisted quite out of recognition. As guiding ideals, they rather tend to mislead. The need for something to counteract this effect is one of the reasons for spiritual reading."[18] This is so true that we can say, also with Boylan, that "there is as little chance of living spiritually without reading, as there is of living corporally without eating!" Doctrine is the food of the soul and there can be no spiritual life without it. If the mind lacks doctrine, if the word of God and his message of salvation do not nourish the intelligence, then inevitably our thinking will revolve around worldly things or about nothing at all. What will become of the priest if that happens? How can he fulfill his ministry of salvation among men? How can he be another Christ if he is so different mentally from his Master?

As we read, our mental prayer becomes progressively easier, at least in the sense that we become more habitually aware of the presence of God, which is the first and most basic disposition for praying. Then, instead of spending part of the time we have fixed for prayer in supernatural considerations so as to prepare the soul to speak to God, the whole period can be spent praying in the true sense, for our daily reading will have more than adequately produced that state of contact with the supernatural which otherwise we should have to stimulate by some preliminary meditation.

Spiritual reading has another effect in that, at least to some extent, it takes the place of study. Apart from the fact that it may sometimes be useful to read theological books—Michael Schmaus's *Dogmatic Theology*, for instance, or Matthias Scheeben's *The Mysteries of Christianity*, or Frank Sheed's *Theology and Sanity*, to name but a few—a large number of strictly spiritual books give ample consideration to points of theology. These include, for example, the writings of Luis de Granada, *This Tremendous Lover* by Eugene Boylan, and the many excellent books by Ronald Knox, not to mention classical writers like St. Teresa and St. Francis de Sales, and especially the Fathers of the Church—St. Augustine, St. John Chrysostom and the others—who should be familiar to every priest, for they should never be totally neglected as spiritual reading.

Devotion to our Lady

A priest's spiritual life will not be pleasing to God unless it includes devotion to the Blessed Virgin Mary. The only begotten Word of God, who was God himself, willed to rely on our Lady's motherly care. How, then, can any priest ignore the help and the company of one whom his Master accepted from the moment of his Incarnation?

There is something very profound and very mysterious in people's attitudes to the Blessed Virgin, something that makes the most sinful, the most indifferent and even the most hopeless find in her some spark of hope, a ray of light in the midst of the deepest darkness, a glimmer of salvation when all is lost. Her powers and her compassion for sinners are not at all exaggerated in those old medieval legends that tell of prodigious conversions that were brought about by invoking her intercession. Her compassionate love can open a breach in the hardest hearts. A moment comes in every sinner's life when he finds himself surrounded by frightful solitude and yet he feels that our Lady has never ceased to watch over him, interceding with her Son, as only a mother can, reminding him of his passion and death "to save the lost" (Lk 19: 10).

Since the priest is a solitary man and a man fighting the Lord's battles in the front lines, he needs the help and protection of the Mother of the redeemed more than anyone else. To serve Jesus Christ, he has given up his right to found a home, to have the company of a wife and children, to enjoy the warmth of a family. Our Lady has a special affection for those sons of hers, other Christs, who have renounced all love other than the love of Christ Jesus, because of their love for all the souls redeemed by the blood of the Saviour. Therefore the Virgin Mother gives warmth to the priest's home, but he in turn must make practical reality of those words from the Gospel referring to children: "to such belongs the kingdom of God" (Lk 18: 16). And it has been said that everyone is a child to the extent to which he continues to need his mother.

It is always a great joy to read what the Fathers wrote about our Lady. It is as if all bounds were broken and all moderation abandoned whenever they wanted to speak about her; as if the gates that restrained their enthusiasm and confined it within reasonable limits all suddenly opened at the same time and released everything the heart had been storing up and feeling about this marvelous creature. The old form of the Church's breviary gives us a rich treasury of what their love inspired them to say, and the third nocturn within the octave of the Immaculate Conception is a veritable outburst of praise and eulogies, affection and piety. When all words and expressions have been exhausted, St. Sophronius explains, "who can describe your splendor?" Paradise of God, St. Germain calls her; Gate of heaven, says St. Epiphanius; Cause of the salvation of all mortals, exclaims St. Tarasius. All these expressions pale, however, when we consider what our Lady really is, the place she occupies in our redemption and in the Church, the bonds that link her with the Father, the Son and the Holy Spirit, her position in the economy of salvation, the part she plays in every Christian's spiritual life. However great the inspiration of saints in the past, however great the inspiration of those who may sing her praises in the future, there is not the slightest possibility of doing her justice, for she is greater than anything that can be expressed in human language.

Mother of the Redeemer and Mother of the redeemed, mediatrix of all grace, co-redeemer with her Son; can anyone doubt her right to occupy a key position in the spiritual life of every Christian? Since the Son of God willed to come into this world by being born of the Virgin Mary, is it too much to suggest that he wishes also to be brought into our souls by his Mother?

We are all sinners, and priests are no exception to this rule. ("If we say we have no sin, we deceive ourselves, and the truth is not in us," 1 Jn 1: 8). If we keep this fact constantly in mind, we shall mistrust our own strength, for we shall realize how weak we are. And then we shall never refuse the Blessed Virgin's help, just as a child who is unsure of himself allows his mother to support him when he is learning to walk. We know that she is the advocate and help of sinners, and thus it should never occur to us to ignore her in our pastoral ministry, where our object is precisely to reconcile sinners with the Father. We know that "we go to Jesus—and we 'return' to him—through Mary"[19] or, as St. Bernard wrote, "For if man fell through a woman, through a woman will he rise."[20] We rise again only through her.

As far as details are concerned, the first thing we have to say is that any devotion in honor of our Lady is good, and it should be practiced constantly. However, taking the reality of the priest's life in the world into account, the Rosary, the Angelus and Marian aspirations are especially recommended, both because they have been repeatedly approved by the Church and because they take up little time.

An aspiration, an ejaculation takes no time at all. It is just an invocation, a raising of the heart to Mary, a call for help, a brief comment made to her silently about some event or other. It is also an act of prayer, of hope, of love. It need not even be pronounced vocally and its very nature makes it easy to repeat dozens of times throughout the day. There are few pious practices that are simpler to perform: we only have to remember to do so—and we can easily get into this habit, with a little time, patience and help from our guardian angels—and few yield such excellent results, for without realizing it we soon acquire a spirit of prayer. Yet few habits are as helpful to make us feel that we are not alone throughout the day.

Saying the Angelus at noon is a very old devotion. There is no harm done if the exact hour passes unnoticed or if, though we remember, we are unable to say the Angelus for one reason or another, so long as we do so whenever we can. Here, too, habit makes things easier, though the ringing of the Angelus bell in the parish church—where this custom still survives— often solves the problem. And if we really pray each time, if we genuinely think about what we are saying, then we are actually recalling and giving thanks for the greatest event that has occurred since the world began. Besides, if we are even a little bit clever, we can easily get whoever happens to be with us at that moment to say the Angelus too, and this is yet another way of helping souls.

There seems to be little point in speaking about the Rosary at any length, if we remember, for instance, that the Church has dedicated a feast day to Our Lady of the Rosary and a whole month, the month of October, to this particular devotion; or if we remember that our Lady herself held the rosary in her hands at Lourdes, passing the beads through her fingers as Bernadette said the Hail Marys, and that, as in Fatima, she insistently asked that this prayer be recited frequently. This is a very old pious custom, it has received countless blessings and commendations and is almost an official act of devotion to our Lady. Certainly it presents no problem for the priest to say the Rosary, if he has a sincere priestly spirit and love of souls. For example, he can say it in his church every evening with his parishioners; otherwise he can easily recite it on his own, especially if he takes the precaution of saying one of the mysteries whenever he finds a free moment if he is extremely busy with his pastoral work, and he can leave the litany until the evening. He will not have recited it all at one time, but on the other hand he will have sprinkled the whole day with Hail Marys.

Of all the devotions we can have, the most lovable and perhaps the most spontaneous and instinctive is our devotion to the

Blessed Virgin. Our heart is made for love and she is the "Mother of Fair Love," the most noble and purest love of all. "And now, my sons, listen to me: happy are those who keep my ways. Hear instruction and be wise, and do not neglect it. Happy is the man who listens to me. . . . For he who finds me finds life and obtains favor from the Lord" (Prov 8: 32-35). The priest especially can find no better counselor, no surer guide, no stronger support, no more self-sacrificing help. The Mother of Jesus, who is the eternal Priest, knows well how hard a priest's work is, she fully understands its dangers, its misunderstandings, its difficulties; she realizes better than anyone else how much heroism is involved in being a mediator. Therefore she softens the harshness of his life, she brings sweetness to his sorrow and company to his solitude, she gives him strength to bear misunderstanding, support in times of trial and hope in the midst of the struggle. She acts as our mediatrix to obtain graces for us that will make our ministry fruitful, and by her intercession she prepares sinners to receive her Son's saving grace. She is the priest's purity, his consolation, his help, his strength and his courage, just as she was for the disciples during the dark hours between the Lord's death and his resurrection. She is the guarantee of the priest's faithfulness, for it was never known that anyone who fled to her protection or implored her help was left unaided. Therefore love and devotion to our Lady are a sign and a pledge of salvation both for the priest and for the souls entrusted to his care, because she, who "believing and obeying . . . brought forth on earth the Father's Son" (LG 63), has shown us how to ensure that Christ will be born in every soul.

6

Milites Christi

İF WE STUDY THE HISTORY OF THE CHURCH in any detail, we shall
see, among other things, that it has been far from peaceful. She
has had to fight at every moment, during every period, to preserve Christ's legacy intact, and to safeguard her independence
from all powers and from all ambitions, for this is essential if she
is to propagate it, while at the same time watching with material
affection over the flock the Lord has placed under her care.

God sometimes permits difficulties to arise; there are times
when "the power of darkness" (Lk 22: 53) seems to dominate.
Satan then prowls around the Church of God and threatens all
those who are not firmly attached to Christ by humility and obedience, by a spiritual life and a supernatural outlook; everyone
who seeks support in something other than Peter, the rock on
which Christ built his Church, is in danger. When those times pass
and calm is restored, the Church emerges purified, and those who
have remained firm are stronger than before. But some are carried
away by the tides of confusion; they fall and are lost. The Church
suffers and ceaselessly laments their loss, but never tires of hoping
that those children will return. Consequently there are certain simple, elementary facts that priests must never allow themselves to
forget, for what right have they to make their Mother suffer?

The Church is divine but her children are all too human. She
is holy but we are not. The world has a strange but natural tendency to judge the Church by the men and women whom she
calls her own, especially those who are her ministers in a public
and official way. Hence, whether they like it or not, as far as the
eyes of the world are concerned, priests are in a kind of show-
case for all to see. And the world watches them, forms opinions,
reacts, judges; they cannot easily deceive people by pretending

to have virtues they do not practice, or to feel warm when in fact they are cold. Priests are really in full view of the world, of angels, and of men.

It would be a grave and lamentable mistake to try to put on some kind of "show" for the outside world because of this—a mistake and a waste of time. It would be a mistake because the world's opinion should not concern us in the least—only God's opinion really matters, because in the final analysis it is the only true and decisive one. It would be a waste of time because if we were as anxious to be as we are to appear, then we should really achieve something; and we all are what we are in the eyes of God, neither more nor less, whatever efforts we may make to appear otherwise.

The priest must really be a man of God, and he will be a man of God if he lives a spiritual life; otherwise he will not—even if crowds throng to hear his preaching. If he lives a spiritual life, then he will be an apostle, whatever his intelligence or his personality, for the apostolate means bringing souls to God and helping them. And in the final analysis this seems to be a question, not of method (although method does matter, things have to be done prudently), but of leaven, and only leaven with great inner strength can raise the world to God.

Anyone who has studied the history of the Church in the first half of the nineteenth century is bound to have been impressed by the contrast between two French priests ordained at about the same time: Felicité Lamennais and Jean Baptiste Vianney. One was a man of talent, brilliant, capable of attracting into the service of the Church men like Ozanam, Gueranger, Lacordaire and Montalembert, but who—perhaps because he had more confidence in his own talent than in the Church's magisterium—ended his life in a horrifying tragedy that culminated in his refusal to have a priest at his death-bed. The other was a rough villager, a dull student, an obscure priest, whose holiness, love of God and of souls made him a powerful magnet that drew crowds to an insignificant little village, where he transformed them. No one who has examined the history of these two men—insofar as it is known—can have failed to reflect on the tremendous mystery of grace and human response to grace. Success in the pastoral ministry is not merely a question of natural talent (apart from St. Paul and St. John, the apostles gave no impression of being brilliant men), but of God's grace, faithfulness to the magisterium and loyalty to Christ. It must be repeated again and again that in the final analysis supernatural results—and these are the type that the priest, as such, is seeking—can be achieved only by supernatural means.

It is true that times change and each period has its own characteristics, its own peculiar features and its own problems. Nevertheless, people remain substantially the same, and the problems that affect them deeply are always the same. This applies even more directly to the priest than to others, for the essence of his priesthood is immutable, as is his mission among men.

It's important to insist on this point, even at the risk of repeating things we have said earlier. We could even say, as St. Paul wrote to the Philippians (3: 1), that "to write the same things to you is not irksome to me, and is safe for you." It is not only safe but also necessary, at a time when technical efficiency and methods are overvalued, that the priest should continually be reminded that one thing alone is necessary (Lk 10: 41), and that, if he has that one thing, then he has everything. We must insist on this point time and again, we must repeat, stress, emphasize, exhort and beg him to live a spiritual life. He cannot impart warmth to others if he himself is not on fire; he cannot spread peace if his own soul is restless and uneasy; he cannot give light if he himself is smothered in darkness and confusion.

"Knowest thou what it is to love Me in truth?" asked the Lord of St. Teresa. "It is to realize that everything which is not pleasing to Me is a lie."[1] Therefore the priest's first and most fundamental concern must be to know what pleases the Lord, and then to go on and do it. But without a spiritual life, without friendship and close contact with God, without help, advice and prayers from other priests—from one other priest, at least— there is no way of ensuring that the soul will have even that minimum of sensitivity necessary to know what pleases the Lord. Instead, the opposite will be the case: he will convince himself that everything pleasing to him will be exactly what pleases God. The blindness that self-sufficiency, lack of humility in other words, can cause in a soul is particularly frightening in a priest. It makes him a blind man leading the blind. And God forbid that what the Lord foretold for such men should befall him! Nor is this, in fact, the least of the dangers besetting any priest who leads his life without spiritual direction, aimlessly, not knowing where he is going.

Milites Christi—soldiers of Christ. The priest in the world is a soldier of Christ. "No soldier on service gets entangled in civilian pursuits, since his aim is to satisfy the one who recruited him" (2 Tim 2: 4). In all times of crisis, of radical and rapid changes, of ideas being crushed by one another as some emerge and others disappear, the priest may find himself under pressure to take up positions on problems and matters of a purely temporal nature—insofar as temporal things can be considered independently of the supernatural. Perhaps his motive is simply to avoid turning his back on the world, and to be better able to fulfill his apostolic mission among the people of his own time. Whatever the reason, however, he should proceed with great discretion and caution, lest in the end he find himself so involved in affairs of this world that he becomes a defender of theories rather than a preacher of the Truth, a social reformer instead of a director of souls. He should give all his attention to the permanent element in people, helping them to know God and carefully avoiding "stupid, senseless controversies; you know that they breed quarrels. And the Lord's servant must not be quarrelsome" (2 Tim 2: 23-24). A stupid, senseless controversy for the priest, in view of his vocation and his ministry, is anything that makes him neglect or abandon his proper place and the work entrusted to him, anything that tempts him to move into other spheres or perform activities that are marginal and perhaps too human, too ephemeral.

Certainly he must influence society, he must transform it, but he must do this as leaven in dough, not as a leader of crowds. He should act, not on society, but on men, on each soul placed by God within his reach, and even then only in the things relating to God, for his vocation is to be a priest, another Christ, a coredeemer, not an economist, technologist, sociologist or politician.

For this very reason he should be open and available to everyone, for the redemption extends to everyone, and Christ shed his blood for everyone. As a man of the universal Church, with a universal mission, he cannot have an insular or provincial view of the Church; otherwise he runs the risk of losing his ecumenical spirit because he would be unable to win over all souls. There can be no parties or factions for him, as there were none for his Master. "Here there cannot be Greek and Jew, circumcised and uncircumcised, barbarian, Scythian, slave, freeman, but Christ is all, and in all" (Col 3: 11). There is perhaps one, and only one, distinction he is allowed to make, namely between those who do and those who do not belong to the Church of Christ, for while he has to evangelize those outside it, he must first and foremost attend to those within. After all, if charity is to be a virtue, it must have its priorities right, for virtue cannot be disorderly.

Like the Church itself, whose representative he is, the priest must be free of vested interests or any type of commitment which could bind him to nonessential, passing forms or structures of society. He has been placed in a particular society at a particular time to act as leaven in regard to faith and morals, the supernatural life, and even of human values and sensitivity. Whether he likes it or not, he has to share in the problems of the world in which he lives, enjoy its advantages, suffer its crises and turmoils. Nevertheless, he must always remain above or outside all those things, for he represents the permanent element in a changing world; in the midst of countless relativities, when all about him passes and disappears, he is the indestructible factor — the rock of Peter.

Since he is a man of all times, he must be very much of his own time, a man of the moment. In this sense, *aggiornamento* is not simply an attitude that came to us after Vatican II. The clergy of past centuries also had to bring themselves into line with the Church's directives after the Council of Trent, Vatican I and every other Council, if they wanted to be faithful to the Church of Christ. They had to practice *aggiornamento* then too. As Blessed Josemaria Escriva has said, *aggiornamento* consists of nothing more and nothing less than being faithful: "The more faithfully a husband, a soldier or an administrator fulfills the firm commitments to love or justice which he once undertook, the better the husband, soldier or administrator he is. That exquisite, active, constant fidelity—which is difficult, as is any application of general principles to changing and contingent reality—is for that reason our best defense against the danger that the spirit may grow old, the heart dry up or the mind become stagnant. The same applies to the life of institutions and most particularly to the life of the Church, which follows, not a precarious plan worked out by man, but a plan imposed by God. The redemption, the salvation of the world, is the work of Jesus Christ's —and our own—loving and filial faithfulness to the will of his heavenly Father who sent him. Therefore the Church's *aggiornamento* now, as at any other time, is basically that—a joyful reaffirmation of the fidelity of the people of God to the mission they have received, to the gospel."[2]

If we regard *aggiornamento* as a process of changing merely superficial points, such as dress, customs, deportment, terminology, language, then we have a very poor idea of what it means and what the Second Vatican Council involved. To think that changes of that kind could win over the masses for Christ would show that we have no idea of what these masses really are and, perhaps, very little of what the apostolate is either. We have to focus our attention on, and place our faith and hope in, much less superficial realities, much deeper things, if we truly want to continue serving the Church and the souls of our fellow men and women.

The Church demands at all times, but more particularly during periods of crisis, which because they are crises, produce a climate of confusion, that the priest devote himself entirely to his vocation, for Christ wants him to serve totally, he needs his efforts and his self-denial, for the benefit of the other members of his mystical body. However, all his efforts and all his self-denial will be of service to nobody unless they are accompanied by humility. Since the object is to serve God, the Church and souls, and not to serve oneself (seeking one's own fame and glory, one's own ideas or theories, one's own success), the priest's function is to pass on the wishes—not just the commandments—of God and of his Church and to be at the disposal of souls. If he is not humble, he will do neither of these things, unless he happens to be personally convinced that each indication is appropriate—a form of discrimination that would say little for his spirit of service—and unless he has a strict obligation to help a soul in a particular way.

Another point is that the priest himself should go unnoticed. Like salt which disappears and is noticed only because of its taste, so the priest's presence should be noticed primarily in the *bonus odor Christi* which he carries wherever he goes. The priestly quality of a man devoted to Christ is measured by the effect he produces on souls: "You will know them by their fruits" (Mt 7: 20). Just as good fruit shows the excellence of a tree, and bad fruit means that it is unhealthy, so a priest's deeds bear witness to his priesthood—not the deeds which are purely human, of course, but those others which, though certainly human, have that special element, that good odor of Christ, which impregnates them with a supernatural essence that comes from grace.

The quality of the priest and his apostolic effectiveness should be seen in the souls entrusted to his care. They should be living a genuinely Christian life that expresses itself in inner peace and good relations with others, in charity exercised in the form of good manners in dealing with people, in meekness and humility, and in an absence of human respect or artificial conventions as far as exercising their faith in Christ down to the last detail is concerned. It is also expressed in a spirit of penance (exercised not in many supererogatory acts, but in joyful and unsophisticated acceptance of suffering or physical pain, without complaining or even commenting, silently offering it to God in atonement and reparation). This Christian life also expresses itself in perseverance in prayer and frequent reception of the sacraments (not as "additional" things or "extras" but as integral parts of life itself, as natural as work, movement or rest), in active love of the Church and of Peter's successor, its visible head, without histrionics, in devotion to our Lady and to Christ in the blessed Sacrament, in a sense of responsibility as a member of the people of God, in honesty and determination to do one's work well in the eyes of God, and in a conviction that personal holiness does the Church more good than any number of speeches.

These are the fruits by which we can know the priest and recognize the mark of his ministry among the people with whom he has been in contact. The other types of fruit—whether he arouses enthusiasm, whether he says things that are worth repeating and remembering, the successful methods he uses, the crowds he gathers around him, the acts and events he organizes —at best will be signs of activity, ingenuity or human worth, but will not necessarily in themselves prove that he has any priestly quality. Apart from, or independently of, these things, he may or may not be a saint. It is the supernatural effect, the changes in human souls, that indicate whether he has been a good instrument or not, a genuine servant of God who has forgotten himself, a "good and faithful servant" (Mt 25: 21).

During periods when people are reluctant to accept supernatural values, the priest should more than ever bear witness to those values, not only by preaching, but also and especially by his way of life. Remembering that the gospel is life itself, not an ideological system, he must adapt to it and shape himself in accordance with it until he is able to say, like his Master, that "the works that I do in my Father's name, they bear witness to me" (Jn 10: 25). Faithful to the teaching he had received, St. Paul told the Philippians: "Let your manner of life be worthy of the gospel of Christ" (Phil 1: 27).

The supernatural must come first, but that must not allow us to neglect our natural ethical duties or human values. These values should constitute the priest's point of contact with the world around him; they provide the common ground, the basis from which he can gradually raise people to the higher level of grace.[3] His human virtues will be perfected and moderated, their tendencies to become deformed or stagnant will be eliminated, by the power of grace.

Once again we return to the same point: the need to live a serious spiritual life habitually and to concentrate on the only thing that really matters. "For what does it profit a man if he gains the whole world and loses or forfeits himself?" (Lk 9: 25). Of what use is it to the priest, to the Church or to the souls of others that he should be very active if he is not living a spiritual life, and therefore his activity neither sanctifies him nor gives glory to God. "Even if Christ should be born thousands of times in Bethlehem," wrote Silesius, "unless he be born in you, you would be eternally lost." Christ must increase day by day in the priest's soul, for there is never any stagnation in the spiritual life: we can never stand still. Either we go forward or we go backwards. The divine life increases or decreases in the soul according to the efforts and regularity with which the priest sustains and nourishes it, and therefore it would be very difficult to find convincing reasons to justify neglecting any of the means by which his grace—and strength—is increased daily. "Believe me," said St. Teresa to her sisters, "let no one deceive you by showing you any other way than the way of prayer."

The Way (82) gives a piece of good advice which any priest, however busy, should consider, for it is worth a whole book: "First, prayer; then, atonement; in the third place, very much 'in the third place,' action." Without this order of priorities, a priest may have more headaches than success, he may be more noisy than useful, and may be more of an embarrassment than a help to the Church. He would also do well to think occasionally about this other point: "If you are not a man of prayer, I don't believe in the sincerity of your intentions when you say that you work for Christ."[4]

Once again today the world is undergoing radical changes, perhaps deeper and more decisive upheavals than at the time of the Barbarian invasions or the Renaissance. The Church is, therefore, once again in a unique position to influence and shape the world which is just emerging, for only she has the word of salvation in its fullness. There is no problem as far as she herself is concerned, for she is the faithful repository of the gospel; it is her servants, the men who serve her—priests, men of the Church, ecclesiastics—who are the question mark. Will we fail her again, as we did at the time of the Renaissance, when the people on whom she relied were incapable of transmitting her message— Christ's message—because worldliness had taken hold of them and had rendered them useless as instruments? Or will she find priests capable, as she did ten centuries earlier, of overcoming the spirit of the world with their solid doctrine, their lives, and their self-surrender?

The answer to this question probably depends on one factor alone, namely the personal *holiness* of each individual priest.

Notes

Chapter 1

The Priest

1. Pope Paul VI, *Ecclesiam Suam*, 4.
2. Vatican Council II, Const. *Lumen Gentium*, 1. (All Vatican II documents are quoted in the translation published by Geoffrey Chapman, London, 1967 edited by Walter M. Abbott, SJ and will be referred to by their initial letters: in this case LG).
3. Alvaro del Portillo, *On Priesthood* (Chicago 1974), p. 20.
4. *On Priesthood*, p. 21.
5. From a discourse of Pope Pius XII, cited by Pope John XXIII in *Sacerdotii Nostri Primordia* 2.
6. St. Thomas Aquinas, *Summa Theologiae*, 3 q 22 a 1, trans. Colman O'Neill.
7. *Summa*, 3 q 26 a 2.
8. Emmanuel Cardinal Suhard, *Dios, Iglesia, Sacerdocio* (Madrid, 1953), p. 235.
9. Suhard, *Op. cit.*
10. Josef Sellmair, *The Priest in the World*, trans. B. Battershaw (London 1954), Chapter 1.
11. Sellmair, *Loc. cit.*
12. From a homily entitled "Passionately loving the world" (preached in 1967) in *Conversations with Monsignor Escriva de Balaguer* (Manila, 1985), p. 137.
13. *Ibid.*
14. Vatican Council II, Decree, *De Apostolatu Laicorum* (AL) 2.
15. Josemaria Escriva, *Letter*, Rome, January 9, 1959.
16. Address, 12 August 1965; the same problem is dealt with by Paul VI in many speeches in subsequent years.
17. Escriva, *Letter*, Madrid, January 9, 1932.

Chapter 2

The Ministry

1. *Address to parish priests and Lenten pilgrims*, February 1966.
2. Josemaria Escriva, *The Way* (New York, 1985), point No. 342.
3. *The Way*, 961.
4. *Ecclesiam Suam* 90.
5. *Didache* IV:1

6. St. Vincent of Lerins, *Commonitorium*, in J. Rouet de Journel, *Enchiridium Patristicum*, 21733.
7. Pastoral Letter of the bishops of Germany, 1967.
8. *Ecclesiam Suam* 20.
9. *Moralia* 30:1.
10. Homily 30
11. Karl Adam, *Christ our Brother*, trans. Dom Justin McCann (London, 1931), p. 45.
12. *Pastoral Rule* III: 33. trans. C, Lett Feltoe, Oxford, 1895.
13. *The Way*, 294.
14. Escriva, *Letter*, Rome, August 8, 1956.
15. *Pastoral Rule, op. cit.* 11:5.
16. Escriva, *Letter*, Madrid, March 24, 1930.
17. *Dogmatik*, VI
18. *Summa* 3 q 69 a 2, trans. Dominicans of the English province, London 1923.
19. M. Eugene Boylan, *This Tremendous Lover*, (Cork, 1946), Chapter XIII.
20. Suppl. q 36 a 2 ad 1, trans. Dominicans, London, 1932.
21. *Summa* 3 q 73 a 3, trans. C. W. Barden O.P.
22. *Mysterium Fidei* 32, trans. A. Garvey, London 1965.

Chapter 3

Training

1. *Divini Illius Magister.*
2. del Portillo, *Op. cit.*, pp 11-18; we base our own views on his treatment of this subject.
3. *Summa* part 4, t 15, c 10.
4. *The Way*, 34.
5. *Palabra* 5, (1966).
6. *The Way*, 357.
7. Escriva, *Letter*, Madrid, January 9, 1932.
8. *Hom. 46 in Matt*, trans. G. Prevost (New York, 1888).
9. Pope Paul VI, Exhortation, August 1965.
10. St. Teresa of Avila, *Way of Perfection*, 21, 4.
11. *Ecclesiam Suam* 26.
12. *The Way*, 196.
13. *The Way*, 172.
14. *Way of Perfection*, 18, 2.
15. *The Way*, 180.
16. *The Way*, 971, 972.

Chapter 4

Sources of Strength

1. *The Way*, 79.
2. *The Way*, 149
3. *The Way*, 630
4. *Ecclesiam Suam*, 54.
5. St. Teresa of Avila, *Way of Perfection*, 2, 5 and 6.
6. *The Way*, 76.
7. *The Way*, 78.
8. *Seeds of Contemplation* (London 1949), Chapter 25.
9. *The Way*, 3.
10. *This Tremendous Lover*, Chapter VII.
11. St. Teresa of Avila, *The Book of the Foundations*, V, trans. E. Allison Peers.
12. *Summa* 22 q 104 a 3, trans. T. C. O Brien.
13. *The Way*, 621.
14. *The Way*, 616.
15. Escriva, *Letter*, Rome, May 3, 1954.
16. *The Way*, 71.
17. Escriva, *Letter*, Rome, August 8, 1956.
18. *The Way*, 28.
19. Romano Guardini, *The Lord*. trans. E. C. Briefs (London, 1956), p. 277.
20. Michael Schmaus, *Dogmatic Theology*, VI, 678.
21. *Sacerdotalis Coelibatus*, 1967
22. Alvaro del Portillo, *Op. cit.*, p. 51.
23. *The Way*, 143.
24. *Way of Perfection*, 7, 1.
25. *Ibid.*, 6, 5.
26. St. Teresa, *Life*, trans. Peers, 37, 4, see also chapter 5.
27. William T. Walsh, *Our Lady of Fatima* (New York, 1947), p. 184.

Chapter 5

Spirituality

1. St. Augustine, *Tract. 30 in Joannem*: trans. J. Gibb (Edinburgh, 1873).
2. St. Teresa of Avila, *Way of Perfection*, 34, 6.
3. *The Way*, 533.
4. *The Living Bread* (London, 1956), p.72.
5. St. John Chrysostom, *Homily 50 on Matthew*.
6. St. Thomas Aquinas, *Summa* 3 q 73 a 2.
7. *The Way*, 90, 91

8. St. Teresa of Avila, *Life,* 8, 4.
9. *Life,* 19, 4.
10. *Life,* 8, 5.
11. Peters, *La Espiritualidad Sacerdotal,* p. 219.
12. Newman, John Henry, "Sermon for Septuagesima Sunday," in *Catholic Sermons.*
13. Thomas Merton, *Seeds of Contemplation,* Chapter 6.
14. Address, December 4, 1963.
15. Escriva, in *Palabra* 26 (1967).
16. Escriva, *Letter,* Madrid, January 9, 1932.
17. Eugene Boylan, *This Tremendous Lover,* Chapter 9.
18. *Ibid.*
19. *The Way,* 495.
20. St. Bernard, *Hom. 2 super Missus est.*

Chapter 6

Milites Christi

1. St. Teresa of Avila, *Life,* 40, 1.
2. Escriva, in *Palabra,* 26, (1967).
3. A priest must try to find the golden mean for his human qualities and virtues. A remark made by Banine, a Muslim writer converted to Catholicism may illustrate this point. She says that, like the French writer Huysmans, "I dislike cheerful priests, or rather those who are boisterously jovial. They should indeed be full of joy, which is the result of inner peace acquired at the price of losing their life in order to gain it, but not joviality, which is often vulgar." (Banine, *Yo escogi el opio,* p. 88 of the Spanish edition.) Likewise, modesty should not be prudery, nor sincerity impertinence, nor loyalty servility, nor boldness temerity or stupidity, nor generosity wastefulness, nor simplicity ingenuousness, etc.
4. *The Way,* 109.

Index

Vatican II *passim*
Vianney, St. J.-B. 72f, 215
virtues 125ff: cardinal 126;
 human 6, 86ff; theological 126

women: priest's relations with
 167ff

world: as good 5, 15;
 opponent 21, 125, 131,
 134ff, 157; two worlds 17,
 22ff, 26f

zeal 40ff, 46